D1625617

Around the World in 80 Pints

Around the World in 80 Pints

MY SEARCH FOR CRICKET'S GREATEST PLACES

David Lloyd

with Richard Gibson

**SIMON &
SCHUSTER**

London · New York · Sydney · Toronto · New Delhi

A CBS COMPANY

First published in Great Britain by Simon & Schuster UK Ltd, 2018
A CBS COMPANY

1 3 5 7 9 10 8 6 4 2

Simon & Schuster UK Ltd
1st Floor
222 Gray's Inn Road
London WC1X 8HB

www.simonandschuster.co.uk
www.simonandschuster.com.au
www.simonandschuster.co.in

Simon & Schuster Australia, Sydney
Simon & Schuster India, New Delhi

A CIP catalogue record for this book
is available from the British Library

Hardback ISBN: 978-1-4711-7240-3
eBook ISBN: 978-1-4711-7241-0

Typeset in Bembo by M Rules
Printed and bound by CPI Group (UK) Ltd, Croydon, CR0 4YY

CONTENTS

Part Three: Hopes for the Future

INTRODUCTION

For those of you who know me simply as 'that bloke off the telly', I have to let you know that being George Clooney's body double, and therefore a renowned international sex symbol, only forms a relatively small part of the Bumble package. And for Nasser Hussain, who for some reason refers to me by an alternative nickname, a lesson in pronunciation. There is no silent 'c' in Clooney, for goodness' sake, show some respect.

Yes, it is fair to say that I have been around a while now, and it was a lovely gesture of the England and Wales Cricket Board to present me with a lifetime achievement award at their annual England team dinner a couple of years ago to recognise the fact – although I couldn't help thinking that receiving such an accolade was the equivalent of being pensioned off. 'Time's up, mate.' 'Put your mic down.' Dare I say: 'Start the car.'

It has been the fullest of lifetimes, too. During my playing days with Lancashire and England, I got the yips, was hit in the pips and suffered the dips (in form). More of that later, as I discuss the game that has been my livelihood since I first meandered through the potholes of Thorneyholme Road to Accrington Cricket Club as a young boy.

During school holidays, that is where you could find me, sometimes with others, sometimes on my own: in the nets, out on the centre pitches cut for practice, honing my technique, practising my bowling. But it is also the place where I first learned about the game, in a manner that so many have before me and since.

Over a drink or two in the bar, matches were dissected, knowledge passed down from older generations to younger, and in this way the game's gospel was spread. For a northern cricketer this was a rite of passage. Cricket sets itself apart from other sports from a social perspective and it starts when you join your first club. In amateur cricket, the hub of the club has always been the bar. It's the place to meet friends, family and opposition. To chew the fat. To learn what is good about the game, what is bad, its etiquette, its rights and wrongs. Even now, these are the principles I fall back on when forming my views for you, the viewer at home. My judgements have been honed over a fizzy pop or a cold pint since I can remember.

Although things have changed a little bit now, traditionally there was a parochial element to this post-match education. Until recently there were 14 clubs in the Lancashire League, and the criterion for playing for one of them was that you had to reside within five miles of the ground as the crow flies. Being from Accrington, I was eligible for 10 clubs. That shows how tight-knit things were from a geographical perspective. The distance used to be measured assiduously, to make sure you represented your local team. All this helped instil the sense of togetherness and belonging from the start. You grew up with lads from your own town, learning the game from folk with similar backgrounds.

Socialising has been part of the fabric of playing cricket in England, and having a beer and a chat is synonymous with all levels of the game. The bar is the catalyst for making friends when you turn professional. You are just used to being in there, discussing the game; there is a social element to competing and in this regard it's a bit like rugby union, I would say. That's not a sport I know well, but the impression I get is that good performances are celebrated by opponents and there is a mutual respect for one another.

The attitude is that two teams play hard on the field, giving nothing, but once the game is over it is time for reflection. Move into the county ranks and you often mix socially both with rival players and the supporters of the two clubs in question. This is the ethos upon which the English cricket system has been founded from grass roots upwards. The bar supplies the social environment as well as the financial capacity for the club and the wider game to prosper.

It's also a place to make friends. There are genuine friendships that flourish year on year. One word synonymous with county cricket is 'circuit'. Quite literally, what that means is that you are off on your travels around the country. Off you go to Hampshire, Glamorgan and Somerset. Sure, there is a match to be won, but there is a renewal of kinship with lads you might have played junior cricket with, been on foreign tours with, or just had some memorable on-field battles with in the past. Each season is like a social catch-up from that perspective.

You don't even have to be bosom buddies to engage in this most civil of ceremonies. Having a drink with an opposition team – and although I enjoy an ale, I am not saying it has to be alcoholic for one minute – reinforces respect. Trek the county grounds in 2018 and you will still witness people sat on balconies, gathered on benches, stood around Long Rooms. For those who have continued the tradition, I salute you.

Particularly in the longer form, of first-class cricket, it is a sport that lends itself to evening chat. You are not going home that night, so you talk. You are there, and so there is a social element that is rich for both supporters and players. I am 71 now and had a very short international playing career, but I still see some of the players I played against. A couple of those in question, Farokh Engineer and Clive Lloyd, became pals through us playing together at Lancashire, but whenever I go to Australia I meet up with Dennis Lillee, for example.

From a work perspective I am often pitched alongside Ian Chappell. There is always a yarn to be had and a beer to be supped. I am always looking forward to renewing friendships I wouldn't have made without cricket. It is a sport of stories. Now, after-dinner speaking is not me. But someone like Geoff Miller, who has an audience in the palm of his hand recalling the memories of his career, is brilliant at capturing the atmosphere we experienced. Cricket is a vehicle for a chat, a beer and a get-together.

It is also one that has helped me form friendships outside of dressing rooms and commentary boxes. I meet up with an actor friend of mine called James Quinn, best known for starring as policeman Phil in the BBC comedy *Early Doors* but who has also appeared in things like *Coronation Street*, *Emmerdale* and *The Bill*, who knows his own industry inside out. But his knowledge about cricket is better than anybody else I have ever met. Whenever we meet up for a drink in Manchester, he will recall a game from the seventies as if it was yesterday and knows its detail vividly. He's just a punter. Some of the games I played in and some of the games he talks about, I remember. Some I don't.

It's a game of opinions. Who is West Indies' greatest cricketer? It has to be Sir Garry Sobers, right? Which one of Sachin Tendulkar and Brian Lara was the better batsman? Who would you rather face on a turning pitch: Shane Warne or Muttiah Muralitharan? How good would the modern-day gladiators have been in the 1970s on uncovered pitches, *sans* helmets? Everybody has got their own opinions. Whether you are a plasterer, an accountant, a lawyer or a coalman, you are entitled to your own and you can argue your case. So-and-so is rubbish, whatsisname never got a proper chance, I'd have played X over Y, John Smith's no good when the ball's doing a bit.

Occasionally, people get too pushy with their theories and I tend to keep my own counsel when someone goes off on one down the pub. 'I've only been involved for 50-odd years, maybe I don't know much. This bloke seems to, though.'

In club cricket, events on the field and after-match gatherings are intrinsically linked. In club cricket, it has been the privilege of thousands of recreational players to have bought a jug of ale for their team-mates to sup in the event of them scoring a hundred or taking five wickets.

In the Lancashire League, we used to get interested in the number of people in attendance, particularly as a batsman when we got into the 40s. At that point you would be trying to work out how many had paid to watch the game. Because you knew that a collection was coming your way. Between overs you would be looking around the crowd, seeing if the buckets were being readied.

Once collected, the money to honour your contribution would go behind the bar, some of it was to be spent immediately on drinks, some would end up in your wallet and another portion would go to the treasurer within the dressing room – the player responsible for collecting the funds for the ride-out at the end of the season. In September, the kitty would be totted up and, typically for us at Accrington, it would pay for a bus to Blackpool and back.

Once there, the remainder of the dosh would pay for several rounds. You'd be staggering around pubs, reliving some of the season's highlights, hours slipping by. When it came to home time, it was everybody for themselves. Someone always missed the bus. During the 1980s, one of our lads could be found the morning after sheltering under a market stall following a late-night liaison with a young lady.

My first senior fifty was against Lowerhouse, whose bowling attack featured the fiery West Indies international Roy

Gilchrist. It was a poor collection because, weather-wise, it was a poor day, but while the sum was modest this was the first dividend on the living I have made from the sport.

It was certainly a different level to when the great Sir Isaac Vivian Alexander Richards turned up for Rishton in 1987, and Accrington drew a 2,000-plus crowd for the fixture. The gate receipts alone were £1,700. Thirty years ago that went a long way. It would probably be worth £5,000 now. People were accustomed to putting their hands in their pockets to be entertained.

The collection for our Indian import Bharat Arun's effort of 72 amounted to three figures. I got a little unbeaten 51, from 48 balls, right at the back end of my first club innings for 23 years and raised £70. In on-field currency, those runs helped set a 182-run target for our visitors, one that was never going to trouble a team containing the world's best batsman. He was only absent from county cricket because of the well-documented bust-up with Somerset that left him in limbo.

Indeed, some of our crowd might have been asking for their Lloyd money back in the second innings when Viv was in full flow, and pongo-ing me all over the ground. My six overs of left-arm ordinary cost 37, including several strokes into the adjacent playing fields. I knew bowling from that end that the ground wasn't big enough for the both of us if he wanted to get serious. And I was right. He did get serious, finished unbeaten on 98 from 87 deliveries, and raised another £400 from his endeavours. People were clearly more appreciative of a bloke averaging in excess of 50 in Test cricket, the scourge of international bowlers, than in a local lad done good.

The seventies and eighties remained a vintage time for the Lancashire League, with the bars rammed at the end of a game. It really was standing room only during that era. The sale of alcohol was what financed the clubs, of course. Clubs would try to put on a good product that spectators would pay to watch and offer the facilities for everyone to wind down and have a natter afterwards.

Some clubs have always been the heartbeat of the community and remain so. Take Haslingden; it's the social scene of the town. A bit further afield, up the road from where I have lived later in life, Alderley Edge in Cheshire is not just a cricket club; it's the local.

Some are not so fortunate. Accrington Cricket Club is ever so slightly out of town, so not as many have tended to go. It has never been a place where passers-by just wander in because there aren't any. So it has been down to those who have been attracted by its charms to spread the word.

Nothing has changed at the club. The dressing rooms, the clubhouse and the pitch are all the same. It's like the place has been spewed through a time warp. Unfortunately, as much as I love it – the smells, the sounds and the history – there are not enough who share my passion. But the reason I have retained mine is because I owe it so much. It was my starting point for understanding the fundamentals of our great game.

Since then I have had the pleasure of meeting so many different characters from further afield, been afforded the opportunity to travel the world several times over and experience such variations in cultures and playing styles. So in part one of this book I will be reflecting on the people that helped form my views on cricket from an early age. How international cricketers landed on my doorstep and provided me with aspirations to progress beyond the cobbled streets and chimney pots of Lancashire; the county team-mates who weren't so different from the kind of lads you might know from your own cricket clubs; the grounds around England that have become like second homes and their neighbouring watering holes where I can be found debating the sport's talking points.

The second section of the book covers my trips around the world, quenching my thirst for knowledge and searching for good spots to lubricate the larynx. Each major nation has provided cricket's evolution with some unique properties that have been incorporated universally. Australia handed us an unparalleled sporting foe; West Indies terrorised with all-out pace; Pakistan were the sultans of reverse swing; India are pushing the game to new commercial levels through Twenty20 cricket; and countries like New Zealand show what can be achieved with great planning and no little amount of natural talent.

To finish up, I try to get across the mix of fun and professional satisfaction a post-career life in broadcasting has given me. It has allowed me to carry on my education and be paid for it. Picking up a wage for having a laugh and nattering with my mates behind a microphone instead of a pint can't be bad, can it? Of course, there is also a very serious side to this privileged position. I have been left agog at some unbelievable skills and in despair when the sport has been tainted. It has made me laugh at the world and occasionally it has made me cry. This is my 20th year as a member of the Sky Sports commentary team, and I am still as passionate about the modern issues as I am fond of viewing the past through the rose-tinteds. So what do I know about stuff? Where do I think the game is heading? Pull up a pew, fill your glass and let's find out.

PART ONE

The Game I Fell in Love With

CHAPTER ONE

When Accrington was Acropolis

April 17, 2018, is a date I will never forget. I could feel a burst of Frankie Valli and the Four Seasons coming on: 'Oh, what a Night'. For those who do not have it etched on their minds, it marked Accrington Stanley's first promotion to the third tier of English football, the biggest achievement in the club's history and the most pride I have felt in my home town. Their best contributed to my best.

Victory over Yeovil was required to secure a top-three finish and an elevation to League One on merit. At the end of the 1957-58 season, when the old Third Divisions North and South became Divisions Three and Four, Stanley ended up in Division Three, but there'd been nothing like this.

Forgive me for starting off a cricket book with a tale about football, but it takes me back to where everything began for me. Accrington's sports clubs provided me with the pathway that would take me from my mam and dad's terraced house in Water Street to some of the sporting world's most iconic venues. Throughout the journey, Stanley have been a constant in my life, as well as the cricket club. Both are minnows in their respective spheres, but they have both offered friendship, warmth and camaraderie and left a catalogue of memories. This night, when a multitude of generations got together in celebration, was one for reminiscing.

Throughout my years of watching those wonderful red wizards and the magic they produce, it would be a good effort if we got 1,200 into the ground. But over the final few weeks of the 2017-18 season we had more than 3,000 per match. Success appeared to have engaged the interest. Those who had been meaning to pop down and watch for ages were suddenly there. The occasional supporters made sure this was one of those occasions. Some were down there, I am sure, to find out what all the fuss was about. It didn't matter. All were welcome.

It meant it was a real squeeze, bumper to bumper stuff on the terraces, and the bloke next to me says: 'David, isn't it?'

'Yes, it is.'

'Christ,' he continues. 'I've given you some kickings.'

As soon as he told me his name was Phil Eccles it all came flooding back to me. Back in the day, Phil played for a team called Whinney Hill. My lot, a team my dad used to run, were called Cambridge Street Methodists. Phil later emailed photographs of both teams.

They were from 1962, the year I made my first XI cricket debut for Accrington. Also the one in which Stanley went out of the Football League, later re-forming in the Lancashire Combination. On the Whinney Hill team were several ex-Stanley players. They'd stayed and played locally after the disbandment, probably because half a century ago your average bloke didn't tend to venture very far.

A few days earlier against Exeter City, those of us who arrived early were told to budge up to make room for 200 more. We were crammed in like sardines. The stewards were told in no uncertain terms that we were staying put behind the goal – we'd been there since 1pm and that anyone wanting a spot should have got there earlier!

This time those 200 appeared to be among us, plus a few more to boot. We'd never had stewards before, let alone mounted police. There were folk on roofs behind the ground trying to catch a glimpse of history. The place was rocking and I have never seen the Crown – or Wham Stadium as it is now – like it.

Football had brought us all back together. Nerves were swirling around the stand, but we needn't have worried. The players came out and put a real performance on. Two up at half-time – such was the roar in reaction to the first that my daughter Sarah texted me to ask: 'Have they scored?' And she lives in Huncoat, the next village – the lads peppered the goal towards the Clayton End after the break, flags were whirling above heads, one even flew off its handle in the excitement. Other than the two goals in as many minutes by our top scorer, and the leading striker in the division, Billy Kee, though, the magic moment for me came right at the end.

The message was transmitted on the electronic screen: PLEASE DON'T RUN ONTO YOUR FIELD AT THE END. The crowd was 3,176 and it looked as if the 176 had listened. The grass was teeming with folk revelling in the 'I was there' moment. Of course, as time goes by there will be 60,000 claiming they were on the pitch. That's the way it goes with football fans.

The key to the club is the sense of community instilled by chairman Andy Holt. Sometimes it is just a tenner to get in, a fiver for concessions, and kids are free. Recently, they gave away free Accrington Stanley shirts to all the Year 3 schoolchildren in the district. It is the be-all and end-all for Andy to get the next generation engaged with the club, and we were absolutely staggered at the number of young 'uns there.

To attract all ages for such an occasion was just wonderful.

There was a buzz about the town. Glory had packed up and left it years earlier. So it was to be cherished upon its return. There is no money to speak of in Accrington; it's a tight area but a sports club doing well unites and gives everyone something to cheer. There was a fan zone, including live music, set up before the match. Afterwards the band struck up again and they were still playing at midnight.

I had gone prepared, travelling to the game with a case of champagne in the boot. Persuading a cheery-looking steward to let me in the dressing room, the place erupted when I entered with my contribution to the celebrations. 'There you are, lads – enjoy.'

How refreshing to see their achievements mean so much. There are not many local lads in the side, but the cheers and merriment showed they cared. And not just about themselves. Three of them were named in the Division Two team of the year: centre-half Mark Hughes (no, not that one), midfielder Sean McConville and Billy Kee. But they seemed to be revelling in their efforts as a collective. Every one of them happy for each other's acclaim.

When it's time for training they have to go looking for Billy Kee. It's not his favourite pastime. But he doesn't lack enthusiasm when there's a task in hand – such as getting up on stage, microphone in hand, to sing for an audience. And the rub of it all was that in the Sports Bar afterwards, these players were drinking, dancing and enjoying themselves mingling with the supporters, still in full kit. It was like time had stood still. Or we had hopped into the Tardis and been transported to another era.

Prices were reflective of this theory too. During 'winning' hour Stanley Ale, made by the local Bowland Brewery, was a pound a pint. Which sounds great. Unfortunately, at those prices you couldn't get near the bar. Those who couldn't jostled for selfies and autographs instead. No one cared.

It was an 'all for one and one for all' atmosphere and one of the musketeers, Scott Brown, a midfielder who joined us in his thirties after serving nine other clubs, certainly enjoyed himself. According to his Twitter account next day, he'd lost his phone, house keys and car keys, couldn't remember getting home but had done so still in his match attire. And he wanted to do it all again!

Supporters of Sunderland were quick to tweet, telling me how welcome we would be at the Stadium of Light the following season. Their relegation from the Championship had yet to be confirmed but I reciprocated by saying the same went for them and the Stadium of Dark. Let's face it, we have so little money that I anticipated not being able to turn on the floodlights when we got round to playing them.

I believe promotion was worth about £800,000 to us – not bad for the league club with the smallest resources in the country. Andy Holt will spend it wisely, and I gather he even wants to reduce the capacity of the Wham Stadium to make it a more intimate match-day experience for the supporters. There aren't many of us but we care. You can take the lad out of Accrington and all that.

During my formative years, Accrington's population hovered somewhere above 30,000, but as far as I was concerned this Lancashire hill town sat at the summit of the sporting world. The equivalent of Athens' acropolis. There were loads of good amateur football teams, and when it came to cricket there were 14 clubs within a 20-mile radius that came together. We were home to the most famous amateur cricket league on the planet. Even now, if you posed the question to the sport's aficionados here or overseas which is the most renowned, they would come back with one answer: the Lancashire League.

In 2018, the world's best cricketers flock to the subcontinent to line their pockets with rupees, but back in the day they arrived on my doorstep to earn their crust. Crowds a couple of thousand strong would turn up to witness the entertainment. Just think about that kind of proposition. That's one in every 15 who lived in the town.

Where I grew up, Lancashire League cricket was the thing in the height of summer. Saturday afternoons were a real social occasion. You didn't just rock up in your scruffs. As a match was a thing to be seen at, you would get people in their finery. The stands would be adorned with suits, collars and ties, top hats and tails, ladies in their best dresses.

And it was the return of one of the superstars of yesteryear in West Indies fast bowler Wes Hall that recently brought it back how significant our little enclave was. During a BBC documentary called *Race and Pace*, chronicling the relationship between the mill towns of our county and the West Indies cricketers who were employed as their cricket clubs' professionals, it became evident that Wes pined for a return to his old stomping ground. Within six weeks, thanks to a willingness to help from several quarters, including among others the Barbados High Commissioner Guy Hewitt, the long-serving members of Accrington Cricket Club and the *Daily Mail*, one of the silkiest fast bowlers ever to grace the game was retracing the steps of his run-up — albeit at the age of 80, with the aid of a stick — from the Highams End.

The likes of Learie Constantine and Frank Worrell had been the Caribbean pioneers on this particular route across the Atlantic, but Sir Wes — his easy demeanour made it more natural to call him Our Wes — was the one who made an impression on me as a youth. Seeing one of the sport's great physical specimens competing alongside the blokes of your town against a neighbouring one, slotting seamlessly into the community, striving to do the best he could for both himself and those he represented, taught me something of the way cricket was meant to be and how the values could be applied outside of the boundary as well as inside. The way Wes conducted himself provided a real life lesson.

Sir Wes was a man of modest means and, although it was a lot for our club to stump up, his £1,000 summer salary was modest too, at least when translated into today's equivalent of about £20,000. He recalled how the first offer he received from committee member Alan Doherty was £500. His negotiations were helped by the 46 wickets he took on West Indies' tour of India and Pakistan in 1958-59. That eight-match haul was followed by a further 22 during England's 1-0 win in the Caribbean on the eve of his arrival.

Other West Indies greats like Charlie Griffith, Michael Holding and Vivian Richards followed him, each buying into the ethos of betterment as individuals and for their teams. Of course, as time passed they were rewarded more handsomely, with Rishton paying Holding £5,000 a summer and Richards reportedly double that sum.

This east-meets-west love affair, of inclement East Lancashire and the idyllic West Indies, began with Learie Constantine's signing by Nelson back in the 1920s at a time when black people were rarely seen in the United Kingdom. His arrival certainly gained folks' interest. They would stare at him in the street. Were they prejudiced? Well, I am not sure about that. Most hadn't seen people from other cultures in their lives and were probably uncertain how to react. So they just fixed their eyes upon him almost in disbelief.

It was certainly something that both Constantine and those he lived among had to overcome. Sadly, there were more disturbing elements that he had to contend with in his dismantling of the social barriers. His daughter Gloria Valere tells a story of how when he first arrived there was a reticence from locals who had been 'fed with the idea that black people are not really people, that they are lesser and they're not very bright'.

My experience was that when these professional players arrived they created a buzz around the area. To see them around town was to be star-spotting. They were our local celebrities. It was just terrific. Wes was known locally as 'the pro'. But Gloria says her father had a tough time as a trailblazer being accepted in the town, that some people would see him coming and cross the street, and that others would ignore him face to face. However, school kids would line up at the front window of the house he stayed in just to get a peek at him.

The novelty aspect of this signing had its upside, though, as it coincided with Nelson being heavily in debt – they had taken the chance on this charismatic Trinidadian both as a cricketer and as a bit of a curiosity to draw the crowds. They gambled on providing the public with a player from an area not witnessed. Previously the professional players had been Englishmen or, if taken from further afield, Australians or South Africans. As a marketing ploy it had a tremendous effect.

And it was not just Nelson that benefited. Other clubs reported bumper gates when Nelson were the visitors. Some that had not attracted crowds of that magnitude before, and some probably since, were able to draw 7,000. People would rush home from working on a Saturday morning, as they did in the 1930s, get their glad rags on and head down to the ground to get a seat. For sixpence you could see some of the best cricket that our country was capable of producing. And Constantine was paid commensurately. In fact, at that time his £800 contract would arguably have made him the highest paid sportsman in Britain.

Constantine provided credence to the theory that your overseas professional was your team. Nelson won seven Lancashire League titles in his nine seasons. Ergo, getting the recruitment of a top-class performer became crucial. All the other clubs were playing catch-up.

The best Australians of their day also plied their trade as professionals in the Lancashire League in the off-season to supplement their income at home. Men like Bobby Simpson – who, until Ashar Zaidi recently toppled it, held the Accrington club record for most runs in a league season – and, later, Dennis Lillee and Allan Border. It was a viable small business model with social and communal overtones. Top players continued to attract the crowds – some at the bigger clubs like Burnley would be pushing five figures – and the gate receipts provided the funds to pay for them. Perform well and there was a bonus in the form of a collection around the stands. Conversely, for those who broke the league's uniform business model there was a penalty. If for whatever reason a club turned up for a match without a pro, there would be a fine imposed. In the event of absence through injury, illness or other unspecified reason, a substitute had to be found, signed up and sent onto the field.

The financial scale of today's elite sport means we will never again see the world's best pitching up in an English village like Rishton again – it was the equivalent of Virat Kohli and AB de Villiers turning up with their suitcases for the summer. Cricket's modernisation has dictated sunnier climes and bigger pay cheques.

It was such a thrill to see Sir Wes back at his adopted home of the early sixties. Not long after we had made the last bumpy few hundred yards of the journey – those same potholes were a feature during his final season of 1962 when I would arrive on my bicycle to play alongside him in the first XI – there was one moment of great mirth when, unnoticed, he bolted under the perimeter rope and made for the middle. Well, okay, it wasn't a bolt in the Usain sense, given that he relies on his stick for balance these days following a car accident back home in Barbados a couple of years ago. Nevertheless, the fact that our guest was no longer as steady on his feet as he once was and had escaped our company proved a mild concern.

Indestructible in his pomp he may have been, but the last thing we wanted having come this far was any slip-ups. Nostalgia had moved him. We caught up with him on this pilgrimage to the middle as recollections of pushing off the sight screen filled his thoughts. The wind was always at his back from the Highams End, he reminisced, and it accentuated the swing he was able to impart on the ball.

'Why you worryin'?' he asked, recognising the concern on our faces.

It was a special moment to witness, as the memories of this artist's work as a young man cascaded through his mind. Sir Wes was a big man at just over six-foot-two, but he possessed a graceful, rhythmical approach to the crease, with his bowling arm gently swaying back and forth. It all looked so natural. Although playing on Accrington's soft turf caused him some trouble, he chuckled, causing him to slide in delivery and send down a few too many no-balls.

You could see the wonder in his eyes at being back in a place he called home between 1960 and 1962. But it was nothing compared to the scene we were to witness when a convoy temporarily left the ground to take Wesley – as he was known to his Lancastrian team-mates – on a five-mile journey up the road to Blackburn. We were off to see Jim Eland, his former new-ball partner. Jim would have been there but for his health consigning him to a care home these days.

To witness this encounter was to affirm all that is good about cricket and its abilities to cross borders, seas, continents, races and cultures. Jim's memory is fading now, but to see his reaction to Wes's arrival was simply priceless. After a warm embrace they squeezed into a sofa together. Alongside each other again after a hiatus of 55 years from a playing perspective, they discussed what made their partnership back in the day so special: Jim's unerring accuracy complemented by the raw pace of our import.

'I'd tell you – "Keep 'em quiet, Jim,"' Wes recalls. 'Be accurate. Don't let any of those great pros take you apart. Just keep it on the spot because then they'll have to push on against me.'

This was an episode that showed you literally cannot beat the memories forged together on a cricket field: the great, the valiant, the farcical, the funny events that happen which are recounted within an hour in the dressing room and a full half-century later. The Eland and Hall families had come together 10 years earlier in Barbados, and Wes used his status within West Indies cricket to take Jim out onto the Kensington Oval outfield, joking when they got to the square: 'You take that end, Jim, this one's mine.'

Back at the Accrington clubhouse an hour later, Sir Wes was hugging all and sundry like long-lost brothers. What a source of pride it was that so many of our former teammates turned out to welcome him back and to extend their friendship. Men I played a lot of first-team cricket with, like Russ Cuddihy – your typical club opening batsman. Not that those sadly no longer with us were to be forgotten. Sir Wes recounted them all.

'I can remember every single player I played with. The experience has remained here on my heart,' Wes said.

He wasn't exaggerating, either. Unstable on his pins he might have been, but he was still as sharp as a tack. The stuff he talked about was amazing. In the audience was one Edward Slinger, an opening batsman from Enfield. He knew him straight away. Addressed him as if they had grown up alongside each other – and in a way they had.

It can't have been easy for a young black man to settle into what was a working-class white town back in the 1960s. Like Constantine a quarter of a century earlier, there were issues to overcome. Yet he managed it with grace and good humour, and he was soon treated like one of our own. I recognised one chap so keen to be reacquainted that night that he had walked down from his house a decent stroll away. 'It can't be,' I muttered to myself when I set eyes on him, collar and tie on, a glint in his eye just from being there.

'Hello, David, how you doing?' he enquired.

'All right, Ted,' I replied. Ted Marshall, a lifelong supporter of the club, was 102. ONE HUNDRED AND TWO! Sadly, he has passed away since.

Doherty, the man bartering over that first contract, was also in attendance. At 94, he must have reflected, on this special occasion, that whatever it had cost it had proved money well spent. During the potato pie supper in his honour, Wes told a tale of one of his early experiences following his arrival from the Caribbean. He laughed off the stares, he said, because it was the only response he knew. 'I was walking to the ground a few days after I'd arrived when I heard a boy shouting into a house: "Mum, mum, there's a black man in the street,"' he told the room. 'It puzzled me, that. You see, we have a surname – Blackman – in Barbados. I told the boy: "I'm Wes Hall. I'm the new professional and if you're lucky you can carry my bags." And he did.'

Just as he had done in his first spell with us, he had everyone captivated when he addressed us. I, for one, idolised him. Not least because of the support and advice he offered to up-and-comers like me. To him, the things you would hope for in an overseas player came so naturally. I came on to bowl on my first XI debut at Rishton in July 1962, taking over from Wes as first change. I was just 15, but he had been lobbying for my promotion from the second XI for weeks. That's the kind of guy he was – a real clubman.

He took me to my first Test match, too. It was at Trent Bridge. I'd never been to one before. And when he came back from a tour of Australia, he brought me my first cricket bat – a 'Norman O'Neill Crocket'. That was Wes all over: helping younger players, showing he cared, full of empathy.

And when you played alongside him, he made you feel an important part of the team. Sportsmanship came so naturally to him. He fulfilled his role in cricket's bigger picture. Somewhere along the line, he himself would have had the knowledge of the game, the way to behave, passed down. Arguably, he was just taking his part in the chain.

He says moving to Lancashire for his first five-month stint was the defining moment in his life. He had to fit in, being thousands of miles away from the comforts of his home, living among strangers, and with the added pressure of performing when he got onto the field. He tried to turn himself into the kind of person others loved to be around.

And how he did. Wes threw himself into Accrington life, and people cared about him because of his attitude. For example, when he lost the gold cross and chain that used to bob around his neck as he bounded in to bowl one Saturday afternoon at Lowerhouse, folk got out onto the pitch to comb the outfield. He still wears that crucifix now. He would turn up with the rest of the team at the appointed meet time to take the double-decker bus from outside the town's Odeon cinema to away games in neighbouring valleys such as Bacup, Todmorden and Rawtenstall. The club would hire the bus from the local council and then fill it, with players upstairs and spectators downstairs.

Twice he took all 10 wickets in an innings. He would keep running in hard for the team, and, as he reminded us over his supper, twice as far as he had for previous teams (for it was during his spell with our club that he doubled his approach from its previous 18 yards in a bid to create a better rhythm). Having fast bowlers like Wes and Charlie Griffith, who played for Burnley, was genuinely good for our league. I would argue that it helped raise the standards of young players wanting to make the grade as county cricketers.

But some older ones would cannily avoid having to face them. At one time there were up to a dozen West Indies players playing in the league, and the seasoned campaigners who batted at the top of the order would scour the fixture list in mid-April and work out when to take their holidays. It was as much a self-preservation exercise as a desire to get a tan or a few days at the coast away from the nine-to-five, and oddly enough tended to coincide with a planned visit to Burnley or an appointment with Mr Hall at our place. Those having to get to work on a Monday morning would be concerned about doing so if their fixture on a Saturday was versus Accrington. Yet they need not have been. Wes's skill was to keep the ball pitched up and use his speed and arc through the air, not a plan to bruise or draw blood, to get them out. Great days for us all.

'I used to think I knew every blade of grass at Accrington and now I've found out that I did,' he says. 'I just so loved that. The feeling that came back. Even though I can't walk well now, I think in my spirit I could take off on my run-up and get a few wickets like I used to do. Thank you. I don't think you could ever envisage what this has meant to me,' he concluded.

It was my job to thank this fantastic bloke for making the trip and reaffirming what a power for good sport, and in particular cricket, can be. 'Wes, thanks for caring. Thanks for coming back,' I said.

Half a century ago cricket was such a huge part of each and every community. Life was so much more parochial then compared to now. Sporting contests were such territorial affairs – real us-and-them encounters. Not in a snarling, frothing-at-the-mouth, abusive kind of way. It was a competitive spirit forged on pride in your own dwelling. You were representing your lot against the best of their lot.

Back in the 1960s, when Wes would be found sipping his Vimto of an evening, a spotty hopeful called Lloyd would be hanging on his every word, with a bottle of Coke or sarsaparilla in hand. This huge athletic man says Accrington has featured in his tranquil moments of reflection ever since, that as a religious man he still prays for the people he lived among.

There are plans afoot in Barbados for Wes to return in the future, alongside Sir Garfield Sobers – who played five seasons with Radcliffe in the Central Lancashire League – and others from the island who supplemented their earnings with spells as cricket professionals in the North-west. A whole region will look forward to that.

The entrance won't be as grand as that of Viv in a helicopter more than 30 years ago – a publicity stunt to add a 'bit of spice'. It also cost a bit more to see iconic players like him on show. Pitches in general would be difficult for attractive stroke play and matches therefore tended to be dominated by the bowlers. Punters could turn up in the knowledge that after their nominal entrance fee there wouldn't be any need for extra brass.

So when a batter was getting close to a landmark, it could lead to episodes of high farce. Team-mates would grab the collection tins quick smart and charge towards the main gate, hoping to catch those clever clogs who were trying to avoid putting their hands in their pockets. If a batsman was in the 40s that would provide a great spectacle in itself.

A high-scoring game – of which, as I say, there were not many due to the uncovered pitches – could prove an expensive business. In the fifties, in addition to an entrance fee, there was also a supplement to get into the enclosure.

That's where the toffs would sit and watch. In that area the seats would have backs on. Different cross-sections of society would turn up and whether you were taking money for sitting on a bench or a proper chair it all added up and contributed to the pot.

For decades, cricket was the main attraction of the area. Not everyone had a car. A family day out was spent locally. There was cricket or nothing else. Not like these days when you can be at the Trafford Centre inside three-quarters of an hour. And be shopping, skiing or abseiling, all within a few hundred yards of each other.

We were so lucky. We got Rishton twice in the Richards season and, blessed with great weather, it meant we got a couple of thousand in to watch on each occasion. Financially, this was to safeguard our club for a good couple of years. The only problem we had with this kind of unexpected bonanza was a trivial and typically northern one: when the best cricketer of his era is coming for the day, how many pies do you get? I guess if that's all you've got to worry about, there isn't a lot wrong. But anyone involved in a cricket club will know these kinds of things matter to those doing the grind at the coalface. The subject of how many pies was debated vigorously by the Accrington committee and dominated our pre-match preparations. There wasn't much time spent on things like health and safety. No, forget that tosh. How many pies should we get? And should they be kidney puddings or beef and onion?

Viv was in his pomp and I was still playing on a weekend, having retired from first-class cricket four years earlier. The boundaries weren't big enough for me and him – well, not big enough for his batting, and not big enough for my bowling. I knew the game inside out by then, but had I witnessed this kind of performance in my youth I am sure it would have had a huge and inspirational influence on me.

When the Australian Bobby Simpson was professional at Accrington, he would coach kids like me for a fee. Along with his technical advice on batsmanship came an edict on how to approach things. That the best way to be was yourself. He used to say, 'This is not a complicated game', and used the example of a young kid coming into a first team. All he does is go out and bat normally, like he always has done.

Ignorance is bliss. You start off playing your natural game and only veer away from it when confronted by failure. It is a trap that captures so many. Ten years on, that same player studies the weather, the light, the wind direction, the pitch and the grass before he goes in. The key message from Bobby is one that has stuck with me, even if I have been guilty of not always adhering to it: remember it's the same game.

In addition to the influx of greats from West Indies and Australia, cricketers from other territories have arrived over the decades to enrich our league. These days southern Africans are prevalent, due in no small part to their own struggles for recognition in South Africa and Zimbabwe, and the weakness of the rand against the pound.

Some fabulous players from the subcontinent were recruited not long after South Asian immigration into East Lancashire began following the Second World War. There was magical leg-spin bowling from Chandu Borde and Subhash Gupte, whom I used to chase for autographs.

The offer of work in the textile factories littering our network of little towns attracted migrants from India and Pakistan to come and settle too, but while social cohesion has gradually happened, things have moved slowly. One of the problems we have encountered in the Lancashire League in recent decades is how to deal with integration when clubs are still relying on the traditional model to be successful. The majority of local cricketers with Asian ancestry often simply play and go, rather than hang around afterwards and be involved in much of the social aspect.

Of course, for Muslim cricketers a bar serving alcohol may not be somewhere they would naturally choose, while for others family commitments may send them straight home, but something is lost for everyone in them not being there. Those who don't stay are missing out on discussing the way the game panned out, on praise from others if they have played well, or hearing different perspectives on the way the game has been and should be played. Many an old sage is worth listening to over a pint in the clubhouse. 'Perhaps you could think about doing this?' Without the post-match camaraderie the game as we have known it becomes splintered. We need a modern fix.

I accept time moves on. For one thing, the Lancashire League is nowhere near the same as it was in terms of attendance. The golden era of great overseas professionals and crowds that lower-league football clubs would be proud of has well and truly gone. Partly, this has been due to a change in the international calendar. Up until as recently as the first decade of the 21st century, the cricket seasons of other countries did not intrude on our own. All that changed, however, with the introduction of the Indian Premier League. Of course, it was not a straight choice between Bacup and Bangalore or Darwen and Delhi, but the altering of the landscape at the very top where the mega money is began to have a direct effect on everything else.

Sure, you still get one or two fine imports to our part of the world, guys who have played for their countries at Under-19, A team or full international levels, but the top players around the world are now busy trying to get into that group of 200 or so cricketers at the IPL, and their jostling for recognition filters down. With the very top bracket no longer in the market, those on the next rungs down are more likely to be looking for a gig at the Caribbean Premier League in late summer or waiting for

the Bangladesh Premier League in the autumn. From a financial point of view, the money on offer at the satellite Twenty20
tournaments has dictated different paths for the modern players
to tread. No question, cricket is a game of traditions and what
a thrill it would be to think you were following in the footsteps
of some of these flipping fantastic players of the past. But there
is also a financial consideration for these guys too.

CHAPTER TWO

Band of Brothers

Talking of wages, Lancashire must have valued me when they handed me my first professional contract because they cut my previous earnings by a seventh! As an enthusiastic young gun for hire, I had been picking up £7 a week in match fees and expenses, but for the privilege of being a permanent member of the playing staff I reverted to £6.

My promotion thrilled me nevertheless, as I was fulfilling a boyhood dream, and living it alongside so many others of similar ages. It is fair to say that the club had been in turmoil in the 1960s and there was a fairly high turnover of players for that day and age. A group of us emerged who would create a very successful period, particularly in one-day cricket. What made the team so special during this decade was that it was Lancashire through and through. We got what it meant to represent the red rose and from one to 11, these lads were absolute one-offs.

The overriding thing about this entire group of men is that they were all naturally funny. This was a band of brothers who could argue like cat and dog inside our own four walls before and after play. The arguments would roll over into the pub sometimes, too. But we would still be the best of mates and as a team we were united. Try taking one of us on and you took us all on.

We had a tight dressing room and in limited-overs cricket we were like a juggernaut – winning six trophies between 1969 and 1975. We were learning from each other on how to be successful in this form of the game and we would leave nothing out there on the pitch. Neither would there be any short-changing on the social front.

Of course, this was a different culture to the one we have become accustomed to in recent times and 1970s fixture lists would either provide you with Sundays off or you would play a Sunday League match. We used to have a saying among the group: 'Saturday night is Saturday night.' In other words, tools were downed and it was every man for themselves once we had finished the week's County Championship graft.

The Bumble Lancashire XI

Barry Wood

My opening partner was an import from Yorkshire. We tried not to hold that against him, though. A technically very correct player who had a massive belief in his own ability. When he first arrived from Ossett, we both had Ford motor cars. But his was one grade up from mine. I had a Zephyr, he had a Zodiac. There were wings at the back that made these things look like the Batmobile.

His prowess in other sports went before him. He played for Chickenley Rovers at football and came over the hills with the belief that he would be the best footballer in the Lancashire team. He was also brilliant at table tennis, apparently. Well, we had a table-tennis table in the dressing room and I can only assume he was keeping his best performances for last because he seemed to be defeated by all-comers. A champion 400-metre runner, he came last in that too. But one thing that cannot be taken away from him is that he has always remained as fit as anything.

His secret to keeping in the best shape? He used to train in hobnail boots. These days you get players wearing these wonderful Adidas and ASICS training shoes, not much more than carpet slippers, which are like walking on air. But Barry swore by the hobnails because when it came to putting his cricket boots on for matches they felt nice and light.

Harry Pilling and John Sullivan

These two were sparring partners, and when I say sparring partners I mean sparring partners. Harry only stood five-foot-three but he must have had circus mirrors in his house because he would fancy his chances against blokes twice as big and three times as wide. He'd also start an argument in a yoga class.

He and John came from up Mossley and Stalybridge respectively. At night, they played in a rock and roll band together and would practise in the showers after matches by singing Everly Brothers harmonies. One night after a game for the second XI they had a gig at a pub, so they both jumped in the communal bath and started warming up their vocal cords. On hearing their ditties, Stan Worthington, the coach, pushed the doors apart and warned them: 'If I ever catch you two doing that sort of thing again, you will both get the sack.' Stan had put two and two together and got five.

After a day's play, they would put their club blazers on, proudly sporting the red rose, then head for the roughest pub they could find. Every now and again some amateur Ali, looking for a rise, would demand: 'What's that poppy?' The standard reply was: 'That's not a f***ing poppy, it's the rose of

Lancashire.' Then it would all kick off, and that suited John just fine. His other after-hours interest in addition to singing was pugilism. He was an amateur ABA boxing champion. But with such a full diary, he sometimes ended up getting his practice in down the boozer of an evening.

Harry made the number three position his own at Old Trafford (don't think anyone dared try to take it off him, to be honest). John was a perfect fit for one-day cricket. He was a real impact player: bowled some decent seam, and when he batted he could be the one to hit 30 off 20 balls in the days when that sort of thing was something pretty unusual.

Frank Hayes

Nicknamed 'Fish' because he could drink like one. There was a pub round the back of Lord's called the Truscott Arms, which is still there but recently reopened as the Hero of Maida after plans to turn it into luxury flats were fought off. The Truscott had 10 hand-pulled beers back in the day and if you could drink a pint of each you got your name up on the honours board. Upon reaching double digits, the imbiber would be escorted by a member of staff to the toilets, ensuring any sickness was contained to Armitage Shanks House. Frank went round twice on the same night!

What a brilliant cricketer. A real touch player as a batsman, he came out of university as a dashing stroke player and kept faithful to his style all the way up to international level, hitting a hundred in his first Test match against West Indies at The Oval in 1973. Unfortunately, all nine of his Test caps came against the powerful Windies, and there was only going to be one winner there in the end. But he remained a supreme talent on the county scene and took Malcolm Nash – made famous by Garry Sobers's full house of sixes at Swansea – for 6, 4, 6, 6, 6, 6 in a single over.

He played rugby for Broughton Park in the off-season and taught physics into his seventies, coaching at Oakham School, where Stuart Broad was a pupil.

Clive Lloyd

He came over from the West Indies and just fitted in from day one – although there was an early difficulty to overcome when the club administrators housed him in the centre of Manchester at 'Unit Two Sauna', an address which should have revealed to them the type of place they were renting. Apparently, they remained oblivious and Clive found himself on what was euphemistically called a 'massage bed'. I am not sure he knew what he was letting himself in for at that stage, but the early difficulty was ironed out and he became a club stalwart. He served as a player from 1968 to 1986 and was responsible for some glorious moments in Lancashire's history.

Like a panther in the field, one of the best I have ever seen, and such a hard-hitting batsman. A little remembered fact is that when we won the Gillette Cup under Jack Bond, Clive opened the bowling with his right-arm filth in the final, a decision that allowed us to play an extra batsman. It was a tactical master-stroke from Jack, as Warwickshire took just 31 runs off his 12 overs, and Clive later charged us home with 126. Away from the field he was an absolute gentleman, and what an ambassador for the game of cricket. If you have a problem with Clive, it's your problem, not his.

Farokh Engineer

An absolute artist with the gloves behind the stumps. As a wick-etkeeper he was a natural. He was also someone who could bat anywhere from one to seven, and if he wasn't opening he would be demanding: 'Get me in, get me in. I'll hit this bloke.'

When Farokh joined us, we had to get used to his different habits and customs. Now, Farokh is one great bloke, one of the best you could possibly wish to meet. But he was a Parsi and they don't use bog roll. (Apparently, the South Africa batsman Neil McKenzie refused to go out to bat unless all the toilet seats were up in the dressing room. He was fidgety unless this superstition was adhered to.)

Well, in the seventies we had to get used to Farokh's habits in what the Americans would call the bathroom. Like most wicketkeepers, he would come off the field at the end of a session and head straight to the loo, where there was always a glass left for the players by the dressing room attendant, in case one required a swig of water.

However, Farokh would come in and take it for an altogether different use. If he was sitting down with the intention to – how should I put it? – shed some weight, or relocate his lunch, he would take this full glass and pour it down the nape of his neck, allowing it to flow down into his nether regions so that he could wipe himself clean.

On one occasion he came out of the cubicle with the glass empty. He's had his fingers all around the inside of it, of course. 'You must have been thirsty,' says John Sullivan. 'Oh, no, it's for my ablutions . . .'

At that point Sully made sure everyone in the team knew what this glass was being used for, just in case anyone else was feeling parched.

Farokh is one of the ex-players who can be counted upon to return to Old Trafford in Test weeks, and you can spot him a mile off courtesy of his odd sartorial choices. One year, he looked as if he had been the victim of an explosion in a paint factory. He was wearing a pink and white jacket, as well as an

MCC tie. He must have been on his way to San Francisco to meet 'flower power' pop singer Scott McKenzie.

David Hughes

Who can ever forget the 1971 semi-final against Gloucestershire when we won in the dark, thanks to David? One-day cricket has been defined by it. When people were ringing up Lancashire County Cricket Club in the days after, the calls included women saying: 'My husband says he was at a cricket ground at 10 to nine last night, can you please confirm this?'

He later became captain and coach of the club and was a renowned organiser. He would literally organise anything. You need dinner? You need a holiday? You need golf? Yosser would do it.

Jack Simmons

'Flat Jack' didn't join us until he was 28. He had been a local pro and absolute kingpin in the leagues, and worked as a draughtsman at the local council in Preston. A few years earlier, he had missed out on a contract with Northamptonshire and they don't know how much money they saved on their tea budget. He could eat a horse, Jack.

He is no different in 2018. What he tends to do now, though, is go on cruises. Not because he likes the scenery, or a life at sea, but because he knows there is a lot of grub. Once, in a match at Blackpool, we were one short on the field, when it came to my attention that Simmo was missing.

'I am not coming on to field until I've had my gooseberry tart,' was his protest. It was always a pet hate when we went to out-grounds for matches that, although you got 40 minutes for lunch, all the dignitaries would get fed first. There was always a bit of pomp and circumstance to such occasions, the lord mayor would be there and the committee from the local club. Cricketers hate that. Especially when they are the ones working. And Simmo didn't like playing on anything other than the fullest of stomachs.

He has been a great mate over the years; talking of which, he played longer than Methuselah. As a league cricketer he ran in and bowled tear-arse quick, but he became an off-spinner soon after joining us. He had this strong, solid, fast bowler's action and turned it into a solid off-spinner's action. Took more than 1,000 first-class wickets with it.

Peter Lever

An Ashes winner under Ray Illingworth in the winter of 1970–71, he sent down big swingers and bowled with great heart. The shop steward of the dressing room, our very own Arthur Scargill, he was forever rucking against the committee. He could be feisty on the field too. Born in Todmorden, which is famous for being half in Yorkshire and half in Lancashire, we were never quite sure if he was one of us or one of them. But we were thankful he was one of us on so many occasions, such was his impact with the new ball, particularly in one-dayers.

Ken Shuttleworth

Another who won away against the Aussies with Ray. He possessed a pure action, very similar to Fred Trueman and was a big specimen of a lad. I will never forget when he arrived at the club for a second XI trial. He was playing for St Helens Recreational. It was a match at Old Trafford. He acted just as he did for the Recs at the weekend: he took his teeth out and gave them to the umpire, along with his comb. At the end of the over, he put his falsies back in and combed his hair on the way back to third man.

Peter Lee

Known to us as 'Leapy' – after the pop singer - he would bowl all day for you and I mean all day, literally. If you took him off after 10 overs he would just sulk. 'I'm just getting going,' he would argue.

He wasn't quick but he possessed a nasty bouncer. He was one of those bowlers – and I would liken him to Glen Chapple in this regard – who would make the most of the conditions. If there was anything in the pitch whatsoever, he would find it. Derek Underwood was his spin-bowling equivalent.

I met up with Leapy quite recently too – along with Clive and Flat Jack – when Lancashire paid tribute to their former players who played at international level with honours boards in the new stand at Old Trafford.

The Shithouse Serenaders

Being a part of this Lancashire group was like rounding up your mates from down the local, dressing them in whites and transporting them onto a cricket field somewhere else around the country. Away games used to follow a familiar pattern in the sixties and seventies. Typically, a County Championship match would begin on a Saturday, there would be no play on a Sunday, and then the match would resume on Monday and finish on a Tuesday. This scheduling fitted in perfectly with our 'Saturday night is Saturday night' manifesto, allowing us a social gathering at the best boozer in whichever city we were in for the weekend.

Of course, lads being lads, there would occasionally be scrapes, although seldom directly alcohol-related. Take, for example, one trek to Hove to play Sussex. Down on the promenade was a roller-skating rink and so we decided to head down en masse. I used to love roller-skating. Had my own skates with bearings that would go like the clappers. I could go backwards, spin round, change direction all at full tilt, with my hands tucked behind my back, like a Franz Klammer on wheels. I thought I was world champion standard and Ken Shuttleworth was another with Olympic ambitions.

Of course, while we were a couple of show-offs, not everyone was as proficient. Take Geoff Pullar, the England opening batsman. To see his lack of dexterity on a rink like this, he looked nothing like an international sportsman, much more like a human Bambi. Anyhow, me and Shut were hurtling around just as Geoff was attempting his first tentative yards. He was a big obstacle to get around and Shut hit him straight up the arse, shot him into the air and plunged him awkwardly into a heap. The end result? A broken wrist for 'Noddy' – so dubbed because he had a red Triumph TR3 like the one Enid Blyton's character drove around Toytown – plus an inquest from the committee at Old Trafford as to what had gone on. They were not best pleased.

There were other hidden talents among our troupe. For example, John Savage, the off-spinner who joined us from Leicestershire, played the trombone. And he would get an urge to play it whenever he had a skinful.

One such evening was after one of the monthly amateur boxing events we used to get invited to in central Manchester. These fine-dining occasions would see one Lancashire player asked to sit on different businessmen's tables. All the big players in Manchester would be at these Sporting Club occasions – including Jimmy the Weed and his Quality Street Gang, the

39

top brass from the police force, and board members from Manchester City Football Club such as Peter Swales, Freddie Pye and Ian Niven.

As I had to go past Sav's house on the outskirts of Bury to get back to Accrington, I would drive and drop him off, allowing him to have a drink. As I did so, he announced: 'Just wait there, lad, and I will play you a tune.' Next thing, he staggers back out of his house and true to his word, starts tooting on his instrument.

'All right?' I asked him next day.

'Not really,' he said. 'The trombone came out last night, didn't it?'

'Yes, and I thought it was marvellous,' I told him. 'Not sure that was an opinion shared by your neighbours, though. They were leaning out of their windows, telling you where they would like to stick it!'

We were quite a musical lot, and would spend time in the dressing room mimicking brass instruments with our mouths. We were the red rose equivalent of the Brighouse and Rastrick Brass Band, and always fancied ourselves to strike up quite a tune, dubbing ourselves the Shithouse Serenaders – as the acoustics in the toilets were much better. During rain breaks that is where you would find us, and the members would debate whether the club had got entertainment in post-match? 'No, it's just those idiots again!'

Cricketers of my era tended to have party pieces they would save for the bar on away trips. Brian Close, of Yorkshire, was notorious for a couple, one of which involved downing a pint in about two seconds flat. The other, drawing a line and taking a beer bottle in each hand. Then challenge an opponent to lean forward and place the bottles upright as far away from the line as possible without either placing a foot over the line or allowing a knee to touch the floor. He would walk out on his hands, stretch out, then walk back. He had such a long reach I am not sure anyone ever beat him.

But he did come off second best on a tour of South Africa in the mid-seventies when a young local player showed off an ability to cleanly hurdle the bar and land feet first behind the counter without moving. It was a bit like the footballer Duncan McKenzie's trick of leaping over a mini and landing perfectly.

'I can do that,' Closey said, after this chap wowed his audience.

He did, too, although his flailing hands cleaned up the entire range of optics.

He wasn't the only English cricketer to come off second best at the hands of a South African. Peter Swart, who played as the professional at Accrington and turned out for Lancashire's second XI, used to hold a block of ice between his thumb and forefinger for 10 minutes, resulting in them turning completely numb, and would then light a cigarette and allow it to burn against his skin until only a stub end remained.

The crucial part of this trick, of course, was the extensive ice treatment – although our hard-nut wicketkeeper Keith Goodwin didn't seem to think so. In taking on Swart at his own game, he went straight for the fag and created the biggest blister imaginable. It swelled and crackled as the grimace on his face grew and sweat cascaded off his brow. He defied the pain, but lost out overall – the damage to his hand rendered him unable to keep wicket the next day.

Goody loved playing up to his tough-guy image and another of his hilarious performances came on a jaunt to the south coast to face Hampshire at Portsmouth's United Services ground. We were out for a team curry and the gauntlet was thrown down for who could eat the hottest dish. I have always loved a curry, but would go no higher than a madras or a jalfrezi. John Sullivan raised the bar by ordering a vindaloo. Not to be outdone by a team-mate, Goody told the waiter: 'Forget a vindaloo, ignore a tindaloo, I want a zindaloo. Or whatever you call your curry three times hotter than a vindaloo.'

When it was served, it attracted quite an audience as the kitchen staff came out front to witness this act of bravery – or, as we saw it, sheer stupidity. The challenge precluded the drinking of water and Goody was turning redder and redder to a deep shade of purple. Incredibly, he won the day.

Unfortunately, however, he lost something the next morning – the control of his bowels. Travelling in from the hotel to the ground as a passenger with Pilling and Sullivan, he failed to make it from vehicle to dressing room before nature called. That afternoon, a repeat attack saw him flee the field fully decked out in his gloves and pads.

Wicketkeepers, huh. Mad as a box of frogs. And some of the greatest characters that I have come across. None greater than one who awaited on the other side of the Pennines.

CHAPTER THREE

Roses are Red, the Roses was Bluey

Of all the journeys you can make as a professional cricketer with Lancashire and England, the shortest is the spikiest. When it comes to rivalries, it's hard to top the Roses. For Lancastrians, those from Yorkshire are the sworn enemy. That certainly rings true in our household. My wife Diana is from the wrong side of the hills, you see.

The best thing about this kind of rivalry, of course, is that myth and reality are poles apart. It's a love–hate relationship in the nicest sense. Of course, those of the red rose persuasion are trying to get one over on the white, and vice versa. It's how we are brought up. It's always been that way. Sporting fixtures between teams from the two opposing counties across several sports are often played to a backdrop of 'YAAARKSHIRE, YAAARKSHIRE, YAAARKSHIRE' or 'LANCASHIRE-LA-LA-LA, LANCASHIRE-LA-LA-LA'.

Often, from my vantage point above the bowler's arm while covering England matches for Sky, I am reminded by the scintillating batting or bustling behind the stumps from

Jonny Bairstow, one of our country's finest talents, that during my playing days my favourite Yorkshire opponent was his late father, David. Whenever a Roses match took place on their turf, it would be Bluey who was the instigator of our post-match drinks. Once stumps were drawn at Headingley, he would bellow instructions to meet at a local pub, in much the same way he would tell fine leg to move 30 yards to his left or Paul Jarvis to take the next over from the Kirkstall Lane end.

Sometimes it would be the Original Oak just up St Michael's Lane, where we'd gather out the back, around the bowling green, watching an early evening game, having a chat, punters mingling among us. Occasionally he would switch choice of venue to the Three Horseshoes up the Otley Road and we would have a couple of pints and then dive into the famous Bryan's restaurant for fish and chips. Hostilities would resume early the next day, but off the field we always had a great craic.

All the players loved Bluey, the crowd did too, and if you were picking a combined Roses characters XI he would be in it, alongside cast-iron selections Fred Trueman and Geoffrey Boycott. David was a social animal who was just good fun to be around.

With his red hair, occasional volatility and unerring pursuit of success, he stood out among the Yorkshire XIs of the 1970s and 80s, channelling his immense fighting spirit and commitment to his team into some pretty impressive personal statistics. His contribution to Yorkshire's cause could be measured in a bounty surpassing 14,000 first-class runs and 1,099 wicketkeeping victims.

Undoubtedly, there were problems throughout his time at Headingley. There was so much dirty linen being washed in public, and I know all of this unwanted and unnecessary friction for a cricketer made a proud guy like Bluey upset at times. All he wanted was the best for Yorkshire. Divisions within the squad were rife and it is fair to say that a whole host of people didn't fully understand Geoff Boycott. Then again, whoever did?

There seemed to be conflicts about how he went about his cricket. Some swore by him, some cursed him, others cringed at the negative publicity it all brought. But it always seemed, to outsiders like me at least, that it was Bluey who was perennially trying to keep a lid on the internal disputes – it seemed that he was forever looking to protect Boycs.

In 1983, after Boycott was sacked by the club's cricket committee, every Yorkshire player was asked whether or not they were happy with Geoffrey in the team. Bluey said he was, and made the case for the team being better for it when Boycott was in it. Another stalwart, Arnie Sidebottom, said pretty much the same thing, and their voices ensured he was reinstated.

The thing about the charismatic Bairstow senior is that he cared so deeply about everything Yorkshire. Pride oozed from every pore when he had his navy-blue county cap on, hovering somewhere above his flame-covered head. He cared so much.

On the field, he was always the same. He simply never shut up. In comparison to the modern day, though, there was never any nastiness. He was just plain funny. He was the biggest caricature in a Headingley changing room stockpiled with them, and that meant there were wisecracks aplenty, often delivered to his own team-mates. One of his favourite put-downs, delivered with a straight face, was: 'You know three-quarters of seven-eighths of sod all.' Deadpan delivery, no malice.

His humour touched all, and he would provide the running commentary behind the stumps while Arnie Sidebottom – a man with a similarly competitive spirit – was charging in to bowl. In Arnie would rush, ball in hand, trying harder and harder to get the breakthrough as each ball of his spell passed.

Striving for that extra pace, though, meant he would push the front line when landing and therefore test the umpire's patience when it came to no-balls.

Here was another wholehearted Yorkie, a truly great soul, but we, as a team at Lancashire, would get a little bit naughty by involving ourselves in a game within the game. We knew that when Arnie was in one of his feisty spells he would get redder and redder with every ounce of effort. So it was a bit of fun for us rogues to try to turn him rouge.

He always got it through at a decent pace, did Arn, but we knew that you could knock him off kilter by offering up distractions. He was not so effective if you could get inside his head, so one of our tactics was to get the non-striking batsman to do exactly that. Subtly, one would examine whereabouts he was landing. Ergo, Arnie suddenly became interested in where he was planting his feet and concentrated on them rather than where he was aiming with the ball up the other end. Said batsman would keep redrawing the line, in the way that some umpires like to, shuffling across and making a point of scraping the studs on the bottom of their boots along it. Or removing a bail and using one end to make an indented line as its extension. Basically, anything to gain attention.

The result of this process almost invariably was that Arnie started to release steam from his ears. And in one of these periods when he was getting faster and faster, and more and more inconsistent on his landing, he was prone to slip one or two down the leg-side. This in turn would lead to our Bluey launching himself full length with a grimace on his face, a whirl of pads and gloves. Emerging from the dust, sometimes with the ball clasped between finger and thumb, and at others with him chuntering under his breath as it nestled up against the boundary boards, he would follow up with distinct instructions to the other half of this illustrious double act: 'Chuffin' rotate,

Arnie, rotate.' A gentle reminder to get the angle of the seam in the right position on release.

As well as being a ringleader on those social nights, Bairstow was a competitive bugger. He always loved the battle and a challenge. He was brave, tough and, when Yorkshire v Lancashire matches were in full flow, you could bet that he would be the one batsman from his side looking to take on our West Indies fast bowler Colin Croft whenever the ball was banged in short.

There are certainly flashes of him to be seen in the way Jonny plays. Neither of them was ever going to die wondering when they were out in the middle with a bat in hand. Both of the mind to take the bowlers on. No suggestion of being careful. How to combat the majority of situations? It is counterattack every time.

At number seven, Bluey was never a player to consolidate; he saw his job as pushing the team forward, more often than not in the company of John Hampshire. Jonny has a similar attitude in whatever match he is thrust into, although I am not sure if he should ever be as low as seven, the position in which he struck three of his first five Test hundreds, when it comes to batting for England. He has already proved himself to be a player well served to hold down a much higher position, and someone of his natural talents is wasted that far down, in my opinion.

It might not have been a talent used to any great advantage had some folk had their way when he first broke into the team. There was no question about Jonny's ability in my mind, yet he was pilloried for the going-over he received in the Trent Bridge Test against West Indies in 2012. Even after standing up with two fine innings in defeat to South Africa at Lord's in the final Test of the summer – after Kevin Pietersen was exiled for texting the opposition – there were still those questioning whether he had the credentials to go on to be an international cricketer for years to come.

The bottom line was that he came in against the new ball in Nottingham and received close to the perfect bouncer second ball from Kemar Roach after a pretty decent first delivery. I don't care if it had been an established batsman on 180, he would have struggled. Yes, an adjustment has to be made because Test cricket is tough, and the challenge for all-comers is to iron out any weaknesses and respond to your mistakes once you get to the top. Some people were suggesting he could never make it because of a problem against the short ball. So I was glad he swatted that accusation off to fine leg with his 54 and 95 against the Safas. It showed he had the character. When the England selectors went back to him again in 2014 he was ready; there is plenty more to come from him, and I am sure it will come, because the boy can play.

Some players don't settle in as quickly as others and the nature of their dismissals can influence thinking. But a good team of selectors will look through that. When Hashim Amla started out in Test cricket, they called him a walking wicket. You'd either hit him on the head or his pads – and he didn't much like either. But he then went away and worked hard on his batting, and turned himself into a world-class player. One thing I would always say is that when a career comes to its conclusion you reflect on it from the finishing line not from the mid-point or at the start.

Fred, Boycott

Certainly, the way we were as opposing teams in the seventies and eighties provided a stark contrast to how the sixties Yorkshire lot acted towards us. Now that was an intimidating team. They liked to make you feel as inferior as possible during lunch breaks; waiting for you to be in the room before making their entrance in a line, blazered up, ensuring you could see that huge white rose badge on their chests. That flower might as well have been a boxing glove. They would stare at you as you tucked into your meat and two veg. The best teams have that superiority about them that makes it clear: you're here to get a good hiding.

They were sociable enough after a game but, unlike their successors, I would describe them as no more than politely sociable. Perhaps once during a game we would be invited into the committee room at Headingley to share a drink. Fred Trueman was always top drawer when it came to entertainment. He would always be up for a chat, but it would be story-telling, sharing gags like a stand-up comedian, rather than a full and frank discussion. He was very funny and some of his tales would even be true.

Geoff Boycott was good value too. But not around the bar. He was not one for having a beer, but he would certainly come into his own in the changing room when chatting about batting – much in the same way as he has done in his media role over the past 30 years. In those days, he was still learning about the art of batsmanship himself: like an undergraduate student, bespectacled, a bit of wispy hair and deadly serious on his chosen subject. He has always been a sponge when it came to cricket knowledge.

A group of us would sit with him, listening to what he had to say in the old pavilion at Headingley which, with its balcony, proved a great suntrap on a summer's evening. He was just an emerging, talented batter in that very Yorkshire mould of 'thou shalt not get me out', but even then he knew he was following in the footsteps of Len Hutton, and it was his single-minded approach that served him so well.

Cricket was to be played at his pace, and it was a sign of how successful his modus operandi was that the occasions upon which he threw caution to the wind by playing aggressive shots stand out in the memory. In one Roses match at Bramall Lane, Sheffield, Brian Statham slipped trying to send down a bouncer. As a result, the venomous brute of a ball he had planned was transformed into a gentle long hop. Of course, any delivery, no matter how rank, still needs hitting and to Boycs' credit he didn't just punish it, he hit it clean over one of the stands. It was an incredible blow which, had it come from the flashing blade of Viv Richards or Ian Botham, would not have drawn a flinch. But this was Boycott: a man devoted to the elimination of risk.

He also struck that memorable 146 in the 1965 Gillette Cup final at Lord's. It helped Yorkshire to 317 for four, the kind of total that teams would need two 60-over innings to chase down in those days. And, to put his efforts against Surrey's seam-heavy attack into context, it was compiled on what was a bit of a sticky pitch. Poor weather delayed the start until after midday and conditions suggested survival would have been the order of the day. But Boycott attacked. I hope he doesn't mind me saying: that was a one-off.

Let's face it, he will be remembered for the high price he placed upon his wicket. He was the type of player you would select to bat for your life, and bowlers had to prise him out. Then, even when he was out, he would be reluctant to go. A typical Yorkshireman in that he was very careful in all aspects of his life.

When cricket is such a numbers game it's hard to be critical of someone who produced the numbers he did at the highest level, although his style wasn't necessarily everyone's cup of tea. He is well stocked with *bons mots* whenever the general pace of his innings is brought up. Take his *Test Match Special* colleague Simon Mann's suggestion on a tour of Sri Lanka in 2012 that his batting used to send people to sleep.

'Aye,' Boycs retorted. 'But I were still there when they woke up!'

Like Boycs, Fred Trueman had extraordinary self-belief. It never left him. In subsequent years, when our friendship was transported into the *Test Match Special* box, you could have some fun with him. It only needed a tiny morsel of bait to get this great white shark of a fast bowler on the hook. Recounting past scorecards, if you brought up any match in which the opposition team had 200-odd for two on the board, his staple response would be: 'Well, to get that many, they must have dropped six off me.'

He had such a positive attitude to what he was doing when-ever he ran in to bowl. To him, dismissing the opposition was simple. His plan didn't need much intervention from anyone else. Fred would be good enough to get the openers out every time. Then he would come back and get either numbers six or seven to break a partnership. Then sort the paupers out, as he would say. By that, of course, he meant numbers 10 and 11. When put like that, bagging a five-wicket haul sounds easy, doesn't it? Like falling off a log. People might see this charade as a protective thing, but he was deadly serious, and that is what kept him going and made him so successful.

In contrast to these two white knights, I have to admit this particular wearer of the red rose wilted when it came to Yorkshire v Lancashire fixtures. Don't get me wrong, I loved the occasions. Both home grounds of Old Trafford and Headingley lend themselves to creating hostile atmospheres, and a Roses match is totally different to any other game of cricket I played in.

For a start, when we played these fixtures in the sixties and seventies they drew five-figure crowds. The atmosphere hummed. When you walked in through the gates in the morning you could smell the tradition of the fixture. That was enough to motivate you to perform to your best before you walked out.

These days, folk in the crowd are swilling down the pints, having fun, chatting away, but back in the day there was nobody laughing. Nobby – 10 sheets to the wind on a stag do – wasn't tripping over in the aisle because his all-in-one body stocking had split at the crotch. Lancashire–Yorkshire was a purist's watch. Dead serious stuff. There was no extravagant cheering, no larks and japes. Those in attendance were studious cricket watchers. Yes, there was an us-and-them element to the whole occasion, and they would have immense pride in the team that represented them. But they were here to witness highly competitive cricket.

On the honours boards in the pavilions you saw the names of those who had gone before you, and the marks they had left. The likes of Cyril Washbrook, Len Hutton, Brian Statham, Fred Trueman. Any player worth his salt would have aspirations of getting their own names up there alongside the greats.

The Rose that Wilted

Unfortunately, though, rather than rise to the occasion, I confess I always felt more pressure in these matches. It meant I didn't respond as much as I wanted to. It is one of my career disappointments to reflect that I never scored a Roses hundred.

With the benefit of hindsight, I would say I never recovered from an inauspicious start against a team of cricket's behemoths. One that claimed a hat-trick of Championship pennants between 1966 and 1968. They crushed all-comers and psychologically, in my formative years, I was absolutely petrified playing against them. Unfortunately, I never shook off this inferiority complex and so, when it came to facing up to Yorkshire, I had baggage I was never able to get rid of. When it came to scoring runs I simply never got any.

My best effort was on a spinning pitch which held Ray Illingworth's interest throughout. I got into the 80s and from there you would hope to convert to three figures. To reveal that I was really pleased with what I had mustered tells its own story. It is still all relative, and the caveat for my minimal returns during that period was that Yorkshire were our best opponents as well as our deadly rivals, but I didn't achieve very much in Roses matches.

In contrast, somebody like Michael Atherton revelled whenever he came up against the Yorkshire attack, hitting six hundreds to equal the Lancashire record set by my adopted brother, Clive. Something clearly inspired Athers whenever he came up against the old foes. He simply raised his game to another level. How else can you explain him claiming a five-wicket haul with those filthy leg-spinners of his. That haul came during a drawn match in Leeds in 1990 when his five for 26 forced the home team to follow on.

No, my trips across the Pennines did not bring much personal joy. Apart from the end-of-season ones, destination Scarborough. I never played a Roses match at North Marine Road, but we would participate in a one-day competition called the Tilcon Trophy in late August or early September. It was serious cricket but compared to Championship or the old Gillette or Benson & Hedges knockout cup matches it was a jamboree. The locals always made these occasions a great event, and the kind of atmosphere they created then became the norm for other fixtures held at their picturesque ground on the east coast. I recall one game up there between England and Young England in which the band played all the way through.

In those days, a post-match routine did not feature warm-downs. In fact, for some either side of a quick shower it was a warm-up. Towards the end of a day's play, the 12th man would be tasked with putting together a drinks list. And Scarborough was the kind of ground where even those who might not have an alcoholic drink elsewhere on the circuit might imbibe. There would always be a bottle of Double Diamond, a bottle of pale ale, a bottle of Mackeson's stout, some Watneys Red Barrel and a pint or two of Tetley's when the tray was delivered to the away dressing room.

Most of the guys would look for a social drink, the chance to close the working day with half an hour of winding down, just like those finishing a shift in a factory would, and for the majority that would include a beer. It was a part of the recreational game that survived despite the players in question moving into the professional ranks. Of course, this migration into the paid elite also influenced thinking on preparation and so, in addition to fancier alcoholic tipples over the years, we saw some players trying to drink things that were good for the body. Some therefore would ask for milk, knowing a pint of it would be good for the bones. Others might not go for the dairy option but, recognising that booze should be limited, they would turn to glasses of lime and lemonade.

More recently, they have moved on to lots of things ending in -ade: Gatorade, Powerade, Hearing Aid and Legal Aid. Some are after any aid they can get. But this is all a relatively recent phenomenon. Even as recently as the 1990s, when I was coach at Lancashire, the practice of taking the drinks order was part of a daily ritual. And certain players weren't daft in ordering their bottle. Take Ian Austin, for example. Oscar, as we called him, upgraded to a bottle of Chardonnay, and would get through it no messing without help from his friends.

Neither would supping alcohol affect his performances. Or perhaps I should rephrase that, before the nutritionists and strength and conditioning coaches take umbrage about the effects of it on performance. Let's just say that in an era when the majority drank, he supped more than most, and performed better than most. He had serious skill as a seam bowler and was one of the most productive tail-enders of his generation. In fact, when I was England coach, as we built towards the 1999 World Cup, I carried out a straw poll of the leading opening batsmen in the country to discover the opening bowler they found trickiest to combat in one-day cricket, and the name most prominent in the compilation? Ian Austin.

The Dreaded K-Word

Relationships between Yorkshire and Lancashire players would become strained at times, without a doubt, but I am not sure they ever broke down; it was always just a fiercely competitive rivalry. When I moved to the back end of my playing days and into umpiring, there were lads like Kevin Sharp, Martyn Moxon and Ashley Metcalfe in the Yorkshire team, all pleasant enough but competitive and ambitious. Same on the other side, with Graeme Fowler, Neil Fairbrother and Warren Hegg. Both sides just wanted to win.

I am absolutely certain the traditions have continued, and there has always been a conscious effort to found the rivalry on traditional core values. The old enemy trek across the M62 for battle and you try to give them one, but it is based on competitive edge not hatred. That's not to say that it is a fixture without tension. Far from it. The very essence of the rivalry means people become passionate about the subject, and that means the occasional flare-up. For example, it wasn't a very popular decision when David Byas moved across the Pennines to Old Trafford after captaining Yorkshire for several years.

And there will always be the odd on-field flashpoint. I remember not so long ago, towards the back end of the 2014 season and his own playing career, Andrew Gale having a stiff difference of opinion with Ashwell Prince. The episode concluded with Gale being banned for multiple matches and he was therefore unable to lift the Championship trophy when the pennant was clinched at Trent Bridge.

The problem was the Yorkshire captain's choice of language. There was a suggestion that Gale used the c-word, which he strongly denied. No matter. For it was the K-word that got him into strife. In telling him to go back to his own country, as a Kolpak cricketer, Gale's verbal abuse was deemed to have racist context. I would see all this as no more than a fired-up bloke within touching distance of a first major trophy getting frustrated by being held up in the pursuit of glory by the deadly rivals.

Historically, the choice words have come from within. For example, this fixture used to carry huge pressure emanating from the committee room. Neither side wanted to give an inch in Roses cricket. It is arguably why there were so many draws during the seventies. And the expectation levels remained high as we moved into the second decade of the 21st century, and not just for this particular fixture. Colin Graves, the Yorkshire chairman, certainly brought a smile to my face when talking about the club's relegation: 'Our players say they couldn't get results at Headingley,' he said. 'Well, the opposition didn't seem to have too many problems . . .'

He has always told it as it is, has Colin. Yorkshiremen tend to be like that, don't they? He threatened to sack all the players after providing them with everything they'd asked for. Then appointed a new captain and hired a new coach in Gale and Jason Gillespie.

Put your hand in your pocket like that and you want to see some reward for it, I suppose. Having lived part-time in North Yorkshire for the past decade I have become accustomed to the way of life, and learned that most Yorkshire-speak revolves around cost. Such as: 'I'll tell you summat for nowt.' Or the classic: 'How much??'

They value things in Yorkshire, and I value things that they have produced such as the Bairstows, Trueman and Joe Root. They have provided English cricket with some fabulous talent. At times you feel like you can't live with 'em. At others, you can't live without 'em.

CHAPTER FOUR

Grounds

I love my job and I love travelling. That's fortunate really, I guess, because even when I am at home I can technically be away. The life of a commentator with Sky Sports replicates that of a county professional. You live your life out of suitcases, from hotel to hotel, media centre to media centre, and pub to pub.

It means spending a few weeks every summer reacquainting yourself, or even learning new things, about the grounds and surroundings of our own international venues. Each has its little attractions, its idiosyncrasies and hidden treasures. Some possess features that get on my wick too, but in the main there is fun to be had, so whenever you're stopping by, feel free to use the Bumble guide to English cricket:

Old Trafford

Bit of local bias here but I am so fond of this ground. You could have flipped it upside down as well as turned it the other way on and I would have still had a soft spot for it. For a while the redevelopment was held up by a court battle with a rival development company that failed with its claim that the local council had applied double standards in the planning process.

There were fears that once the square was turned round it wouldn't regain its old zip, but although we got slow pitches during the first 12 months, as it bedded in, it was back to full working order in time for the 2013 Ashes. It featured everything you could wish for: pace, bounce, batsmen scoring hundreds and turn.

Old Trafford has always been a great venue with a great pitch – and it's staged some memorable matches. Snapshots are etched in Test cricket's fabric: Richie Benaud going round the wicket to instigate a win for his never-say-die Australians of 1961; Bobby Simpson's triple hundred in 1964; Shane Warne's ball of the century in 1993 which unfathomably spun more than the width of Mike Gatting. It's a rich list, and in keeping a quality playing area there will be further entries – of that I have no doubt.

The realignment has meant the old pavilion is no longer in use as it was, with the new dressing rooms and media complex now housed in the new stands opposite. When the pavilion was side-on to the play, they used to have the Pit of Hate, where spectators used to bawl at the opposition and umpires. They should be more refined now they're behind the bowler's arm. And less vociferous than the heyday gang from my playing days.

I remember one chap called Ken Dean. We called him 'Bullet Head' on account of the size of his noggin. He used to shout words of encouragement to batsmen like: 'You'll never die of a stroke!' Or: 'Better to be a lucky one than a good one.' It never got nasty. But, by 'eck, Ken and Co. let you know if you'd not played well.

Not sure what the POH crew would make of the 21st-century reworking of their old haunt, with its new Point conference centre and Hilton Garden hotel. The club seemed to like the red letterbox look so much they posted two. But that's the modern way for cricket: you have to maximise your earning capacity and bring people onto the site who won't necessarily come for cricket.

At 25,000 capacity, England matches produce great revenue, but Old Trafford is a perfect example of combining cricket with a commercial enterprise. During the summer of 2016, there were two major pop concerts – Beyoncé and Rihanna – where the whole ground was taken over. It was during monsoon weather, but luckily Rihanna (she was in the same class as Chris Jordan at school, you know) brought her umbrella with her. Boom, boom.

All joking aside, though, the problem with such ventures is that shows like this have to take place in the summer and even in the driest spell possible the outfield suffers for having folk trampling all over it. In this instance, the ground staff worked day and night to get things back to normal for the Test against Pakistan. Similarly, in 2017, when Ariana Grande and Radiohead played before the South Africans provided the opposition. It was not great on either occasion, but the club made plenty of brass from the 2016 gigs, then did their bit for the city with its post-Manchester Arena attack benefit show. There was some scarring left on the outfield, but the Tests passed without too many problems.

As a local man, everyone tends to ask me where to go in Manchester when the mics are put down. Look no further than three old favourites shoulder to shoulder on Portland Street: the Grey Horse, Circus Tavern and Old Monkey. Further afield, there's nothing better than Marble Arch on Rochdale Road. If live music's your bag, there's the Band on the Wall. And if you like laughing, go to the Comedy Club, or the Illusion Club. It's magic!

But because it's a home fixture for me, while my chums and

colleagues are out and about, I tend to be stuck at home. Getting a pass-out from Vipers is not easy in weeks like these.

Headingley

What a culture shock if you arrive in Leeds straight from Lord's. To be honest, though, I tend to stay up at Harrogate. Which for the uninitiated is posh Yorkshire. There are designer shops, Bettys tea rooms and a district called Montpellier. Nothing in the town, though, compares to two fabulous pubs. The Old Bell Tavern has more real ale than you can shake a stick at, while Hales Bar is the only gas-lit pub in the UK.

When you get to the ground, there is no bubbly on show like in St John's Wood. No, the drink of choice in the media centre at Headingley is Bovril. It goes down well, as sub-zero temperatures are standard for its Test matches.

Not that the locals are right bothered about what they drink. It all goes down the same plughole as far as they're concerned and it can all get a bit fruity on the Western Terrace. To be fair, the club have cleaned it up a bit. It used to be mayhem over that side of the ground. Who can forget the pantomime horse that invaded the pitch during our nail-biting win over South Africa in 1998, when I was coach and had a shoulder dislocated by a burly security guard?

If you want to get into the spirit of things and ensure the best possible start to your week, there's the fabulous Ugly Mugs cafe just outside the ground on St Michael's Lane, where you can get a full English and a pot of brew for a fiver! It does the best egg and bacon barm cake (with brown) in this corner of the county, which is ideally washed down by a pint – of Yorkshire Tea. It ceased trading for a while but has recently had a second wind. You can't keep a good thing down, you see.

Trent Bridge

Trent Bridge is lovely, one of those grounds where you feel at home and very content with life. It's more of a stately ground than a stadium. It reminds me of Woburn for its tranquil hum and sense of occasion. It's got its own atmosphere, will be less raucous than its Midlands rival Edgbaston, yet the supporters will still be right behind England. It's a bit smaller, at 18,000 capacity, but that makes it a bit more intimate.

Traditionally, the ball has swung here but the locals reckon it hasn't swung as much since they built the new stands. I think it's all a load of balls – the balls are what it's to do with rather than the atmosphere, in my opinion. Some batches swing and some don't. It's the luck of the draw, I reckon.

Mind you, when I was on the circuit as a player with Lancashire, it's safe to say us batsmen did not look forward to a trip to Trent Bridge. The groundsman, Ron Allsopp, used to say he liked his pitches to be 'interesting', which basically meant he used to leave a load of grass on it for Clive Rice and Richard Hadlee to wreak havoc. The thing was, it used to turn for Eddie Hemmings, too, so even if you escaped the perils of the new ball it was tough.

Pitches are different now, with something generally in it for everyone, meaning that things tend to happen quickly in Nottingham – so if a batsman gets in, the scoring rate rockets, and if a bowler gets on a streak then a team can be shot out for next to nothing.

Allsopp's successor Steve Birks has done a good job when it has come to producing surfaces to promote exciting matches, although the only way was up after 2014. Anything would have been an improvement on the effort in the Test against India, which was just unbelievably slow and low. There was no base to the pitch, but Steve is a terrific bloke and he came right out and apologised for what he had produced. And we have witnessed some crackerjack action since – like England's first ever successful chase of 350 in a one-day international, versus New Zealand, and Stuart Broad's ransacking of Australia in the 2015 Ashes.

It's a ground of rich heritage and its changing face this decade saw the old scoreboard removed and a modern giant electronic screen erected in its place. Must have cost a fortune, that thing, and the fact that they auctioned bits of the original gave the game away. It was at a black-tie dinner during 2013 and one of the Australians, Ed Cowan, who spent some time at the club as overseas player, started bidding down the phone. He wanted the board with 'AUSTRALIA' on and paid £300 for the privilege as sole bidder. If only he'd waited until the end of the night, he could have retrieved it from the skip out the back.

All the refurbishments have been carried out with a touch of class, but one area of the ground does make me chuckle. Cricket clubs tend to honour their high-class players and Nottinghamshire are no different in recognising two of their own greatest, albeit cricketers from further afield, in Sir Garfield Sobers and Sir Richard Hadlee.

However, while round the world stands are dedicated to the top-notch performers – these days Jimmy Anderson runs in to bowl from his own end at Old Trafford, for example, and Marcus Trescothick doesn't so much show the bowlers the maker's name as slam them into seating emblazoned with his own name at Taunton – the powers that be at Trent Bridge have been groundbreaking in their service awards.

In two dungeon-like enclosures in the Radcliffe Road Stand, with a couple of IKEA chairs, is the Sobers waiting area and the Hadlee waiting area. Can only think that the broom cupboards behind the bar area in the pavilion had already been bagged by Harold Larwood and Derek Randall.

It was almost as strange a decision as to ban the Barmy Army's Billy the Trumpet from attending with said instrument. Fancy dress is permitted, so you tend to get bands of Robin Hoods chasing Maid Marians all over the aisles during the final session of play, but no tootin' Billy? Bit harsh that. A comb and tissue paper just doesn't sound the same, unfortunately.

You get some real outlaws out and about in Nottingham after play and it's a city that offers a cracking night out. I like to spend a bit of time at the Lincolnshire Poacher and the Castle, and a visit to Ye Olde Trip to Jerusalem is always worth it. Then, of course, there's Ye Olde Salutation Inn up Maid Marian Way, which is said to date back to 1240. And if you are into throwbacks when it comes to music, a little pub called the Dragon is a gem, serving decent beer as the resident DJ plays the likes of the Clash, the Fall and the Jam on vinyl.

But don't drink too much as there will be no room left for this city's fantastic cuisine – because, if you were not aware, Nottingham is the curry capital of the English cricket circuit. Head to Maid Marian Way and take part in the original Grand Slam of Naan – a curry every night for five nights in five different establishments.

First on my list of curry houses on that stretch is Cumin, which does a mean lamb jalfrezi. It sets the standard for the others to match. If you want it posh, go to MemSaab, and if you want value for money head down the road to Chutney. There used to be one right over the road from Trent Bridge called Slumdog. You could pop in there and indulge in cricket chat with the owner: Usman Afzaal, formerly of Nottinghamshire and England. But trust me on this, when it comes to the GSN in Nottingham, Laguna is the best.

Lord's

This place is just different to anywhere else in the world. The Lord's pitch is unique for a start, with its eight-foot slope down to the Tavern Stand. Players new to playing here find it difficult, because you feel like you're being pushed down the hill. The groundsman, Mick Hunt, seemed to run the operation. He always knew everything that was going on, and so he should because he has literally lived in the shed at the nursery end for 50 years. He was so respected for his pitch preparation that no one would dare ask him to prepare it in a certain way, perhaps to help seam or spin. You'd get what you were given.

The slope has thrown plenty of people over the years. It's simply not a level playing field and, as we saw in 2009 with Mitchell Johnson, you have to get used to it and get used to it quickly or risk the game running away from you. Historically, Australia tended to cope pretty well with the challenges it presents. Until that particular match, they had not lost a Test there for 75 years.

For other visiting teams, the grandeur can be inspirational. The dressing rooms are fantastic. People pay just to come and sit in them. The lovely balconies, which the players crowd onto during matches, are very special, and then there's the honours board, which everyone wants to get their name on. And the smell of the place. Nostalgia fills the nostrils.

It demands respect when you turn up, as I did in my England blazer for my Test debut back in 1974. Even then the meals were a veritable feast (no wonder Mike Gatting was so content at Middlesex). There were even bottles of beer available during the 40-minute break for lunch. I had a pint of lager and, unsurprisingly, I was dismissed shortly after lunch four runs short of a 50. I never did get that elusive hundred at headquarters. It's the lunches, you see.

The Lord's dressing rooms are totally unchanged from how they were 44 summers ago, too. You've got these lovely sofas, the honours boards and a huge table in the middle of each room. It's a special feeling for players to be sitting where all the greats of the game have sat over the years. Then there's the little balconies where there's only room for about five people, so most of you are peering at the game from the inside. It's almost a time warp.

Few get to experience the splendour first-hand, of course, and the famous Long Room has remained off limits for all but members of the MCC. Even filming inside it was restricted in days gone by, so it was wonderful when Sky Sports were given privileged access in 2017 to be able to share television pictures of it, to actually bring the viewer right into the action and help them imagine what it must be like to be walking out to represent your country amid all that tradition and pageantry. That moment has featured in so many dreams, and it's fair to say it's one occasion when all us ex-players wished that time stood still and we could be out there again.

Being involved at Lord's in just about anything feels like a real honour and bell-ringing, or campanology to the more educated among us (I am talking to you here), is quite an event. It happens every morning to provide a five-minute warning that play is about to start, and they even let me loose on it for South Africa's visit one year.

Shaun Pollock had also been asked to do it that week so he was very excited. But the way it worked out it looked like he was going to miss the chance of fulfilling his lifetime ambition. Every morning he seemed to be shunted down the queue by someone or other. First Yohan Blake, the Olympic sprinter from Jamaica, rocked up, then another Olympian, the British shooter Peter Wilson, took the honour on the second morning. Wouldn't have been a good idea to argue with a bloke like him. Then yours truly was asked ahead of day three.

When Polly got the gig 24 hours later, I could only imagine that the British musical chairs champion Basildon Farg wasn't available. He couldn't stop smiling: he's clearly a man who enjoys the sense of ceremony. It was all rather a contrast to another former international captain's response. When it was the turn of Steve Waugh, the legendary Australian, his expression barely altered. In fact, rumour had it that he sledged the bell! It would have been something along the lines of: 'You're not good enough to be here! How come they've picked you? Is there no one else? You're not even the best bell in your family.'

You have to see and be seen at Lord's. It's quite formal in one respect because you have to behave yourselves. There's a buzz, a hubbub, rather than real noise. If Cardiff and Birmingham are rock and roll then Lord's is opera. It oozes class. The Grace Gates, the Compton and Edrich Stands. I love it.

As do bundles of other folk. When I am at a match down there I tend to stay in the hotel across the road and you can bet, whatever time you choose to get up, that upon opening the curtains on the first morning of a Lord's Test, you will be confronted by MCC members queuing all the way up to St John's Wood tube station. And some of them will have been there since five in the morning!

I'm always intrigued as to what happens when someone needs the toilet in that situation. The trick would be to walk straight to the front of the queue at five to nine and say: 'Thanks for keeping my place, Percy!' I have been egging on a few of my mates from Manchester to try this one year. Trouble is, the accent and lack of egg and bacon tie would blow their cover.

They can see northerners coming a mile off down in the Smoke. For example, I had a Friday-night jaunt in Hampstead one year, and met a couple of likely lads who'd clocked my 'Circus Tavern Manchester' T-shirt. Turned out they were hairdressers. Now, up in Cheadle Hulme, Sir Alex Ferguson and I pay the pensioner's rate of £8 for a trim. These two were offering their services for a cool £91. 'A snip,' I reckoned, and passed on the business card to a bloke called Nasser.

You know your clientele have got a bob or two when stewards are removing champagne corks from the outfield just after the start of play, rather than just after the close, and there is a high proportion of red trouser sightings. But there are some lovely little secrets around Lord's too, at more affordable prices.

Round the back of the ground is Abbey Road, as in the place the Beatles made famous, while further along is Clifton Hill. Hidden down there, cunningly disguised as a terraced house, is a pub called the Clifton. It's a great little place, and it's within comfortable walking distance of the ground. Then there's the Star, just off St John's Wood High Street, a six-hit from Lord's. I used to drink there with a rather posh actor by the name of Ronald Fraser. He was very upper class, so I'm not sure what he was doing in a proper London boozer like the Star.

A group of us, including Ian Ward, Michael Atherton and a producer called Mark Lynch, are always looking to expand our extra-curricular activities in this part of the capital and have now discovered Hampstead. I can recommend a couple of lovely pubs there, too, the Greyhound and the Flask, stopping off for a couple of snifters before moving up to Primrose Hill and popping into the Queen's Head, a great Young's pub.

When working with Channel Nine, my Australian colleagues stay in Covent Garden, so I like to take them out in the Ho. That's Soho, if you're not down with the kids. One weekend in 2017 we branched out the other way and finished up in Notting Hill, where I bumped into football manager Alex McLeish, who regaled me with cricket stories about none other than Alex Ferguson.

Apparently, Fergie once organised a match at Gordonstoun involving the Aberdeen players and insisted on opening the batting. One of the reserve players demolished his stumps in the first over, so Fergie put them back together, and insisted the laws stated you can't be out in the first over! Rather reminded me of WG Grace's insistence that 'they've come to see me bat, not you bowl' as he replaced the bails.

Grace was an amateur, of course, yet made a handsome sum from his playing activities. That world of gentlemen and players seems an age ago, but I was reminded of the fact it was one I frequented at the start of my career during a trip down Lord's recently. I was having a nice little tipple one Thursday night in the Lamb and Flag in Covent Garden, when I was asked for one of those infernal selfies by a pair of ladies. It transpired they were the daughters of Ian Bedford, the last amateur captain of Middlesex in 1961! Selfies tend to go down with me like a cup of cold sick, but I was happy to oblige on this occasion for posterity's sake. When I first joined the playing staff at Lancashire, Old Trafford still housed separate dressing rooms for amateurs and professionals, and teams would enter the field of play from two different gates.

I've always been a spit-and-sawdust kind of bloke and so, other than if Athers is with us – and signs us into the Groucho Club – it's into Soho for a livener in the French House, then a nip round to the Coach and Horses, followed by a flit to Gopal's for an Indian and back in the hotel for 11pm. I'm a creature of habit.

Thankfully I am not a cake lover. And no longer work for *Test Match Special* as I would be the size of a house during weeks at Lord's. Keen *TMS* listeners will be aware of the large number of home-baked delights that get sent to their commentary box on a weekly basis. Lord's seems to be their favourite destination. No such tradition exists at Sky, but just in case you are feeling sympathy at this juncture, could I reiterate that I am not so much of a cake man. Pork pies? That's another matter.

Occasionally, though, something does turn up to cause a stir. An intriguing package arrived one year in the form of a beautifully framed, crocheted portrait of one Andrew Strauss, looking anything but a cricketer. The former England captain, spending a couple of years with us on the Sky Sports commentary team before taking over the top job with the ECB, was virtually unrecognisable. My first thought was that it was meant to be a Russian astronaut or a Metropolitan Police photo-fit of Mr Big! I'm sure Mrs Strauss found the perfect place for it – perhaps above the fireplace to scare the kids away.

It's amazing what you get sent through the post in this job and I opened an envelope last year stuffed with £50 notes. 'Kerching!' I thought. Alas, though, as on closer inspection it became apparent they had my face on them instead of the Queen's. Rumour has it they might be made legal tender in Accrington.

The Oval

Synonymous with gas holders is this place. As it's t'other side of Vauxhall Bridge, if you like a walk there's all sorts you can see along the Embankment, such as the London Eye and the Houses of Parliament. And you can buy a flat that's a snip at around £2 million. MI6 headquarters are down there too – but don't tell anybody.

I stumbled across a place called Chelsea one year on a River Thames foray. Flower shows and Russian roubles, isn't it? There seemed to be lots of four-wheel-drive tractors driven by very petite ladies. I was standing outside the Pig's Ear one night watching a lady spend 25 minutes trying to reverse-parallel park one of the monsters. Gave her a round of applause at the end of it all. She weren't impressed.

I had to send a pint back in the local, though. All that cash sloshing about and they can't even serve a decent pint. I told the barman it was off and he said, 'It tastes all right to me,' before reluctantly accepting that a customer ought to be satisfied with the product and poured another. If it had been any flatter they would have to serve it in an envelope. Get your sparkler working, capital boozers.

You won't find such trouble in the Fentiman Arms, round the back of the ground behind Archbishop Tenison's School. It's a cracking place, but it can get packed on match days and there's a high quota of red strides in here too. If you want somewhere a bit different, head for Waterloo, where you'll find the Windmill on the Cut. But things have never been the same since the Queen Anne closed down. It was painted a vivid orange and there were no windows. Now it's a tea room, naturally.

Sadly, my top curry spot for Oval matches is also a thing of the past. It was all in the name, to be honest. Across Vauxhall Bridge and into Pimlico was the Top Curry Centre. Now that was a proprietor not lacking confidence. The fact that it had a huge picture of Lady Diana in the window was worth the trip alone. She happened to be passing the joint when the paparazzi appeared, and the photo took pride of place in the restaurant.

Surrey are also the most progressive club when it comes to sustainability issues. Last year, I got involved with their Ocean Rescue initiative – basically, there's too much plastic knocking about on this earth of ours and no way of disposing of it, so I helped spread the message by dishing out reusable and biodegradable bottles. Oval punters could then help themselves at water stations around the ground if they got thirsty, although one clever gentleman was seen behind the Bedser Stand filling his up with gin.

Have your wits about you with The Oval, though, because from my experience there always seems to be an obstacle either on the way in or on the way out of the ground. One year I got near the Chelsea Bridge, where I was staying, to discover a right old commotion. Traffic was stopped, the police were in attendance and cyclists dismounted. What could have caused all this mayhem? None other than a juvenile royal python curled up on the pavement. I can never understand people running towards these things. Shouldn't you be going the other way?

It is chaos too when they shut the roads and bridges for Ride London. The England team travel on the tube in such circumstances, as, surprisingly, does David Gower. I was shocked to learn he knew what an Oyster card was. Roughing it with oiks on the Underground, how Lord Gower's standards have slipped.

Edgbaston

There is nothing quite like a Brummie-filled Bullring cheering on their matadors. England get fantastic support here, particularly against Australia – just ask David Warner.

They have never let him forget the Joe Root incident in Birmingham's Walkabout bar back in 2013, taking every opportunity to goad him. There is always a terrific atmosphere, not least from the Eric Hollies Stand, and they love to poke a bit of fun at the Aussies, stretching back to 1985 when Jeff Thomson snapped and flicked the V-sign in response. Aaron Finch also got a bit hot under the collar with the attention they gave to his boundary fielding during the Champions Trophy match against England in 2017. Play along with them, though, as Justin Langer did in removing his boots and walking about on his knees pretending to be a dwarf, and they are putty in your hands. Suddenly, you have got 4,000 best mates.

The Hollies habitually has a good selection of Elvises. There is the Indian Elvis – Patel Vis – in addition to the One-Legged

Elvis, who has been known to frequent these parts, and sings 'Don't step on my blue suede shoe . . .' And it was all hands to the pump when an overzealous steward confiscated a beach ball during the 2017 Test match between England and South Africa. Superman and Wonder Woman had a go, but in proving that not all heroes wear capes it was Jesus and his disciples, with a little help from the Big Bad Wolf and the Three Little Pigs, who swung the deal.

That lot don't need any topping up post-stumps, but I always like to stretch my legs and I've found a cracking little boozer in Birmingham off the beaten track just behind the Mail Box. It's called the Craven Arms and it's got 11 hand pumps with some interesting craft bottles. My colleague Michael Atherton indulged in one weighing in at 6.5 per cent and for some reason started shouting at everybody. The Wellington has its own scoreboard: they've got about 20 beers on draught, all chalked up with their strength and other vital statistics.

At the bottom of Broad Street, and backing onto the canal, is the Tap and Spile. Beware, though, that as you move into the weekend it's not a place for the faint-hearted. And if you are up for a curry then you've got Shimla Pinks or the Blue Mango, where they boast the celebrated bullet naan, a fiery thing that Nasser invented. If he hasn't got copyright, he really should.

Cardiff

Talking of lively: 'Bore da, sut wyt ti?' I always feel a part of me is going home when we head to Wales because my grandad Arthur was from there. I used to be able to recite that long place name – Llanfairpwllgwyngyllgogerychwyrndrobwllllantysiliogogogoch – but I can't for the life of me remember how to spell it now.

The Welsh capital is one of the newest Test match venues in

Britain and is quite an intimate, quirky place. Although Sophia Gardens has been transformed over the years with the erection of new stands and a brief flirtation with an electricity company, it's nice that one side of the ground has remained undeveloped, so we still have a picturesque view of the trees that line the River Taff.

The people worked damn hard to create a friendly atmosphere when the Ashes first came to Cardiff in 2009, and when the weather is set fair it's a pleasant walk from the city centre through the park. A more unusual mode of transport – a water taxi – is also available at a price. Arriving at a ground by boat was a new one to me, but you know what they say about variety.

As for a snifter or two at stumps? The Cambrian Tap back in town lives up to its good rap from the locals. These craft beers are all the rage and, as Peter Kay once said of garlic bread, 'I've tasted it. It's the future!' Another belting nightspot, tucked in right next to the Millennium Stadium, is the City Arms. I bet that's absolutely rammed on big rugby days. Bags of atmosphere.

PART TWO

The Gospel of Cricket

CHAPTER FIVE

Beware of the Flora and Fauna (and Warner)

I cannot claim to have watched every ball of this one – must have been something good on the telly – but the Ashes started as a box of explosives back in 1882 and has been full of firecrackers ever since.

The match that is considered to be the origin of international sport's greatest rivalry, and the historic forerunner to thousands of us invading Australia every four years, sounds like a ripsnorter. Australia were dismissed for 63 in 80 overs and England roared back with 101 from 71 overs. England were then set 85 to win but could only muster 77, prompting the famous *Sporting Times* obituary and the start of the Ashes legend.

The relationship between Englishmen and Australians is a bit like one between a Yorkie and a Lancastrian, just a bit spikier. We're the same yet completely different. Not much separates us, yet we are poles apart. We can get on famously, then next minute we can't agree on anything.

An episode during the Olympic summer of 2012 encapsulated the love-hate relationship the two countries have. I ended up on one of those boat bars on the Thames while covering one of the London Test matches, and got chatting to a young Australian lady. She proceeded to tell me that Englishmen were boring, and how she preferred Polish blokes. London was dull, she said, and our weather's terrible. I am not sure why she bothered coming – and to think they have the nerve to call us whingeing Poms!

Most of the English adventures in Australia have contained that familiar ending. It's been painful more often than not – particularly so for me personally on my only playing trip in the 1970s, when I was almost neutered by an Exocet from Jeff Thomson – which makes the memories of triumphant winters like 1970-71, 1986-87 and 2010-11 all the more special. What I have come to appreciate during my time in cricket is that even winning down under takes a huge emotional and physical toll.

It was interesting listening to Andrew Strauss talk about the gruelling nature of these five-Test series when he worked alongside us, post-playing career, on the Sky commentary. He basically said it's seven weeks out of your life once the first ball is sent on its way (preferably into the wicketkeeper's gloves rather than the hands of second slip). Nothing else matters. The wife and kids take a back seat, and the outside world is shut off. He said the Ashes is the series that defines you as a cricketer. And there is the mental challenge of coping in foreign climes.

It can be hard for Englishmen in Australia. After all, it's a country that has some of the most poisonous creatures on the planet within its perimeter. And that's just those that seat themselves in the stands. My tips for avoiding further mishaps if you ever tour the place are to avoid going in the bushes (snakes) and the sea (sharks). Oh, and keep an eye out for spiders. They're flipping everywhere.

It is also a land in which I have plenty of friends, like Ian Chappell, Jeff Thomson and Dennis Lillee. When I have been over there with Sky Sports I have regularly worked with Channel Nine, and it always gives them all a good laugh to show reruns of the time I copped one in the you-know-wheres from Thommo. Brings tears to my eyes does that. And tears to their eyes too. Particularly Chappell! He thought it was hilarious!

A Rare Bloom

The series of 2010-11 coincided with a vintage year for England and a time when Australia were on the decline. At that time only South Africa came close to touching Andrew Strauss's team in Test cricket. In my career as a commentator, this was the one England team that has gone to Australia and stood out.

What shone for me was not only their batting and their bowling. Their fielding too was out of sight from what it used to be. They genuinely enjoyed stopping the opposition scoring runs. In the past, discussions around England selection would include lines like, 'He can't field but . . .' That team under the guidance of Andy Flower showed that if anyone couldn't field, they didn't get into the side. Simple as that.

One feature of that 2010-11 vintage was how adept Andy Flower was at distancing himself from the team. He called the captain 'Andrew Strauss' or just 'Strauss', and referred to all players by their surname. It was an old-school respect thing, echoing days between the two world wars, and the players had to refer to each other as 'Mr' at their pre-series boot camp in Bavaria. Once they got through that few days camping in a remote forest, a tour of Australia didn't seem so bad after all.

There was hardly a glimpse of Flower throughout the series and in particular afterwards. He's a very understated kind of guy. And he allowed the players he asked to take responsibility to take the credit. It was the same with David Saker, an Australian who paid his way to England for an interview as bowling coach because he wanted to be part of that set-up. Thing is, Troy Cooley did an equally good job with England's bowlers in 2005, but struggled for immediate success with Australia's once he switched allegiances. It comes down to the ability of the players. Flower and his back-up team understood that, doing everything they could in preparation to try to get them performing at the optimum level – like splitting the bowlers up, sending those playing in the first Test at the Gabba to Queensland early and allowing the reserve attack to play in the final warm-up match against Australia in the completely different climate of Tasmania.

England were just so professional on this trip and it was the one time I have seen the Australian media, normally such parochial tub-thumpers, turn. Newspapers and television stations became hysterical once the Ashes were retained by Strauss's team in spectacular manner in Melbourne. It was as if Australia were the new England. Ricky Ponting was a great captain, head and shoulders above the other players Australia had at the time, but even he was under pressure for his place in a country hungry for a cull.

No one was safe from criticism. Michael Clarke, his long-tipped successor, certainly wasn't overly popular and so when Greg Chappell, the then full-time selector, said Clarke wasn't ready to lead, it probably went down well in some quarters. Then they made him captain in Ponting's injury absence for the final Test, and his permanent successor four months later. It was all a bit of a mess.

In contrast, everything about England was certain and clinical. Alastair Cook was such a strong character, piling up 766 runs at the top of the order. People have said over the years that he's not good to watch. But I always thought he was terrific.

Jonathan Trott, in the crucial anchor position of number three, was a machine; Kevin Pietersen rediscovered his best and, at his best, he was a cut above, a special player. Ian Bell always oozed class and Matt Prior had become the best wicketkeeper-batsman in the world, answering his critics by going away and aiming for the top. Such was the depth, I reckon some of these players' contemporaries, like Ravi Bopara, must have felt they were born at the wrong time.

In James Anderson, they had a bowler who showed he could get under opposing batsmen's skins and get them out too. In tandem with Tim Bresnan and Chris Tremlett, his wonderful bowling complemented the total domination of England's batsmen, whose nine hundreds on that trip were followed by a combined four in the following two Ashes tours.

England had underrated players like Bresnan, who snuck in with 11 wickets in two matches and then followed up with 16 wickets at 16 runs apiece which took the team to number one in the world by the following summer. Australia had overrated players like Shane Watson, a fine all-rounder but no more than a makeshift opener in Test match cricket. He just didn't possess that opener's mentality of 50 being only a start. He looked as if he had spent his whole career on the bowling machine, lunging at straight balls. Unfortunately, you need a bit more than that against the new ball, and Anderson in particular appeared to enjoy aiming at that thick front pad of his.

In the end, a 3-1 scoreline was reflective of the gulf between the teams, but it could have been a closer-run thing. The spectacular storms – thunder and lightning all over the place – in Adelaide shortly after victory was secured reminded me of 1998 when I was in Australia as England coach. We were six down on the final day with plenty needed, and we knew the storm was coming as we could see it on the radar. Sure enough, the heavens opened and there was soon a river running right down the ground and the match was drawn. It was a pity really because, with Angus Fraser and Alan Mullally to come, I fancied our chances of winning . . .

We Were Warne-d

Australia's tactic for beating England held a familiar pattern for two decades – put a total on the board, then throw the ball to a bloke called Shane and ask him to single-wristedly finish things off. No wonder, following England's 2010-11 Ashes win then, that reports emerged of him coming out of retirement specifically for the back-to-back 2013 and 2013-14 Ashes.

Those plans were shelved, however, around December 2012 and Melbourne's Big Bash League derby. A 43-year-old Warne – still holding his own in Twenty20 cricket at this stage in his extended career, I might make clear – was miked up and providing the running commentary on what was coming next, saying things like: 'I'm going to bowl the slider now.'

Problem was, it appeared as though Aaron Finch had an earpiece in 22 yards away because he kept lining him up and depositing him into orbit.

The slider disappeared 12 rows back into the stands. Unperturbed, our blond hero continued. Next ball he said, 'Right, I'm bowling the googly', and that went even further! Ever the showman, he took his cap from the umpire and said: 'Think I'll go and hide now.' At least he retained a sense of humour. His two overs cost 41, and those Ashes comeback plans were on ice.

You could tell why Australia would have wanted him back. They totally dominated Ashes contests while he was around, and spin always plays a major part in the outcome one way or another. Look at how the tables turned when Warne retired and England picked their own world-class spinner in Graeme Swann. One of the intriguing things for me in cricket's modern gadgetry is the spin-revolution counter. Swann used to get 2,400 revolutions a minute. His baggy green oppo Nathan Lyon proved himself a pretty useful rival with 2,300 revs, but the guys Australia turned to in 2010-11– the likes of Xavier Doherty, Michael Beer – were not in that league.

When Swann pulled up stumps himself midway through the following tour, Australia were back in the ascendancy. As a coach, I always preferred it if blokes who didn't want to be around anymore were out of the way as quickly as possible. I also don't buy the argument that Swann deserted a sinking ship on that 5-0 thrashing of a tour. For one thing, the ship had already sunk. It was just a matter of how far it would plunge. For another, it seems to me he was supremely unselfish in going straight away, and not hoping for one last salute from the crowd. These guys who announce they are going to play one more series always seem to struggle with their motivation levels. Swann knew his elbow was cooked and did the right thing. An international team must always be selected on ability and Swann no longer had the ability to spin the ball as he once did.

I'll remember him as England's most exciting spinner since Derek Underwood. The number of times I was on commentary and said: 'And there's another wicket in his first over for Graeme Swann.' He made things happen from the start. That's a priceless knack for any kind of bowler. It means you are regularly bowling at players just arrived at the crease. The fact that he spun it like a top meant he was also quite successful at getting the set batsmen out. You'd see him bowl to the very best Indian batsmen – and they'd struggle.

The lack of back-up meant England ended up with Moeen Ali as Swann's successor. The cupboard was pretty bare at that point in time and so all credit to Moeen for taking his chance. Swann was a good all-round package too – a decent slip fielder and an extremely productive tail-ender, but he was 85 per cent bowler, 15 per cent batsman. In contrast, Moeen was 80 per cent batter, 20 per cent bowler when he was selected, and worked at altering that balance towards 50:50 over time.

But unfortunately on his first trip to Australia he was not able to emulate his world-class performances of just a few months earlier in the summer of 2017, when he claimed 25 wickets and struck telling runs down the order to finish as man of the series in the 3-1 Test win over South Africa. When class batsmen like Hashim Amla and Faf du Plessis were making things look easy in the sunshine, he would come on and prise them out. In contrast, the Australian batsmen milked him.

When England have had a decent spinner against the Australians we have had half a chance. Take my personal favourite memory of success against them. I will never forget the final Test match of 1997 when I was England coach and Phil Tufnell and Andy Caddick bowled us to an extraordinary victory when they needed only 124 to win. Mark Waugh had said that Tuffers couldn't bowl, so it was great to see the Cat come to life. It may not have won us the Ashes but it was a great win, narrowed the margin of defeat to 3-2, and we had a fantastic night down at Chelsea Harbour to toast the success.

He Bowls to the Left, He Bowls to the Right

More often than not, however, it is the overall strength of a bowling attack that will decide a series. It is why I was so confident that England would defeat Australia in the home summer of 2013. Bearing in mind you need 20 wickets to win a Test, the following stats I believed would prove crucial: at that stage

Jimmy Anderson had 307 Test wickets; Graeme Swann, 222; Stuart Broad, 195; and Steven Finn, 88. As for Australia? Peter Siddle, 150; James Pattinson, 40; Nathan Lyon, 76; and Ryan Harris, 47. The winning team had to be the one with the proven track record. It also happened to be the one that was more adapted to English conditions.

Considering the feisty nature of matches between the two countries in the past decade, 2013 was all a bit meek, the tone being set by England's 48-run Champions Trophy defeat of their Ashes foe. I was on commentary with Shane Warne and neither of us could believe how passive the Australians were at that time. They were just so un-Australian.

'I expected this game to set the tone for the rest of the summer,' Warne said. 'I expected a bit of argy-bargy and a really good contest. It was [Australia's] lack of intent that struck me. The very first over from Mitchell Starc looked a bit gentle.'

Ironically, Australia had the firepower but were afraid to use it: in the return series Mitchell Johnson was bowling at 95mph and Ryan Harris wasn't far behind. While England were nowhere near that. Pace can do funny things to the mind – it did to me when I faced Lillee and Thomson in 1974-75.

Mitchell Johnson's preferred line during the 2009 and 2010-11 Ashes had appeared to be about a metre wide of leg stump, but when this enigmatic character got it right he was unplayable, no doubt about that. Like Thommo, there was no thought of worrying about his technique or how he was gripping the ball or whether he was swinging it, when he was in the groove. They just wound Thomson up and watched him go.

Four decades later, Johnson went through a similar process. When he got it wrong, he looked innocuous, as the Barmy Army were only too fond of reminding him with their refrain: 'He bowls to the left, he bowls to the right, that Mitchell Johnson, his bowling is shite.'

But when he got it right? Pure dynamite. A pantomime villain to English supporters, the reaction to him when he walked to the crease at the start of the 2015 series said it all. Johnson was booed on the way for his short visit to the crease just before lunch. That was actually a sign of respect. He is a lovely polite lad, Mitchell, but he was an absolute warrior for his country, a champion fast bowler of his generation, and a captain's dream.

Fast bowling puts an enormous strain on the body, but the thing about Johnson, a man not without his injury problems early in his career, was that he would bowl anytime, any end. I was always impressed that at five o'clock of an evening he would still be steaming in and hurling that leather sphere down at close to his optimum speed and in the most hostile manner. That hurts.

The WACA, What a Cracker

It can also be painful from a batsman's perspective if you happen to be struck a blow from one of these fast nasties, and I played a lead role in the Nutcracker in late 1974. Due to a neck injury I felt myself getting too square on in my stance when I faced up to Jeff Thomson at the WACA, but there was no alternative. It was the only way I could stand and keep my eyes on the ball. Being felled by a delivery that smashed my protective pink box was only marginally less humiliating than having to go and buy a new one, with the female sales assistant asking me what size I was after: large, medium, or small. How do you answer that?

Sadly, we have already witnessed the last Ashes Test staged at the WACA, and it's a great shame because it's a super venue, steeped in history and great stories. I've dined out on mine, and had blokes cringing over their coffees for more than 40 years.

One of the things I've always enjoyed about the place is that you can walk to and from the ground. At the end of a day's play, you can fall into step with the fans and hear all about their views on the cricket. It felt like part of the community.

But it was also inhospitable to visiting teams. Even the acronym WACA has a chilling connotation, with its faint promise of violence. At the start of every Ashes series there is talk of 'Fortress Gabba', and an unbeaten record against all-comers stretching back to 1988, but it has been in Perth that England's Ashes hopes have often foundered.

In 14 Tests there, England's solitary victory came in 1978-79, a series lost to the memory banks due to the absence of Australia's best players to Kerry Packer's World Series Cricket. When Joe Root's team relinquished the Ashes in December 2017, it was England's eighth consecutive defeat on the west coast. Even in 2010-11, when Andrew Strauss's side won three games by an innings, they left the WACA defeated after running into a hot Mitchell Johnson.

So what are the factors that have made Australia so dominant? Those old bedfellows pace and bounce. When they get together they are enough to psych out the best batsmen. I don't care what anyone says, no one likes facing the kind of chin music that has been Western Australia's tune. I got away lightly compared to Alex Tudor, who damaged an eye after ducking into a bouncer sent down by a Fremantle Doctor-propelled Brett Lee in 2002-03.

But the characteristics of the pitch also make it a ground for strokeplay if you can get yourself in. For example, four years later, England arrived at the WACA already two-fifths of the way through what would become the first Ashes whitewash for 86 years and were only 29 runs behind on first innings. Enter Adam Gilchrist, who thrashed a hundred in 57 balls, the second fastest in Test history at that time, to leave England needing a notional 557 runs for victory. The urn was back in Australian possession in a flash. It was here that George Bailey took 28 runs off one James Anderson over in the other 5-0 home win, in 2013-14. To see the premier bowler in Anderson being taken apart just before the Australian declaration would have hurt the team enormously. In contrast, even when English batsmen have flourished in Perth, such as Ben Stokes and Dawid Malan with their maiden Test hundreds, or Jonny Bairstow with his first in Ashes cricket, they have lost.

Home and Away

All this goes to show what a part home conditions play in a major Test series. England's ongoing struggles down under are mirrored by those of Australia in the UK, particularly when there is lateral movement on offer. The pace of Test cricket now is extraordinary (as a way of comparison, I refer you to the scoring rates and length of innings to which I referred at the start of this chapter), and particularly Ashes cricket. When one team gets on top things can deteriorate for the other very quickly. The modern batsman doesn't like to hang about.

Take the Edgbaston Test of 2015. It was like a gunfight at the OK Corral, with punches being thrown all over the place. There were some astonishing shots played, too, in total disregard for the conditions. Steve Smith has marched to the summit when it comes to Test batsmen, but even he was out to an absolute hack at Steven Finn in the second innings. And there were several hoicks across the line accounting for the tourists' batsmen during the match. The ground staff in Birmingham have a contraption for measuring the firmness of their pitches called a Clegg hammer, and the pitch upon which Steven Finn took a man-of-the-match eight wickets on his recall to the team measured

275 gravities. The firmness reading dictates the pace and bounce bowlers are able to extract and the quicker the ball is travelling off the surface, the harder it is to combat any deviation. This particular one was in the premium range for the Birmingham venue of 260–80 whereas the pitch used for the following year's Test versus Pakistan came in at 230, giving the batsmen that precious extra time to adjust their shots if necessary.

Edgbaston is a place England tend to get on a roll, due to the atmosphere of the ground. If it was possible to bottle that up and take it around the country, they would. But for action on the field Trent Bridge was similarly astonishing. As a commentator you have hardly time to catch your breath when a team is dismissed in a session. It was like the Whitsuntide wakes, it was a procession.

Stuart Broad led the attack brilliantly in the absence of the injured Jimmy Anderson and enjoyed being the main man. It was a perfect storm – ideal conditions and the captain won the toss. However, seam bowlers are judged on their performances when the cloud cover is in and there is dampness in the pitch. They had to deliver before the sun came out in the afternoon, and figures of eight for 15 for Broad in a total of 60 all out told the story of how they did.

Supported by some stunning catching, Broad produced one of his spells. He is what they call a streak bowler. When he's on a hot one – as he was at The Oval to turn the 2009 Ashes in England's favour – he is a major force. It is almost taken for granted that Broad, charging in with the bit between his teeth, will unleash a spell like this annually. Think of his rout of New Zealand at Lord's in 2013, or the lung-busting 10-over spell in the altitude of Johannesburg to seal the series victory over South Africa in 2015-16. Most bowlers are blowing after five overs off the reel, so it was a sensational display of stamina in addition to skill.

There was a lot of talk about Australia not doing this and that from a technical point of view but Broad, Mark Wood and Finn were absolutely awesome in making them play at stuff they didn't really want to, and the work put in by England, ridiculed when they went to Spain seemingly on a jolly, under fielding coach Chris Taylor paid off.

I have to say that in all my years in the game I have never seen an Australian team rattled like that. They were all over the place. Mesmerised. Spooked. They just couldn't cope. In English conditions you've got to be like a musician – and play tight. They were sloppy and out of tune, Michael Clarke for one a shadow of his old self. The theory is that the ball hoops about in Nottingham because of the new stands they have put up during the redevelopment, but after spending most intervening years swinging like a 1960s suburban key party, it proved as straight as a die on Australia's previous visit in 2013.

While highlighting the disparity in Australian batsmen when the ball is moving around to when it is not, it also made for another cracking encounter. England knew nothing of a chap called Ashton Agar before the match in question and, it seemed, neither did Australia. Had they done, they would not have given him the opportunity to hit a world-record score of 98 for a number 11. He would have walked in at three down. This was a 19-year-old on debut with three half-centuries in 10 previous first-class matches and a technique so good that Nasser Hussain and Michael Atherton, in their Sky TV analysis, couldn't find any faults in it.

To be fair, England have played it by the book over the years, with the likes of Phil Tufnell, Peter Such, Devon Malcolm and Alan Mullally bringing up the rear. I remember Shaun Marsh as a kid hanging around the Australian nets when his dad, Geoff, was my opposite number on the 1998-99 tour of Australia. Marsh senior and I had a drink, as you do, after the final Test and we asked each other for an honest appraisal of each other's teams. I recall Geoff's response about my XI: 'Six out, all out,' he replied.

Successful teams seize the moment. Looking at the statistics alone at the end of the 2015 series and you would have been hard-pressed to explain how England had won, so heavily did they favour Australia. So how did they? With four telling bowling performances from Anderson, Broad, Finn and Ben Stokes across a fortnight in the Midlands. Anyone will tell you that you have to take 20 wickets to win a Test, supporting the claim of the old gnarled pro that it is 'batsmen for show, bowlers for dough'.

Less is More

What the 2017-18 Ashes defeat spelled out is that it is time for English cricket to prepare its players better. As productive as our bowlers are on familiar territory, they are struggling to be penetrative on the flatter surfaces in Australia where genuine pace and variation, such as wrist spin, are key.

The attack on duty in the 4-0 defeat was crammed with workmanlike seam bowlers capable of top speeds of 85-86mph. Anderson at 35 years of age was quicker through the air than the emerging duo of Craig Overton and Tom Curran, and to exacerbate the problem Broad, the one man capable of slipping himself and putting in a hostile spell, was totally out of rhythm. Lessons have to be learned. For bowlers who rely solely on movement through the air or laterally off the pitch, big things just will not happen on those types of surfaces. We simply cannot travel to Australia with that make-up of bowling unit again.

So what is to be done? The fact of the matter is we are not

producing enough fast bowlers. It's all very well scheduling cricket across six months of a domestic summer, but it's not helping the England team. Two of our quickest guys – George Garton, of Sussex, and Yorkshire's Liam Plunkett – aren't even guaranteed to get a game in the County Championship.

Arguably, that's not surprising when so many fixtures are scheduled for April and May when the spring weather makes pitches a bit nibbly. No disrespect to him because he has shown fantastic career longevity, but Darren Stevens shouldn't be taking the volume of wickets he does at the age of 42. He is cute enough (wouldn't you agree, ladies?) to keep hitting the seam and allow the surface to be his ally.

Don't get me wrong, I love county cricket, I am a massive believer in it. It has given me everything I have ever had – I was totally besotted with it as both a coach and player, but we have to get real. The system must change. We can't keep playing 14 four-day matches and expect to produce anything other than worthy seam bowlers. We are encouraging the counties to pick the dobbers when the bigger picture is calling out for something quite different. We need quality, not quantity, but it will require a change of mindset from club chairmen. And from the county member who just wants to see cricket wall to wall.

Our administrators have a choice to make. Do we carry on with all this county cricket, with too many games across all competitions, and a fixture list that has four-day matches in winter and autumn and none in the heart of summer? Or do we play less cricket to help improve the Test side? I suspect I know the answer, unfortunately. I will continue to crusade for turning county cricket into a better product via a greater emphasis on rest and preparation. Then, bang, you are going to get a great game.

The change I would make is to revert to three divisions of six, and 10 games per team per season. That way the quickest bowlers might have a chance of getting through the summer, and be at the forefront of thoughts when it comes to selection.

Why are we so special and different that we have to play 16 – as we did until a couple of years ago – or 14 games a season as is the case now? Australia don't do it, South Africa don't do it, New Zealand don't do it; in fact, no country in the world with an established first-class system does it, to my knowledge.

I know for a fact that during an English domestic season the fast bowlers go through stages where they are running on empty. That's in the short term. In the longer term, the effects reveal themselves in a gradual drop in pace. Let's think of some-one like Tim Bresnan – a multiple Ashes winner, one of the crack attack to guide England to the one victory in Australia in the past 30 years – who was always a lively seam bowler. What a wonderful cricketer he has been for Yorkshire and his coun-try. Even now at 33 he is not old, but a system that means he is playing every week across a season spanning six months means his bowling pace has shown a steady decline year on year. It's all to do with workload.

Another example is a guy who has just retired. For his won-derful period with England between 2007 and 2010, Ryan Sidebottom was a big, strong, left-armer, bowling 86–87mph and proving himself an absolute handful.

Talking to coaches now, they actually want a nucleus of quick bowlers that they can rest and interchange without losing any-thing from the overall quality of their attack. But it's difficult to do that because you need to educate the players that it is not a slight to be overlooked in selection and that resting is beneficial. England have done that brilliantly with Jimmy Anderson, and even then he has rucked a couple of times when he has been omitted, such as for the Lord's Test against Pakistan in 2016, because he is from a culture in which the best players always play if they declare themselves fit. Over his final few years at the top I think we will come to consider that him playing less has preserved his skills. County squads are creaking by the middle of summer, they have played so much, and towards the back end spare a thought for the groundsmen. They have run out of pitches.

In contrast, I reckon Australia's powerful performance, particularly from their bowlers, was in the planning for two years. I didn't expect Mitchell Starc, Josh Hazlewood and Pat Cummins to make it through, but the preparation was excellent. They were pulled out of one-day series in advance, wrapped in cotton wool on the eve of the series, and to stunning results. Starc was the only one to miss a match – the drawn Boxing Day Test – and each broke the 20-wicket barrier, as did their support act Nathan Lyon.

Everyone was talking about the Aussies' pace at the start of the tour and whether it would fizzle out. Well, it didn't, and Lyon showed there were many ways to skin a cat. He ended up skinning Moeen Ali in every Test. And he was on a hiding to nothing after summoning his inner Dennis Lillee on the eve of the series. Back in the seventies, Lillee would do television interviews in which he would peer into the camera and address an England batsman personally, warning of what was to come next day. It adds to the menace when a fast bowler does that. It's not quite the same look when an orthodox off-spinner shoots from the hip, but Lyon promised to end careers, before a ball was bowled, and but for the lack of obvious alternatives in James Vince's case he might have been right.

Vince's batting smacked of a loss of concentration. He'd be in for a while, have his eye in, having customised himself to the pace and bounce of the pitch. The stage would be set. And then he would go and spoil it all by playing something stupid. I remember Bob Woolmer once giving a lecture and asking batsmen in the audience when they thought they were 'in'. Some said after 10 runs, others after a quarter of an hour. Woolmer's reply was that you're never in, because it only takes one ball to get you out. When you're batting, you have to focus, otherwise you won't last long at Test level.

It's also important not to lose sight of the bigger picture. Take the case of Michael Carberry in 2013-14. Make no mistake: in county cricket, he was a wonderful, bossy player. He had been made to wait for his chance, barring a solitary appearance in Bangladesh three years earlier, due to the form of Andrew Strauss and Alastair Cook over a sustained period of time. He was prolific and played in a dashing style. Indeed, in the warm-up matches in Australia he was batting like Matthew Hayden. Then he goes and scores 12 in 81 balls in Melbourne, having got scratchier with each passing innings. I was staggered. He had been selected to play his way but something stopped him doing so. As Michael Slater put it on commentary: 'That innings has just batted him out of the Test team.' Sadly, one match later, despite Carberry finishing as England's second top scorer behind Kevin Pietersen, he was right.

Smudger Leaves His Mark

Due to Sky Sports no longer holding the rights to international cricket in Australia, the most recent Ashes series was the first one in years I did not have the privilege to cover live, and it was strange following from afar.

I am not quite sure how, but between days two and three of the first Test I ended up in Soho, central London. When I woke up the following morning there was a vague recollection of me wearing a wig, spending all afternoon doing Neil Diamond covers in an Indian restaurant. A figment of my imagination? Well, I also had it in my mind that Steve Smith was now the best Test batsman on the planet. Yes, that Steve Smith. The one who, when he came into the Australian side eight years ago, was being touted as the new Shane Warne – batting at number eight, bowling leg-spin, and taking three wickets against Pakistan on debut at Lord's. Yes, the Steve Smith who was recalled for the 2010-11 Ashes with a remit to bat a bit, bowl a bit and tell a few jokes at slip.

Smith's ascent actually goes to show that you do not have to have a technique straight from the MCC coaching manual to reach the pinnacle of batting, and he has followed a similar route to that which Kevin Pietersen took. KP was an off-spinner who came in down the order with Natal, of course – but both developed into world-class batsmen through natural cricketing ability and nous. Their methods may have looked at odds with orthodox practice but, wherever the rest of their bodies ended up, the one common theme they shared was that their head was always still when bat made impact with ball.

By the end of the series, England were left wondering: 'How on earth do you bowl to him?' Among batsmen with 1,500 Test runs, he was second only to Don Bradman in terms of average, which says it all. England tried all sorts – including hanging the ball outside off stump, but he proved equal to almost everything. Where they might have had a bit more luck was with off-cutters. At Adelaide Craig Overton got one to nip back through the gate, but Smith's ability to adjust his stroke at the last moment got him out of subsequent trouble against that particular delivery, and just about every other variety England sent down at him.

My concern about Smith after he became Australia captain was never his impact with the bat, but how he would handle the position of responsibility. He had a hell of a lot to live up to because of the legacy of Australian captains – from the Chappell brothers to Steve Waugh to Mark Taylor, Ricky Ponting and

Michael Clarke. Perhaps he got sucked into trying to cultivate a tough-guy persona to emulate some of those men despite it not being a natural fit. He appeared at least to be more of a leader who was going to score a shedload of runs and look for his team to respond.

Steve Waugh was what I would call 'hard', a niggardly old sod who would give you nowt; Taylor was a tough competitor but one of the nicest people you could ever wish to meet away from the field; Ponting had a bit of mongrel in him, while in my opinion Clarke tried to live up to a reputation.

Smith's demise (more of that later) was sad, but there were tell-tale signs that he did not have full control over his team way before his one-year Cricket Australia ban was imposed. There is a way to behave and he didn't always act in a manner becoming of his position. I was not very impressed with Smith telling Craig Overton that he was too slow out in the middle in Adelaide. Don't get me wrong, there's nothing amiss with a few verbals, and if it's someone like Jimmy Anderson he's fair game because he's been round the block a few times, but for an Australian captain to say that to a young lad on his Ashes debut lacked class. There is no way Richie Benaud or Ian Chappell would have acted in that way.

And I am not sure he had the best choice of deputy in David Warner. All this talk of being a reformed character, and earning a nickname of 'the Reverend', was codswallop. He seems the kind of bloke who could start an argument in a morgue. The slightest provocation and he is off on one. Take his scrap on Twitter with a couple of respected Australian journalists, Robert Craddock and Malcolm Conn, in 2013 over their criticism of the Indian Premier League, where he was playing for Delhi Daredevils. Despite a fine and two-match ban for his altercation with Root mentioned in the previous chapter, I don't think he has changed.

There are shades of Mario Balotelli with Warner, and you half-expect him to rock up in a T-shirt saying: 'Why always me?' The lad never seems to learn. Even in 2017-18, when he broke a blank sequence with a fine hundred at Melbourne, he had to scream at the England slip cordon. The conclusion I draw is that he's not wired up right.

The Gloves are On

More often than not, England have run into trouble on the field of play down under, and if it's not the batsmen and bowlers giving them a working-over it's a bloke in huge gloves. Throughout the 1970s and early 1980s there was Rodney Marsh, one of the toughest competitors I ever came across.

Later came Ian Healy, who combined so brilliantly with Shane Warne throughout his career. It all came so naturally to him when Warne was bowling, despite the fact that the bloke releasing the ball bamboozled all-comers when it came to opposition batsmen. Even in later life, Healy showed he still had it when Channel Nine did a feature on leg-spin. Warney just stood there wearing a T-shirt and rolled them out, spinning it yards, landing each ball on a sixpence, and there was Healy gobbling everything up without a fumble in sight.

Then there was the game-changer Adam Gilchrist, with his feats such as the 57-ball hundred at the WACA in the Ashes whitewashing of 2006-07. Whenever he got into full flow the wheels tended to come off for England.

And Brad Haddin maintained the tradition with the most brilliant of series in 2013-14. England seemed obsessed with engaging him verbally, but he absolutely loved that. The number of times England totally lost their discipline when Australia were five down was incredible. He would walk to the crease with fewer than 100 runs on the board and was suddenly faced with a smorgasbord of short and wide stuff, followed by a collection of deliveries that were full and wide.

His record is right up there with that of Gilchrist in Ashes cricket courtesy of that series when he proved so influential. At 36 years of age as a no-nonsense dasher with the bat and a feisty character behind the stumps, he proved absolute gold dust, passing 50 six times in eight innings – more than anybody else on either side managed. Rumours were rife that he would retire after that and although he continued he never again reached those heights.

Never Too Old

There has been much debate recently over how a visiting team prepares in an Ashes series, with the quality of opposition in the warm-up matches at the heart of the issue. The boards of both countries are keen for this to be addressed in future following the lack of first-class experience within the Cricket Australia XIs England faced during the 2017-18 tour. Gone, it seems, are the days of facing the state sides, as was the case as recently as 2010-11.

However, it did make me think back to 2013 when England's own preparation included a match against Essex (all out for 20 against Lancashire less than a fortnight earlier). It all seemed a meaningless exercise, but the pitch at Chelmsford was antici-pated to be the nearest England could get to the dry, flat surfaces with spin to the fore that Graeme Swann and Co. would have been expecting during the Ashes.

Experience in the conditions in which you are going to play is vital. I was a massive fan of Ryan Harris, the kind of guy Duncan Fletcher would have called a solid citizen and a bowler who would have played many more Test matches had he been blessed with a more robust body. He was well suited to operating in English conditions because, as well as a short stint with Sussex, he had a spell of league cricket with Lowerhouse near Burnley. He returned there to catch up before the Old Trafford Test of 2013. It's great when someone knows where they've come from, and I know how much he would have picked up from bowling on nibbling surfaces in the North-west.

Similarly, when Chris Rogers was called up at the age of 35 that summer, he had done the rounds in county cricket, and therefore knew what it took to combat the seam and swing bowlers extracted with the Dukes ball. At Chester-le-Street, I was willing him to get his maiden international hundred. He'd made loads of first-class hundreds before, of course, but having waited so long to enjoy regular Test cricket, to prosper on what was a spicy pitch meant I was thrilled for him. And he proved there was life in the old dog two years later when, after a spate of 50s, he made his eighth first-class hundred at Lord's. Like Harris, one of the more lovable souls Australia have produced of late.

The Bumble Tour Guide to Australia

Brisbane

Bris Vegas, as the locals know it, has returned to its full glory thankfully after being badly hit by flooding at the start of the 21st century. It's a great stroll down the Eagle Street boardwalk, with all the restaurants now rebuilt and back in business. It can get a bit lively in your average Brissie nightspot. So much so that we were asked to pay for our pizzas in one joint – before we'd eaten them! I was recovering from a knee operation at the time, so it wasn't as if I was about to do a runner. It just shows how careful some folk are. I was half-expecting the owner to wander out from the kitchen to introduce himself with a bellow of, 'Hello, I'm from Yorkshire.'

The Story Bridge Hotel is typical of an Australian pub. The thing about your Aussie establishment that I like is that, no matter how dark and dingy they are, you can always purchase food. This one's like five pubs in one. The bogans at the front. You know the type: those with six fingers, two heads and webbed feet. The larrikins of life. Then inside there is a properly nice restaurant where serious bottles of wine are served and there is a high level of sophistication. Folk are dressed in their best clobber.

Then there is the Port Office Hotel in central Brisbane. There's no smoking allowed, not even on the pavement out front, and in typical Aussie style they have staff patrolling the area to make sure this rule is upheld. If you want a fag you have to go and stand in the middle of the road. I'm all for it myself, filthy habit. Although it might just be a way to manipulate a few figures – don't die of smoking, get run over instead.

Adelaide

Traditionally, you always think of spin when considering the characteristics of Adelaide Oval. More recently it has become synonymous with floodlit Test matches.

Undoubtedly, it is my favourite place on the Ashes beat. It is a more sedate city in general, surrounded by wine regions. Hindley Street is where you want to go for a bit of life. There's plenty of it. Especially at the Crazy Horse, where women clearly can't cope with the 40-degree heat. They're forever taking their clothes off. Now, if anyone says they have seen me in there – particularly if they claim the clock had struck midnight – they're telling fibs.

The Exeter pub down Rundle Street is time stood still. It's got three rooms, none of which gives off the impression it's been touched. If you haven't got rings in every orifice or tattoos top to toes you are not going in. Luckily, the staff are only too willing to take my word for it that I have a kuno piercing. I never seem to get much further than 'it's just down here' before the doormen wave me through, which is great because there is always a cracking atmosphere inside.

Just around the corner is the Oyster Bar. As Mike Atherton is my witness, my world-record sitting is 48. After that I felt like I could march on Poland. Oysters, they say, put lead in your pencil. Unfortunately, though, on that particular trip I had no one to write to.

North Adelaide is a gem of an area. Go straight up O'Connell Street to the Royal Oak, where there'll always be a live band on at weekends. It has a bottle shop behind it at which you can buy wine from both ends of the market. There's lighter fluid at a couple of dollars, and if you have got the budget the very best at a hundred times more expensive. To get into the pub you then pay your corkage and pass through a football-style turnstile. It always makes me chuckle, that.

There's a bloke who has been in there every time I've visited with the best comb-over I have come across – it sweeps around in five different directions and is quite something to behold. It looks like his hair has been flamenco-dancing across his scalp. He must be about 105 by now. But he is consistent and one thing you can be sure of is that he always has a partner in tow.

There's also the Oxford, and then closer to the ground is a classy place called the Queen's Head, behind the cathedral. It's a wonderful little crawl back into town, past the churches and the parklands, ending back up at the Metropolitan Wine Bar.

Get a tram down to 'Glenelg and you are at the beach.

England had their academy base there from 2001 to 2004 under Rodney Marsh. Adelaide's got a great stretch of coastline, although I wouldn't recommend going for a dip as the water is full of sharks and you'd probably get eaten. Aussie sharks like nothing better than taking out a Pom, you know. It's in their DNA. So I wouldn't even go paddling.

It's also the Australian capital of great wine. Geoff Merrill, a wine-maker pal of mine, has produced a new one and called it Henley. Named so it's one up from Grange. Just as it is in Adelaide's map of beaches.

Perth

I don't have such fond memories of the WACA because that's where Jeff Thomson rearranged my furniture during the 1974–75 tour. Thankfully, it was all returned to its rightful place.

These days it's full of English folk, and Sir Ian Botham tells me it's the fourth most expensive city in the world. He didn't tell me what the other three were. But wherever they are, I can guarantee they will have drinks lists and menus to make your eyes water, Thommo-style.

For a night out, look no further than a pub on the river with the interesting name of the Lucky Shag. Shags are coastal birds, apparently, so expect to see a few twitchers on the scene. It's also where the Barmy Army like to set up headquarters in Test match weeks.

Melbourne

What an iconic ground the MCG, or 'the G' as the locals know it, is. With 90,000 in on Boxing Day, it is a venue to rival any other in any other sport anywhere. As a player you can hear the drone and buzz of the crowd of this raucous place. Noise is a constant. The notorious Bay 13 is no more, which is a shame. They used to chuck empty beer cans at you at third man and then, as the day progressed, full ones! Tony Greig used to throw it all back at them, with interest. And who could forget the day a live pig was sent onto the outfield with 'Eddie' and 'Beefy' written on either side of the poor thing.

In spite of this cross-section of Melbourne society, it's a sophisticated city. Very European. And I like going to Fitzroy, its most bohemian district. It rather reminds me of Camden Town in London or Chorlton in Manchester.

The Labour in Vain is a good boozer but nothing tops the Standard. Warney put me onto it. It's got a huge picture on the wall of David Boon, with the words: 'Boonie for Prime Minister!' I was in there one night when the doors opened and in shuffled a horse. He drank a bucket of water and, when his thirst was quenched, he reversed out again. Name of Royston. It is a raw old place. There is not much talk of cricket here but it provides a great study of real life. Real jeans and T-shirt territory.

Wander into your average pub in Melbourne, in fact, and they are likely to have reruns of Australian Rules football on their array of oversized tellies. As far as I can see, there are no rules. The players just kick it and run. And if you are in range of the goals you simply cannot miss. The umpires look like ice-cream sellers stood by the posts. They have got those white jackets on but they don't really look like they know what they're doing.

You can score either through the posts, or if that target isn't big enough for you and you miss, fret not because you get something for having a go. It's a bit like a school sports day where everyone gets a prize. Even little Johnny who forgot his kit and didn't want to run in vest and pants because he was too cold. If the ball ends up in the crowd, some young 'un kicks it or punches it back and extra points go on if it goes through the middle. Your average score is something like 121–108. It reminds me of Michael O'Hare's commentary on Gaelic football: 'It's a goal. It's a goal. It's a goal.' Can't recall him ever saying much else.

Sydney

The SCG is my favourite ground in the world. It's class. There's the tradition, the pavilion and the dressing rooms. It smells of cricket. Sydney's a fabulous city. I love nothing more than going down to the Harbour View Hotel right under their big old bridge to people-watch. Hundreds of silly sods climb it all day long. I prefer to kick back and chill.

Just down the road, if you walk along George Street into the hub of the city, is the Fortune of War. It claims to be Sydney's oldest pub, having been established in 1828, and can be known to goad its potential Pommie punters during an Ashes tour. Take the most recent trip, in 2017-18, when they marked rare English resistance with the bat with a billboard outside the premises that read: 'Finally Jo [sic] Root got some runs. Shame it was gastro in a hospital!'

They say Sydney on New Year's Eve is spectacular and I agree – I tend to watch the darts on TV. No fireworks for me, just room service, a glass of wine and a catch-up with happenings at Ally Pally. Most years it was Phil Taylor picking up the world crown, although all champions have to lose sometime, just as the Aussies have discovered. Neither won in 2010-11 ...

Once the New Year's Test gets going there is only one colour on anyone's mind. The McGrath Foundation day is when all are required to wear pink in honour of the great Glenn McGrath's wife Jane, a Birmingham lass. One member of each commentary team is expected to wear a pink suit for the day. Michael Atherton was always my choice from us lot at Sky – he got him out often enough. But having donned the thing myself I have to say it looked rather natty. Not that I could compete with some of the guys in the Caribbean when it came to sartorial elegance.

CHAPTER SIX

Chicks and Gravy

One of the best trips you can possibly go on when it comes to international cricket is West Indies. Ten thousand England fans can't be wrong, you know. That's how many you can expect during a winter in the Caribbean, slumped across the stands as red as tomatoes, having a grand old time.

With all that Reggie music you simply can't stop dancing. He's produced a lot of songs, has our Reggie. Prolific. And the dancing? Well, it's as synonymous with that particular part of the world as fast bowling used to be. Back in the day, folk would be winding and wiggling in the stands as the batsmen bobbed and weaved to the chin music in the middle. Yep, a Caribbean tour is great fun. Cricket is razzmatazz, so much so that it used to make personalities out of individuals in the crowd. There would be characters familiar to you on every island.

In Antigua, the centre of the amateur dramatics, you would be regally entertained by Labon Kenneth Blackburn Leeweltine Buckonon Benjamin. Well, that's how his mother knew him anyway, until she gave him the nickname 'Gravy'. He of the eye-catching outfits designed to draw attention to himself, who during breaks in play would dance outlandishly on a platform in front of the Double Decker Stand – spinning on his head, that sort of thing. Gravy tends to go lumpy after a while but this particular one was like whisky, getting better with age until he retired in 2000, donning a bridal dress on his farewell appearance. As you do.

Then, at the other end of the ground, Mayfield used to stand and mimic his rival. He may not have garnered as much attention as the gyrating Gravy, but he did get involved in a significant piece of cricket history when, in 1994, he marked Brian Lara's passing of the previous Test best score of 365 held by Sir Garfield Sobers, by entering the field of play at St John's and smashing up records. Just as the Trinidadian had done with his bat.

Vinyl was all part of the show, although mainly due to the influence of another Antiguan. Chickie became a household name in 1986 when, on hearing the news that Viv Richards was plundering England for what would turn out to be the fastest Test hundred in history, he rushed to the Rec and set up a party stand that was to become famous not only inside the ground but around the globe. He began, cheekily, by playing 'Captain, the Ship is Sinking' to poke fun at David Gower – the man presiding over what only a matter of hours later would become a 5-0 whitewash – and never looked back.

Redvers Dundonald Dyal, aka His Majesty King Dyal, was the nattiest dresser on Barbados and would turn up to the Kensington Oval to bellow his royal approval, continuing a tradition of crowd commentary dating back to the late 19th century. Like his predecessor Britannia Bill, being from an island nicknamed 'Little England', the king would support the touring team, responding to heckles from other locals by taking a drag on his pipe and delivering an answer to the serfs.

Dyal would often change his coloured suits at lunch and tea, ensuring that his accessories of hat or crown, pipe and walking stick matched. He also wore white gloves more often than not. Mac Fingall, a band leader, would head down to Kensington Oval with a suitcase full of percussion instruments, such as cowbells, whistles and iron drums, in the belief that the Bajan crowd wasn't animated enough. As part of his show he would spray magic voodoo dust on the outfield to jinx the opposition. Across in Trinidad and Tobago, a bandana-clad chap by the name of Blue Food would whip up a frenzy of noise in the stands with his blowing of a conch shell.

These iconic individuals added boundary-line entertainment to cricket – and Test cricket at that – long before Twenty20 came riding into town with an army of dancing girls, acrobats, flame throwers and hot tubs. And they provided a unique flavour to Caribbean cricket that you simply could not taste elsewhere. It made going to Test matches an interactive experience; one long party. Anyone who thought they were going to studiously watch a game of cricket was in the wrong joint. They are very knowledgeable people who watch but react differently to its events.

Speed Freaks

What I found when I toured as England coach was that while it was fun off the field, the business on it was serious. That's because we were up against Curtly Ambrose and Courtney Walsh, two greats upholding the region's wonderful tradition of producing fast bowlers. It was one of the big disappointments of my tenure not only that we lost that series but that we didn't win it, and the main reason we didn't was being confronted by those two. Ambrose took 30 wickets and Walsh, although not at his prolific best, claimed 22.

They had come out of the golden era when blokes were

queuing up to pull on that famous maroon cap. What a who's who they could provide: Joel Garner, Michael Holding, Andy Roberts, Colin Croft, Malcolm Marshall, Wayne Daniel, Sylvester Clarke, Patrick Patterson, Ezra Moseley, Winston Benjamin and Ian Bishop. It was a conveyor belt.

The majority of them were enormous men, which meant they possessed these great long levers and were therefore releasing the ball from great heights, accentuating the bounce they were able to extract from pitches which until the mid-1990s were like lightning. Indeed, the thrill of playing West Indies was taking on their pace.

It might not have been very subtle, and curmudgeons would try to detract from what West Indies were doing by fielding four fast bowlers, but equally they were ahead of their time, and their primary mode of attack was the short ball/yorker combination. These are classical pace-bowling principles: shove the batsman back to test the back-foot game and then follow up with the full delivery, hoping their weight is going the wrong way.

Everything was within the laws of the game. As my good friend Michael Holding says: 'People weren't accustomed to change. We didn't ever bowl above shoulder height. Some got hit on the head, yes, but a lot of them ducked into the ball.' He reckoned the infamous delivery that struck Andy Lloyd at Edgbaston in 1984 was almost lbw!

Now, on Caribbean soil if you took the hook shot on as a visiting batsman the ground would erupt with a cacophony of noise. They wanted to see a genuine contest between their fast-bowling heroes and visiting batsmen, not just the waving of a white flag. The ball would be propelled at differing velocities (even the slowest speeds would have incurred a driving ban in the UK, mind), trajectories and angles. For example, compare the size of Marshall and Garner, or the fact that Holding would glide close to the stumps while Croft would be aiming in at the body from his release point wide of the crease to the right-hander. Because his deliveries tended to follow the batsmen, he was considered by some to be the meanest of them all.

But Croft just saw this as offering a variation to his captain. 'We may have been scary to the batsmen and spectators but we were just doing what we were supposed to do – get people out,' he says. 'All Clive Lloyd did was look at what he had and recognised he could use us as a weapon. We all had a purpose and role in the team.'

During the 1980s it seemed every other English county had a West Indies fast bowler as an overseas player. Sylvester Clarke, of Surrey, was an absolute beauty. Here was a fast bowler who didn't like bowling. But he was savvy enough to work out that the faster he got the opponents out, the less bowling he was doing. He could then get his feet up and have a sleep. Some blokes back-pedalled from a challenge with excuses like 'the pitch is no good', 'the wind's in the wrong direction', 'the ball needs changing', and ended up just going through the motions. But once an opposing team reached the back end of an innings, 'Silvers' just went faster and faster and faster until he'd knocked down all the pins.

From within that overspill of fast bowling talent, if you carried out a straw poll of those who played against them, the majority would tell you that Balfour Patrick Patterson was the quickest of the lot. He was immensely powerful and, to add menace to his bowling, his unusual action didn't allow you a sight of the ball until very late – the boot on his raised front leg obscuring his right hand.

Jeffrey Dujon, the West Indies wicketkeeper throughout the 1980s, was the best person to make a judgement and he says: 'I reckon that when you get into a certain pace bracket, one or two miles an hour doesn't really make too much difference. But the one who made a marked impression on me on one or two

111

occasions was Patrick Patterson. I had never kept to anything as quick.'

Twice, Dujon reckons, Patrick got just about everything absolutely right. The first was against England in Kingston in 1986 when he claimed seven wickets on his debut. As West Indies wicketkeeper, Dujon was accustomed to the ball thudding into his gloves but he still recalls that performance as 'rapid'.

Patterson's other excessive indulgence came when the Australians pissed him off in 1988 at Melbourne. Merv Hughes and Co. had him hopping up and down, and the close fielders were chirping at him to get behind it – 'to have some balls'. After being dismissed, he returned to the dressing room and began huffing and puffing. At the MCG, the two teams change adjacent to each other and so he paid a visit to the home team during the interval. 'You, you, you and you,' he said, pointing around the room. 'I am going to kill you.'

The Australians went unmaimed, but Patterson was at the heart of a crushing West Indies win, with his best match figures in Test cricket of nine for 88. But make no mistake, this plethora of West Indies pacemen carried menace with them. Around this time I was back at Accrington as the professional, captaining the first XI, and we headed to Todmorden for a bank holiday cup match. Todmorden's overseas professional was Ravi Ratnayeke, the Sri Lanka all-rounder, a capable batsman and canny bowler at the top end of medium pace. A decent cricketer. However, Ratnayeke was injured for this particular match and the Lancashire League regulations of the time stipulated that if the professional was otherwise indisposed another must be recruited. Enter onto the outfield as we all warmed up a hulking young lad called Ian Bishop, who had taken the world stage by storm with his ability to take the ball away from the right-hander at express speed.

As Robin Smith among others will attest, his short one was

a venomous brute, and as he bowled like lightning, reaction time was minimal. To most, facing Bishop in his pomp would have been the height of intimidation. Not to Billy Rawstron, though, a solicitor on weekdays and wicketkeeper-batsman on weekends. When it came to it, this made for a dangerous combination. He certainly didn't lack confidence, and declared before heading out to bat that Bishop 'doesn't look very quick to me', choosing to do his combat without a helmet. What happened next had a certain inevitability, I guess. Bishop unleashed a bouncer which struck Billy flush in the mouth and sent him careering off his feet and into the stumps behind him. Always one to argue his case, he wasn't going to miss an opportunity to do so now despite being on his haunches, claret flowing from his mush.

'I can't be out hit wicket,' he said. 'I'd finished my stroke.'

'Don't be daft, lad,' we informed him. 'You hadn't even started it.'

Later, he kept wicket with a crepe bandage wrapped around his head, making him look like the Invisible Man, Peter Brady. You could just see this pair of eyes and his mouth. Some would have said the mouth should have been covered too, but give Billy his due – yes, he'd talked the talk, but he wasn't the only one to come off worst in a confrontation with a West Indian behemoth.

The thing about these superhuman specimens was that they were all absolute gents. Quite religious were some of them but all very nice people. Their ability and conduct put them on the map and for two decades solid they were the world's box-office team.

Unfortunately, though, these pitches would transform over time from the fastest in the world to the slowest and lowest imaginable. In terms of pace, they have gone completely and – not unlike many you find in India – turn prodigiously. The only way of getting them back into their previous states would be to re-lay them all. The problem, of course, is that they have no money to speak of.

So, recent generations have been given no encouragement to hurl it down as fast as they can. Instead, they have adopted a more leisurely approach. In fact, bowling is about the only thing that has ever happened fast in the Caribbean. They have a different outlook on life in general. Any more laid-back and they'd be horizontal.

On the 1997-98 tour, when I was England coach, we had a practice match at an out-ground in Jamaica called Chedwin Park. At grounds like this it's customary to have a perambulation, a bit like you do at league matches back home. Anyhow, on this walk around the ground I get a whiff of this pungent aroma and follow my nose. It is coming from a lad who is sat in the middle of some bushes set back from the boundary edge, puffing away, as high as a kite.

'All right, pal?'

'Yeah, man.'

'You just want to be careful,' I warned him. 'Because this is the England cricket team playing here and with the England cricket team comes a lot of security. And when I talk about security, I mean a lot of police.'

Nonplussed, he took another drag and said: 'Chill, man, I supply the police.'

What West Indies cricket has been chock-full of over the years is players capable of individual brilliance, guys who can turn a match in a decisive direction. The film *Fire in Babylon* celebrated their collective drive for recognition as black role models in sport, but equally as important was a professional drive to be paid commensurately with their status as the best team on the planet and they could only get somewhere near by pocketing regular win bonuses.

The formula for success in the 1970s and 80s was pretty much bombproof: four of the world's best-ever fast bowlers backing up a batting line-up you could argue has never been repeated. They were just a cut above what anyone else could get on the park, and for me they were not only the best Windies team but the best Test team that has ever been.

It wasn't only in their ability that they hit heights unmatched by their peers or those who have followed. They had great leadership, great senior players, pride in performance and an addiction to showing the world what they could achieve. For two decades no bar was high enough for them. They were relentless, fit and had everything that they needed to win matches.

A low basic wage is not a particularly modern phenomenon for West Indies cricketers, you see – 30 years before the likes of Chris Gayle, Dwayne Bravo and Andre Russell began prioritising Twenty20 cricket around the globe to earn the kind of living enjoyed by their Indian, English and Australian counterparts, a multi-World Cup-winning Windies group were playing World Series Cricket for the same ends.

It's always been this way because there is no real TV deal with which Cricket West Indies can develop an infrastructure. From being the hottest ticket in town, they have been left behind when it comes to funding. Without the numbers in terms of the Caribbean's combined population there is no market for a substantial deal. They are trying to compete with India, England and Australia, countries that rake in millions, but cannot do it through regional pride alone.

Well, it's about time that the fat cats of world cricket helped this sporting phenomenon out. As Michael Holding says, there are people from islands yet to provide a Test cricketer who still feel passionately enough about the West Indies to refer to them as 'we'. They need help and they deserve help for what they have done for the sport over the years. Talk about punching above your weight.

Everybody hopes that they'll turn the corner, but their Test match cricket is suffering because of their attention to white-ball cricket. In Twenty20 they are as good as anything going around and it is reflected in two world titles during their troubled times. Equally, without the kind of television deal to remunerate the players, their recently appointed chief executive Johnny Grave will need to use all of his experience of dealing with England's top players while at the Professional Cricketers' Association to get things right.

The modern West Indies are not going to emulate their predecessors because quite simply they were the best Test team I ever had the privilege to watch. No, their like will never be seen again, because the power game they pioneered has disappeared and spin has become the dominant force in their domestic cricket.

Their natural flair suits the condensed game, and that is why they are continuing to produce cricketers worth a fortune in auction prices. Equally, though, they are having to work hard to persuade their players to maintain international ambition. The global domestic Twenty20 scene continues to be an Achilles heel in luring their leading cricketers away. Money talks, I suppose.

When Lara Met His Match

On the tour of 2003-04, we were staying at the Hilton Hotel in Trinidad, which has a rather strange arrangement in that you head down from reception into some dungeons that serve as bedrooms. This upside-down establishment, constructed on a hillside, had the louche Pelican Bar at the bottom which everyone attends at night.

The clientele one evening during our stay included none other than a Mr Brian Charles Lara. Unsurprisingly, seeing as he is the equivalent of royalty on the island, he seemed to hold sway. At that time our statistician at Sky was Richard Lockwood, a very eccentric guy whose devotion to cricket numbers was only one of his idiosyncrasies. The other was that he liked to go dancing on his own. Nowt wrong with that, I suppose. He wasn't doing anyone any harm, or at least he wasn't in principle.

However, he had a nasty habit of not only occupying a dance floor but launching a hostile takeover, drawing particular attention to himself by completing a move that would become known as 'the Locky' – effectively a frenzy of arms and legs. Most of the time during this whirlwind of limbs he was bent over, staring at the floor, but every now and again he would spring up, rather like the courtship strut of the bird of paradise. Swooping down low, then flying up randomly. It was mesmerising stuff.

Unfortunately, though, one of these indiscriminate thrusts resulted in a loose arm swinging out and clattering the aforementioned BC Lara on the head. Now, that's not something you want to be doing when you are in the Caribbean. This is a bloke that owns Trinidad. A melee ensued and the pair of them were pulled apart. The important thing to report here is that the music played on, and eventually we all danced on. But I think it was the first time I ever saw Lara flustered by an Englishman on his own manor.

He is a pretty chilled-out kind of guy, and proved himself to be a great host when it comes to putting on a shindig in his lovely house overlooking the savannah. Michael Atherton was a big mate of his, their friendship stretching back to their school-days, and he very kindly invited all of us from the Sky crew over one day. It was a typically Caribbean barbecue, sitting around at outdoor tables, watching the world go by.

During his playing days it was said that Lara could appear aloof, that he could get quite moody. That's fine by me. Everybody can be a bit like that at times, and don't forget he carried that particular West Indies team. They had Ambrose and Walsh with the ball, then Lara with the bat, and that brought a lot of pressure to deliver. When great players do so they tend to have a trait that sets them apart from the rest and Lara was no different in this regard. So what was his trait? From my observations it was his canny ability, whenever he struck the ball, to miss the field. His placement of it through gaps was what gave him his edge.

He was a guy driven to be the best of his time when it came to batting and he undoubtedly had a God-given skill when it came to picking up length. He would judge so early where the ball was pitching – that split-second earlier than anyone else could manage – then the bat would come down in that lovely flowing scythe of a swing to propel it through the field. It would fly through the air at head height and as a commentator you would think 'gone'. No chance. He was a con artist. 'Gone' was actually 'four' every time because he kept it away from where the catchers were positioned. Forget that the ball had travelled aerially, any danger of it being caught was diminished by such exquisite placement and timing. He had this flowing, high backlift and his co-ordination of brain, eye and hands was just something else.

Lara also had this insatiable appetite for scoring runs and he liked to do it in enormous chunks. Three hundreds, four hundreds, five hundreds; what an ability he had for compiling big innings on a regular basis. Others would dominate with their aggression and take games away from opponents, but what made him different was that he did it for such prolonged periods of time. There was no let-up.

You got a sense of when he was set fair and I was commentating when he broke the Test record score for the second time with 400 not out in Antigua in 2004. You just knew it was one of those occasions when he was in for the long haul. I was on-air with Tony Cozier when he got to three figures and I thought things were looking ominous for England.

'There's a lot more to come from him yet,' I warned.

He just gave off that aura of 'you're never getting me out'. Gareth Batty was only playing in what was a dead rubber because Ashley Giles was suffering from an illness, and by the end of the innings he himself must have been feeling rather unwell. Every time he came on to bowl, Lara's welcome was to pump him to the boundary. An off-spinner would normally offer a threat bowling against a left-hander but not a left-hander of this quality. It was a real case of Groundhog Day at the start of every spell, as he picked him off for boundaries at will to keep the scoreboard ticking and the rhythm to his batting.

To possess both the artistry in your hands of a genius and the work ethic and discipline of a craftsman is unusual, but they are the traits that served Lara so well. Other people have got double hundreds but triple hundreds now seem to belong in a bygone age. Someone like Hashim Amla could do it, although the way of the game seems to be to get things done quicker. Score your runs, get the opposition in, get them out. The way of Lara's era was to be ruthless, to grind opponents into the dirt.

He certainly didn't have any weaknesses that I could detect. Or that Angus Fraser could detect, for that matter. He famously said to him during his 375 a decade earlier: 'I would like nothing more than to sledge you but you're just a bit too good.'

There was a period in his pomp when an England attack could have bowled when he was not ready and still not got him out. When he was in form he was nigh-on impossible to stop, and I guess the one thing when you have made such huge totals in the past – he made the world stop and take note when, six weeks after his Test record 375 against England's 1993-94 team at St John's, he broke Hanif Mohammad's 35-year-old record for the highest first-class score with 501 not out for Warwickshire versus Durham at Edgbaston – is that you know what you are capable of.

He dominated bowling attacks for such a long stretch of time at the highest level and to retain the ability to bat for nine- and 10-hour spells was just incredible. He barely broke sweat. He signalled his appetite for such huge individual totals with 277 off an Australian attack boasting Shane Warne, Craig McDermott and Merv Hughes in just his fifth Test appearance in Sydney. The powers of concentration to bat for that long without making a mistake against bowlers of that calibre were phenomenal. He didn't get a lot of sleep, either. He liked a good time.

In this regard he was following in a grand tradition. Sir Garry Sobers used to say in the most matter-of-fact tone: 'I never go to bed before three o'clock.' It was the Caribbean way. The West Indies lads I knew would grab a bit of shut-eye sometimes between seven and 11 in the evening, and then it was time to get off out. That's when the action would be happening for them.

West Indians have a very carefree attitude to life. Nothing much troubles them. They do things at their own pace, and in Trinidad they even have their own expression for not doing much other than eating, drinking and sharing conversation and laughter. They call it 'liming'. If someone says to me, 'Let's go lime', I am all for that. I love that laid-back vibe they've got going.

It's not such a clever tactic to be hanging out in Manchester at that kind of time of night, though. Well, not on 360 of our 365 days a year. Heading down Deansgate Locks late on? That's a totally different kind of chilling. You'd be freezing your nuts off.

Sobers, Lara and Viv Richards were all calypso cricketers and my three favourite players to watch. They shared that effort-less cool. No one was hurrying them, ruffling their feathers or knocking them off their games. Cricket was to be played at their pace. Great midfielders in that other ball game are said to be able to dictate the pace of a match whatever the situation, to suit themselves, and this trio ensured that quality came out in three generations of West Indies cricket.

Remember these three were just the best of the best. They had other fabulous talents who played with a similar ethos. Who can forget Collis King and his part in their 1979 World Cup win? England were in with a sniff when he strolled to the crease at 99 for four. Time for consolidation? Viv, who greeted him at the non-striker's end, certainly thought so.

Of course, a World Cup final at Lord's is supposed to be a big-pressure occasion. King, still playing and breaking batting records in the York District League into his sixties, wasn't having a bar of it. This match, he decided, was going to be played at an altogether different tempo – his tempo. You would only have backed one other player of the generation to smash 86 off 66 balls in that situation, and he was watching on from the non-striker's end. The vivacious Viv just seemed happy to stand on his bat handle in his iconic and idiosyncratic way and take in this wonderful spectacle.

Goners to a Goesoner

When it comes to first-class wickets, and I managed 237 of them, Brian Lara is not in my bag. But somehow both Garry Sobers and Viv Richards are.

Although I began as a bowling all-rounder as a youth, it is fair to say I was known as a stroke-making batsman among the professional ranks with Lancashire, partly due to the fact that

I got the yips at the age of 20 and became a nervous wreck at the thought of bowling in a competitive match. With time I overcame this, but I was no more than someone who filled in a few overs, really, for the majority of my career. Alternatively I was used to entice the declaration.

So how would I describe myself as a bowler? Simple. I was a non-spinning spinner. Sure, any spinner worth his salt has his speciality delivery and I was no different in this regard. You've no doubt heard of the doosra (the second one or other one, as it is translated from Hindi or Urdu), that goes the other way to the orthodox delivery, the teesra (translated as the third delivery but nothing more adventurous than a traditional back-spinner) and the carrom ball (a delivery flicked out of the front of the hand by a combination of a mystery spinner's thumb and bent middle finger, designed to rush on and hurry the batsman off the pitch)? And another delivery of deception – the zooter or flipper – sent down by leg-spinners in a similar manner.

As a slow left-arm orthodox bowler I was always looking to get the ball fizzing towards the batsman on a perfect arc, curving and drifting from a height just above his eyeline and then dipping as it got towards his pads before biting beautifully into the pitch and spinning just enough to take the edge as he played forward. I never stopped looking for that, to be honest. I just never found it. So it was the goesoner that accounted for most of my victims. What's the goesoner? That would be a trade secret, but seeing as it's you I will share. It's a bit of a round-arm delivery that just *goes on* a bit with the angle.

The Strut

It makes me chuckle to think that anyone in this age of verbal diarrhoea might have deemed themselves tough enough to take on Viv Richards. Here was a guy with such an intimidating presence that I couldn't imagine even the hardest nut telling him that he was about to get a broken arm, as Michael Clarke did to James Anderson in the 2013–14 Ashes. In fact, I would have loved to have seen any of the current serial sledgers have a pop at him. He would have scared the living daylights out of them. The same went for the great West Indies pace attack. For them, there was never a need to say a word.

With Viv, his batting persona was an act but boy could he act. I always used to say that people should pay to watch him walk to the crease. That strut was telling the bowlers that a superior human being was about to enter this match of theirs and that they'd better watch out. He would saunter at a leisurely pace, hips wiggling, arms gently windmilling, allowing the opposition bowler time to ponder what was coming. I always reckoned if I had been able to walk like that I'd have got thousands more runs.

Even then the dramatic entrance was only part-complete. Once arrived at the crease to take guard, he would be banging the top of his bat with the palm of his hand and snorting. Part-gladiator; part-lion; part-bull. Then, after a thrust forward to pat the pitch, the head would be tilted back and the dreaded eye contact made with his direct opponent. He was always full-throttle and aggressive, Viv. Never did he let up. Some players would come out and you would make the judgement: he's not interested today. That was never an accusation you could level at this guy. He was interested every time.

Hope for the Future

Shai Hope gave us a glimpse of the quality of batsmen West Indies used to produce with his wondrous twin-hundred performance at Headingley in 2017. That extraordinary win for West Indies saw him become the first man in 534 first-class matches at the ground to make three-figure scores in each innings. And a bit like Leeds buses, local folk had been waiting all that time for a batsman to be able to break that duck and then two came along at once.

Kraigg Brathwaite, 12 months Hope's senior at 24, fell agonisingly short but his performance was enough to earn a contract with Yorkshire for the end of the summer, as well as highlight the potential for these young players. They had never played at Headingley before but quickly worked out the vagaries of this most unique of grounds, and countered everything an experienced England attack could throw at them. It was a quite extraordinary display of discipline and skill from two lads still in their early twenties, and from players from a region no longer associated with any degree of success at the longest form of the game. They adapted to conditions very quickly and it went to show the benefit of persevering with young talent. Before his double bubble, Hope averaged 19 in Tests.

West Indies have been in the doldrums for so long, but coach Stuart Law can be very proud of the young team that's developing. It seems their best players continue to pick and choose when they play for the region, which puts a heavy burden on the younger ones. This has become the established way, unfortunately, and it has never been clear which players will fall back into line and when. Take the 2012 tour to England, for instance, which started with a toast to absent friends. Three years earlier, they had defeated England in the Caribbean, but for their next assignment there was no Chris Gayle, Ramnaresh Sarwan or Dwayne Bravo, due to other commitments, while Jerome Taylor, instigator of the infamous 51 all out match at Sabina Park, Jamaica, had disappeared from the international scene.

It would be foolhardy to expect them to replicate the same

skill level, but it would be a step in the right direction if at least they could develop a group with the drive to be successful that the ruthless 1976 team possessed. I can still see the parched Oval outfield at the end of a long summer. West Indies recorded 687, with Viv Richards hitting 291 – and it wasn't even Richards' match. That accolade belonged to Mikey Holding for a 14-wicket display on an absolute featherbed. For some reason, he seemed to bowl with particular venom at Tony Greig, and the pitch invasion afterwards was like a South American football match. That's passion for you.

They have some canny cricketers, none more so than their captain Jason Holder, but they don't need nice-looking seamers. They could really do with developing more like Shannon Gabriel, a big, strapping fast bowler of the old school. He reminds me so much of Charlie Griffith. Charlie was once the scourge of the Lancashire League and in 1964 took 144 wickets at 5.2 apiece for Burnley. It left my hero Wes Hall's effort of 123 at 10s look positively pedestrian.

Remember the Name

There are times as a commentator when you have to let the other guy take the lead role, and the most obvious example of this was when I was on-air with Ian Bishop for the final over of the 2016 World Twenty20 at Eden Gardens. England's Ben Stokes had the ball in hand and West Indies, with Carlos Brathwaite on strike, required an unlikely 19 from six balls to win the title for a second time.

Sorry to shatter any illusions of amateurism you may have had, but the scheduling of who works when and with whom is not just done on a whim. It can be a very elaborate, long-winded process to make sure the best men for the job are with each other to call it at the business end. For that special moment. The moment. Bish and I were paired together in the calling chairs as representatives of the two teams contesting the match, and for all the world it looked like it would be me waxing lyrical on the events of those final deliveries at Kolkata, calling home an England victory.

'Oh, heaved into the leg-side. Oh, West Indies. That helps,' I said, as Stokes sent down a full delivery outside the line of Brathwaite's pads that was helped on its way into the stands at long leg.

'Thirteen from five.'

I could sense that England were not comfortable with their situation and in that split-second you have to react and call what you see. Pressure appeared to have transferred from one team to the other.

'It's all gone back onto Ben Stokes. All that chatting, the field change, they're all over the place.'

Of the two of us, although Bish is interjecting, I am the lead commentator.

'Oh, big shot. Huge shot,' I exclaimed, as another ball, angling into the giant Brathwaite's pads, was hoisted over long-on.

'Into the stands! Seven from four. What a start to this final over. SIX! SIX!'

At this stage, the game has completely changed but I still called the third delivery: 'Stokes to come again. Oh, it's high in the air again. Oh, it's three sixes and that's his 18 gone.'

It was an astonishing passage of play. Bish, getting more and more animated, came back in with: 'Look at the West Indies. Look at England. Let's see Carlos Brathwaite. I said he was a superstar under construction. The foundation has been laid.'

At this point, I advised Bish that he should take over for the remainder of the innings – be it one ball, two or three. When the commentary team has been assembled from all over the world, it is nice to have expert knowledge on-air to describe the tournament-sealing stroke.

I whirled my hands in a signal to him to switch, while adding: 'Brathwaite, breathtaking.'

Therefore, this time it was a different voice that met Stokes being clubbed over the ropes.

'Carlos Brathwaite, remember the name,' Bishop demanded. 'History for the West Indies. What a match we've had here at Eden Gardens.'

He'd taken the entire world by surprise with his career-defining moment of monstrous ball-striking, not least the Star Sports commentary team.

A Rum Time

West Indies players like to make fashion statements. Long-term opening bowler Fidel Edwards used to have stars shaved into his hair, while his new-ball partner Kemar Roach lugged some serious gold round his neck. Andre Russell favours a similar look, with lots of earrings, too, but I'm old-school on these sorts of things. They should only go with high heels.

Tino Best was a different sort of character. He was on the receiving end of Andrew Flintoff's 'Mind the windows, Tino' jibe at Lord's, and the same man who kept opponents amused with running commentaries. During his astonishing innings of 95 in a Test match at Edgbaston in 2012, he kept countering: 'Graeme Swann cannot get me out!' Then would yell: 'Don't bowl there!', as he crashed another ball through the covers.

Talking of characters, you meet plenty during time spent on Tino's native island of Barbados. None bigger than the late Hans Grootenboer, who sadly passed away in late 2017. Groot's Bar, near Speightstown, was not much more than a shed. Although he held Dutch ancestry, he previously lived in Warrington and was a massive rugby league fan.

Looking at him, you would have concluded that he was lived in, and he certainly got very thirsty while at work, encouraging his customers to take the same attitude. You'd see the likes of Cilla Black and Cliff Richard in his joint but there would be no star treatment. Everyone was forced to sit on stools and, to give him his due, Hans would treat everyone with the same mild disdain.

Once, when I took my wife Diana for a drink, he was sat in his customary place at the wrong side of the bar. I had my usual of a Banks's and asked for a pina colada for my beloved Vipers. To which my host replied: 'Oh, for fuck's sake. Pina colada? I've got to go and make that stuff from fresh, so if you are having one, you're having four.'

Who were we to argue? That's how he was, bless him. Simple and up front like his bar menu of fish and chips, sausage and mash, and steak and kidney pudding.

Then, there's Nancy's Bar. Now, she's a big lady, Nancy, and there's not enough room for her behind it so someone else pours 'em from a huge fridge. There's not much room anywhere in there, as it happens, so instead of sitting in you sit outside. And you'll find lots of famous faces talking cricket in the open air. I've seen the likes of Desmond Haynes and other old-timers yarning about the game.

Afterwards, it's down to St Lawrence Gap, although I wouldn't recommend bothering until midnight. There is something for everyone there, from a roti for a few dollars to a hellish-posh meal with the waves lapping up a few yards away and a live band playing.

Opposite Tamarind Cove, where we tend to stay, is Croc's Den. It was actually a massive shed but den was a more appropriate description, for this was a real den of iniquity. Ten dollars to the little fella behind the bar, sporting a long ponytail and brandishing a baseball bat, gets you in. Anybody who oversteps the mark leaves with the baseball bat close behind them. It is not much of a deterrent, though, and the stars of the world could be in attendance at what you imagine a 1950s youth club with perks to be like. As you walk in, there is an air hockey table on your right, then at the front a pool table and karaoke machine. It's been a who's who list when I have been in there. The supermodel Jodie Kidd, Gary Lineker, even Bob 'the Cat' Bevan frequents the place.

I was very lucky on my last Caribbean trip to get asked to host a cruise for 80 people on behalf of a company called ITC. We had a ball circling the Caribbean. I am not a big cruiser but it was a great scene. Steve Smith and Fran Cotton, two rugby union guys I have got to know over the years, were on too, along with Bob the Cat, who was regaling us with his stories of derring-do. For some reason he kept losing his wife.

'Has anybody seen Laura?'

'She's probably avoiding you, Bob,' I thought. And I did have the heart to tell him.

CHAPTER SEVEN

The King of (Reverse) Swing

Pakistan, land of the doosra, is also the birthplace of a more devastating bowling phenomenon. Reverse swing is now an established part of cricket but for decades it was looked upon with scepticism – at least by those unable to extract it themselves. Then again, ignorance and suspicion tend to be natural bedfellows.

Developed by Sarfraz Nawaz in the seventies, the practice of getting a ball of two contrasting halves – one smooth and/ or shiny and the other roughed-up – to swing the opposite of its conventional way via the use of a similar wrist position has become common the world over. But for many years it was a maligned practice, as if those capable of mastering this dark art were somehow bending the rules. As if this nation of wonderfully gifted cricketers, following the teachings of the godfather Sarfraz, could not possibly be producing such logic-defying bend on their deliveries without cheating in some way. Absolute codswallop.

Pakistan were global leaders in its execution and their extremely dry playing areas gave them ample opportunity to experiment. Imran Khan was a fine reverse-swing bowler, but the world hadn't seen anything quite like the combination of Waqar Younis and Wasim Akram when they bowled in tandem with a scuffed-leather sphere. Scorecards throughout the 1980s and 1990s were littered with periods in which this fabulous duo would scythe through an opposition's batting order. They were a handful with the new ball. With the old one they were simply knockout.

Of course, there has been all kinds of innuendo about the use of third-party objects to catalyse the deterioration of one side of the ball – such as bottle tops, spikes from boots and concrete. But having seen all this at close quarters I must tell you that these boys didn't need any of that. Once one side of the ball was roughed up through general wear and tear, they were in business.

Knowing about the skill is one thing but administering it is another, and not many have been able to do so. There have been teams who have profited from its use. Of England's 2005 Ashes-winning attack, Simon Jones, in particular, tormented the Australian batsmen. But the best English exponent of reverse swing I have seen is Darren Gough, and that I believe was because he could get his body into a similar sling position to that which Waqar managed in delivery.

So what other characteristics make for a good reverse-swing bowler? Well, there is no doubt you have to have extreme pace for it to be truly lethal, and that means top-end 80s to 90mph. At something like 79mph, it is neither here nor there because there is enough time for the batsman to react. At that pace it's not really anything other than drift.

As reverse swing only comes into play in the last third of a ball's journey – it sets off dead straight and only veers when it's half a dozen yards shy of the batsman – an increase in speed accentuates its devilry. One of the features of the two Ws getting it ducking and dipping at express speed was hitting batsmen on the boot. It was incredible how often batsmen were just unable to get their feet out of the way. Those in for a while would naturally have a much better chance of lining it up, but if new to the crease you were there for the taking.

As a tail-ender – and a half-decent dancer later in life, according to Alesha Dixon and Len Goodman – Phil Tufnell was not averse to a quick step to square leg when he came in to bat against the hostile stuff. But he simply couldn't get away from a Waqar delivery that seemed to have a homing device in it during the first innings of a Test match at The Oval in 1992. This heat-seeking missile began its route going down the Bakerloo Line and then took a sharp right onto the Jubilee, leaving poor old Tuffers between stations as it crashed into his boot. Ouch. It's a classic bit of footage as our England hero hops about, rather appropriately given his nickname, like a cat on a hot tin roof.

Others blessed with greater batting ability would not have got their feet into such a position. Not that getting them into the perfect place helped the extremely gifted Brian Lara when he faced up to Waqar in Rawalpindi in 1997. Having struck the ball three times into the gaps on the off-side for a combined 10 runs earlier in the over, a boomerang of a ball slid straight through his defences and left him on all fours as he tried to make a late adjustment. The ball missed his toes but knocked back leg stump.

Garry Sobers used to argue there was no such thing as reverse swing, that swing was swing any road up and the ball was either swinging in or swinging out. He didn't care much for theorising on the methodology and perhaps it was because, while Pakistan were ahead of their time in this art with a dry ball, and absolutely brilliant at it, a variation with a soaked one (bowlers using the sweat from their brows to make one side so) was prevalent in Barbados club cricket in the 1950s. But what is clear is that Pakistan had every right to guard their own blueprint from their rivals – it was the tactic that would provide them with an advantage over the rest and coincided with their 1992 World Cup win.

Wasim delivered the two quickfire blows that swung the final back Pakistan's way after England had reached 141 for four, chasing 250. Again, it was all in the planning. At the start of a new spell he wanted to bowl left-arm around the wicket to Allan Lamb and bowl outswing because, he reasoned with his captain Imran Khan, Lamb had never faced him in county cricket when it was reverse swinging, as he usually batted number three or four.

In this match, Lamb was in at six and, as Wasim reflected: 'He must have thought, "Left-arm, round the wicket, going away? I don't think so ..."'

The delivery that broke the 72-run partnership between Lamb and Neil Fairbrother started on middle stump and went away from him against the angle. Wasim refers to it as one of the top five balls he ever bowled. Then, when Chris Lewis came out to bat, he was about to bowl a yorker. But Imran said that was what he would be expecting – an outswinging full-length ball – so to send down an inswinging length ball. The right pace, the right swing, a little bit of inside edge onto his stumps, and England had lost two wickets without addition.

During his time with us at Lancashire his preparation on a run-of-the-mill day was as meticulous as his planning of a match-winning spell in a major match. I remember one particular occasion at Old Trafford when he wanted to practise but the entire first-team squad had been granted a day off. So to accommodate his request meant arranging a net to be prepared by the groundsman Pete Marron. I was in my office anyway, so popped out to watch.

It was a tragi-comic scene. At one end there was this hugely impressive physical specimen gliding in towards the crease like a big-game cat. His prey was sporting a tight pair of jeans and his attire was reflective of his ability. Wasim was peppering a guy that cooked for his family, in turn striking the stumps or an ill-protected body. This chap didn't seem to realise that the bat should be the first line of protection.

'He's only there to throw the balls back,' smiled Wasim. That was him all over. A dedicated practice session for an hour and then away.

His nickname in the Old Trafford dressing room was 'King'. The others simply idolised him. It was our responsibility to protect him from breakdown, too. Because of the saturated nature of the county fixture list we had to map out his matches carefully and look for him to play 10 to 12 in the County Championship per season.

It was a good team, with a decent attack including Peter Martin, Glen Chapple, Phil DeFreitas and Ian Austin. Wasim was not only our go-to man, though, but also the perfect foil to Mike Watkinson, who was just changing over to spin from medium pace at that stage of his career. Wasim, bowling left-arm over, would develop these rough areas where his spikes landed and Winker would aim his quick spinners into them. It was a really good combination.

He was such a natural all-round talent, comfortable batting at number six or seven, with Warren Hegg and DeFreitas occupying the places behind him. But it was his bowling that placed this enormous bloke ahead of his peers. He had one of the fastest arms the game has ever witnessed and his run-up was the best of both worlds: economic and explosive. He didn't need to lengthen it because doing so would have simply wasted energy. He had the necessary speed through the crease from his measured approach and so he would have bowled no quicker with an extension.

His injury problems tended to occur in the groin because his legs used to open up and splay to get his body through. But his wrist was monstrous. We used to joke it was as big as some people's thighs. His strong wrist position meant he controlled the ball for inswing and outswing, utilising the knowledge he'd picked up from the masters, Sarfraz and Imran.

Wasim and Waqar were a wonderful combination and absolutely deadly in tandem once the ball was old enough to start dodging about in unconventional manner. They were compulsive viewing. In fact, Reverend Andrew Wingfield Digby thought that much of them he named his two Labradors after them.

My one experience of these dogs ended up like most encounters with the human equivalents – a couple of Englishmen in the shit. Literally.

A fishing trip in Scotland had been arranged, also involving Michael Atherton and John Barclay among others. But it soon became clear that there wasn't enough accommodation for us all where we were headed. So I got in touch with Don Amott, the king of caravans, and the then chairman and chief sponsor at Derbyshire County Cricket Club. Telling him of our plans, I asked to hire a caravan off him for me and the Reverend to sleep in. Andrew picked it up on his way up from his diocese in Oxford, starting spectacularly when he knocked a wing mirror off before exiting the drive. That was nothing, however.

Having parked up in the wilds of north Aberdeen, we all got together for a long dinner, Andrew having fed his two hounds before we left. This information was significant later when we returned to our hired vehicle at two in the morning. Wasim and Waqar had, not to put too fine a point on it, shat all over it. To the extent that we were still pulling mats out, washing covers in the river and generally disinfecting two hours later.

We even built a camp fire to keep warm while we worked. As I say, they caused carnage, did that pair.

For Lancashire, Wasim was our game-changer. Not that his influence was always appreciated by our opponents. Take June 1993, when we were playing Derbyshire and the contest was going nowhere for us – if anything Derbyshire looked like they were on the way to winning at 216 for one, chasing 379 for victory – when Was announced, 'I'll bowl.'

His demand for the ball proved inspired. Boom, boom, boom, straight through them he went, as 243 for two deteriorated rapidly from the moment John Morris was dismissed for a magnificent 151. In an incredible implosion, the home team mustered just 267 all out. It was one of Wasim's devastating spells and Derbyshire were left seething. He claimed six of the eight wickets to fall, including the last one as number 11 Ole Mortensen's stumps were demolished like a deck of cards. You can probably visualise the delivery in your mind: a heat-seeking yorker right on the money.

While his team-mates congratulated him on its execution, though, Mortensen was off like a shot, pegging it down to fine leg to retrieve the ball. Putting it straight in his pocket, he marched off to give it to Bud Hill, who was coaching Derbyshire at the time, for further inspection. I'd never seen a batsman seek the match ball as a memento after getting nought before.

Relations between the two teams were still heated during a six-run defeat to Derbyshire in the Benson & Hedges Cup final at Lord's the following month. It hardly helped cool things when early in the first innings a beamer slipped out of Was's hand and thudded into the back of Chris Adams, taking evasive action.

Unfortunately, there was always a stigma when a ball suddenly began misbehaving but it was primarily about the skill of the individual, and part of that skill was knowing when it was in the right condition for it to dart about like one of Harry Potter's snitches. Wasim and Waqar were great bowlers and whispers of skulduggery always made me chuckle. If it was purely about altering the condition of the ball by foul means, why then didn't they do it sooner in the innings? Why weren't opponents 50 all out?

They would certainly be trying to dismiss top-order batsmen with the new ball, and they were pretty successful at that, lest we forget, but there were no international rivals quite like them once they returned later in the innings. The movement they managed at such electric pace made them devastating.

Wasim was a great lad with a tremendous sense of humour. He embraced everything Lancashire. He wasn't one of those overseas players with a superiority complex and, despite the regal status of his nickname, he didn't want to be any different to the other lads. As an all-rounder, he was as good as I have seen, and if you were picking a World XI in a modern era he would be in it. Nobody would argue with that.

I first saw him in late 1982 when Graeme Fowler and I were involved in the Qasim Umar Benefit double-wicket competition in Qatar. I had left the playing staff at Old Trafford the previous summer but partnered up with Foxy for an event to help my old Cumberland team-mate Qasim earn a bob or two. It was here that we played against Imran Khan and this spindly 16-year-old kid with the brightest of futures.

Later we saw what a fantastic player he was at first hand. It was the previous coach, Alan Ormerod, working with then club captain David Hughes, who signed him but I was glad to see the benefits. There were some occasional downsides, as he liked to do things his own way at times, but, crikey, they were outweighed by the positives.

As I say, his arrival at Old Trafford pre-dated my time. He embraced the club straight away and the players embraced him. He was just one of the lads. People like Neil Fairbrother, Michael Atherton, Paul Allott, Fowler and Hughes became mates. Ormerod had picked him up from the airport upon arrival, dropped him off at his digs and instructed him to be ready within the hour as they had a meeting in the bar that evening.

'What? In the bar? That can't be right! I come from Pakistani culture!' Wasim thought. When he walked in to meet his new playing colleagues, they all raised a pint to him to toast his arrival and despite the culture clash he felt like a Lancashire player from the get-go.

Occasionally, he would be challenging. For example, we had a club rule when travelling to away matches that if we went south of Birmingham we went on a coach. For fixtures north of Birmingham, the players could take their own cars. It was just the practical way of doing things for long-distance drives, such as those to Bristol, and we had an agreed departure time of 2pm.

'I'm taking my car,' Wasim declared.

As first-team coach this was a bit of a tricky issue. The entire squad, including Wasim, had agreed on the protocol for road trips and there should be no exceptions. On the other hand, I knew our overseas import could win a match for us in a flash and I realised how important it was to keep him sweet.

'I really need you to do this. We are going on a coach,' I told him, before walking off, allowing him to mull things over.

I made eye contact with several players as I did so, and wondered what they were thinking. If he doesn't turn up now, I thought, they will know he's defied me. Thankfully, at two o'clock the next day, Wasim hops on board with the rest of the lads and all is well with the world. A diplomatic incident has been avoided and I take my place at the front to read the newspaper. Card schools have formed towards the back and all is calm as we set off. Not long after getting onto the M6, though, around the Knutsford Services area, the driver pulls up on the hard shoulder.

'What's up? Have we broken down?' I ask.

'No, he's getting off.'

'What do you mean he's getting off? Who's getting off?'

I arched my neck to look down the aisle and of course it is Wasim striding towards me.

'I got on bus. Now I am getting off bus.'

A mate of his had been tailing us from Old Trafford and the pair of them were intent on having a night in Birmingham before meeting up with us next day. As I say, within reason, you have to make allowances for your superstar player, and the important thing was that he hadn't disobeyed me. Well, he hadn't totally disobeyed me, anyway.

Once with us he was as good as gold. The trouble was getting him there in the first place. I remember playing in a knockout cup match at Leek early one season. Staffordshire had named their XI but we held off handing in ours while we phoned Old Trafford for confirmation Wasim would be turning up. Yes, came the reply. Of course, he didn't, and still hadn't done so 10 days or so later.

In the pre-mobile phone era, communication with Pakistan was a far different proposition and we were reliant on contacting him via a landline. When eventually he did arrive, I went into a meeting with the club and the committee members were adamant – he has got to be reprimanded. A disciplinary was required. That kind of thing. They wanted him to be suspended for a couple of matches. But he had already missed some and as he was our best player it was my priority as coach to keep him happy.

'Leave it with us,' I said.

We used to have a dressing-room court to decide the fate of transgressors. Ian Austin would be in chambers, and instead of a wig he would place a box on his head, and the other players would make up the prosecution, defence and jury. Up in front of Judge Austin, Wasim pleaded not guilty.

'Did you or did you not say you were going to be here 10 days ago?' Austin asked, through a collection of coughs, splutters and wheezes.

'Yes.'

'But you never arrived, sir.'

'I couldn't get a flight.'

'You, Wasim Akram, couldn't get a flight from Islamabad. The most famous man in Pakistan – grounded?'

With that the jury filed out of the dressing room and then immediately filed back in and retook their places on the cinema-style seats.

'Do you have a verdict, foreman?' Austin enquired.

'Yes, your honour. Guilty.'

'Right. Take him down.'

Taking him down actually meant a trip into the lavatories while Austin deliberated the punishment. Upon his return, he was told he had one of two choices: either eat a ham sandwich or roll the practice pitches. This was a bit of a Hobson's choice for a Muslim, so off he toddled to the groundsman's shed.

When Wasim practised he always did the same thing. Complaints about the quality of the balls available for net sessions were prevalent among county cricketers nationwide. He took a drastically different approach, simply waiting for all the moans and groans from his team-mates to die down – 'These balls are rubbish', 'Why can't we get some new ones?', 'I can't bowl with this' – before choosing his own from the bag.

Of course, we used these balls until they were like cloth rags because of the cost. We simply couldn't afford to be buying new practice balls every week. He delved into what remained and would settle on the oldest, filthiest, dirtiest piece of leather with bits hanging off it – and that is what he would use. He was quite happy to bowl with that because he was practising reverse swing all the time. Mastering it was what set him apart from the rest of the fast bowlers in the world at the time.

Overstepping the Mark

Pakistan have always unearthed wonderful bowlers and one of their brightest of recent times has divided opinion. I understand the argument that Mohammad Amir served his time, went to prison, completed a ban and the slate was wiped clean after the spot-fixing affair of 2010, in which he delivered no-balls at designated points of the Lord's Test. But I don't necessarily agree with it.

Let me explain my rationale. Say you're driving a car at 38mph in a 30mph zone. You might be fined £60 and given three points on your licence – but if you're going at 120mph, you face the consequences, and Amir, to use an analogy, was driving at that speed when he opted to wilfully do something he had never done before and overstep the mark. Never before had he bowled a no-ball in his first-class career.

Yet here he was fabricating the game for financial reward for himself and others. What he did was an enormous offence against the game of cricket and I don't buy the 'he was only a kid' line. We've all been kids and we all know what is right and what is wrong. He had total disregard for the sport no matter if he was leant on by his captain Salman Butt or not.

Every player in the world is told what to do if you get an approach from anybody suggesting corruption and that is report it. They are briefed on it by the International Cricket Council's anti-corruption unit and by their own board. They know very clearly what they must do, and those rules applied in 2010 when

Amir committed his offence just as they do now. Amir chose not to report his team-mates – he did what he did for cash and for me there has to be the ultimate deterrent of a lifetime ban from the game. I accept the decision made by the ICC and I have done what I have always tried to do in commentary when analysing players in a match – provide a fair and balanced assessment of their performance. But I have very strong opinions on this. Having served his time, he should have been able to take part in educating younger players about the dangers of corruption, not making a Test match comeback for Pakistan at Lord's in 2016. It just didn't seem right.

I experienced a similar feeling in The Oval Test match between England and Pakistan in 2006. This was a match memorable for all the wrong reasons. Pakistan refused to carry on playing when the Australian umpire, Darrell Hair, decided the ball had been tampered with. England were awarded the Test by forfeiture, then the ICC said it was a draw, before deciding England won it after all. Grown men cried that day and the whole sorry saga ended with Hair losing his job. Ridiculous.

Home from Home

What Pakistan have gained my admiration for in recent years is their adaptability. They are unable to play at home but they have turned the United Arab Emirates into a real fortress, and have been far too street smart for England on the past couple of tours. Beating England 3-0 and 2-0 in consecutive 'home' Test series was a fantastic achievement.

Slowly, top-level cricket is returning to Pakistan, but I fear it will still be quite some time until that includes all their bilateral international fixtures. Several England players, including Dawid Malan, Samit Patel, Chris Jordan and Liam Dawson, went to participate in the finals of the 2017 and 2018 editions of the Pakistan Super League in Lahore and Karachi respectively, and West Indies flew in for three Twenty20 internationals in as many days.

Security was at a presidential level and it seems the Pakistan Cricket Board are that keen to return cricket to their homeland that touring teams are whisked in and out under similar blankets for short trips. It is hard to promote the sport if your population never sees the country's best players first-hand.

Fact is, they had all the tools to win in the desert. Spin obviously plays a part, as you would expect in a place which is so dry, as does genuine pace through the air. Yasir Shah, the leggie, is a real handful who really comes into his own in the fourth innings, with sharp turn. With experience, he has learned to bowl at the perfect pace for the pitches in question. He is very aggressive to the crease, with a big follow-through, and he gets plenty of energy on the ball as a result. And Wahab Riaz showed just how dangerous a bowler of his speed can be when he puts a shift in.

Meanwhile, their batsmen have the combination of skill, concentration and staying power to fatigue visiting attacks in heat that can get quite oppressive. Two old stagers, Younis Khan and Misbah-ul-Haq, provided regular exhibitions of how it is done with their calm and well-organised games, getting in big strides, sniffing the good ball out, and staying in that sideways position. They dropped anchor when they were trying to get rid of Jimmy Anderson and Stuart Broad from the attack. At others, Misbah in particular went the other way – he could be a barnacle but he could hit sixes, as we saw when he launched Adil Rashid and Samit Patel into the stands in 2016.

Generally, though, it's hard work. Just, as I imagine, is climbing that Burj Khalifa, the tallest building in the world at 828 metres. It might be a big 'un but it's got nothing on the

Blackpool Tower. There's no ballroom dancing, nor Reginald Dixon on the organ. And I bet it doesn't have an oyster bar or a Harry Ramsden's chippy. But I do know it has got a restaurant on the 122nd floor because Sir Beefikins, from our commentary crew, has told me so. You'd probably cancel your reservation if you turned up to find the lift was broken, wouldn't you?

Everything is big in the Emirates, in fact. In Abu Dhabi, they have the widest roads that I've ever seen. There are about 15 lanes on the highway from Yas Island to the ground. And the cars! Bentleys, Rolls-Royces, Mercedes. Didn't spot a Fiat Punto in two dozen shuttles from the hotel to the ground and back. Not that there is much to see as you cruise along. There's more sand around than at Jewson's. Down the road, buildings are going up left, right and centre in Dubai. I'm not sure who's going to fill them as it's an expensive place. The one exception – the taxis. And there is a good reason for that, the one thing that is cheap in this part of the world is fuel.

It's a different kind of tour when you are in the UAE and one of the main events over there appears to be shopping. Not Sainsbury's- or Tesco-style, mind. No, this is an altogether different experience and so I took the chance to go to one of the splendid malls they have there, in the company of Michael Atherton. These places include everything from giant fish tanks to ice-skating rinks, but we were taken by surprise by a sign on display as we made our way inside. It told us to avoid showing shoulders and knees and not to kiss or show any outward signs of affection. We've worked together in various capacities for 30 years, and I can assure you we are not going to start any of that kind of stuff now.

There tends to be only a smattering of the Barmy Army present on these trips, but no matter the number they still like a singsong. And that, of course, makes them very thirsty. Yet even in a dry state like Sharjah they are very resourceful, so trust them to suss out the only licensed premises in this particular emirate. It's called the Wanderers Club and it was set up by some tarmac engineers years ago by kind permission of a local sheikh. Cheers!

Holly, the Elephant

Wherever I go I always like to get involved in the local culture and it is a shame that for security reasons tours of Pakistan no longer take place. It used to be a brilliant trip when we toured there in the late 1990s, made so by the intrepid voyagers we had in our group.

Someone like Adam Hollioake was brilliant at rounding up a crew and encouraging us to head out downtown to the markets. People like him and like-minded souls such as Dougie Brown wanted to get out and see what local life was like, get their hands dirty so to speak, rather than sit cooped in hotel rooms for weeks on end. One day, I walked round the corner on one of our forays and there was Hollioake, heading towards me on the back of an elephant. During his time as an international cricketer here was a lad who embraced everything that went on and seeing the world is part of that.

In Pakistan, their cricketers have always been treated like national heroes, and for a touring team it was great fun to see how cricket mixed with everyday life. In cities like Rawalpindi and Karachi you would wind your way through narrow streets, past communal drains, and find yourself greeted by familiar scenes: open shops with crackly television pictures showing somewhere in the corner. Wires dangling across rug-covered floors and the picture of a cricket match flickering on and off. Dozens of people gathered round with cups of coffee and samosas to chat about the match they were watching and the game in general. Wander in and you would be made to feel most welcome. In the hinterland between the hustle and bustle of the road and the relative calm of the shop, some bloke is sat having his hair cut.

Experiencing everyday Pakistani life was a real thrill and showed that, however you do it, cricket is a game that is celebrated the world over. Like India, Pakistan breathes cricket and the maidans of Lahore are as populous with bats and balls as their equivalent in Mumbai. Unfortunately, though, it does not have anywhere near the finance to match.

Games are happening everywhere. Occasionally, it is like a farmyard meandering through the streets of one of their big cities, an on-foot safari in which you regularly pass goats and sheep roaming on their merry way. They pass impromptu games of street cricket and no one seems to bat an eyelid. Some of these young lads don't even need proper equipment to express their talents, substituting a piece of wood for a bat and a taped-up piece of paper for a ball. But it is enough for them to get a game going and offer them a chance to showcase their skills. This improvisation highlights their devotion to what is *the* game in Pakistan.

One of the features of their main stadia is the open expanse of land around them. Inside, the national team will be playing and outside there are knockabout matches being contested as far as the eye can see. It is slightly chaotic at times, as games tend to overlap and a fielder at mid-wicket can find themselves nursing a blow to the back of the head from someone crashing a cover drive into the vacant offside on the pitch next to them, but it is a wonderful spectacle to behold. It shows you what cricket is worth to the ordinary man.

Pakistani cricketers tend to play with great flair and freedom of expression, and part of the reason they have adapted to the UAE conditions so comfortably is that pitches in their own country have been so unforgiving to bowlers, failing to deteriorate like ones elsewhere in the subcontinent. Because they are unresponsive, it means they have to work extra hard to make things happen. The same struggle to get the ball to deviate is true when they play in the dusty streets, so they experiment to get it moving through the air. It is this ability from their youths that has helped so many of their top internationals break open matches on flat pitches.

In Pakistan, just about everyone wants to have a go at being the next Imran or Waqar or Wasim. In contrast, I am yet to walk down Oxford Street and witness someone chalking up some stumps on the wall of Selfridges. Sure, there is a deep love of the game shared by many in the UK, but in Asia cricket's in the air that they breathe. A part of their daily routines. In places like Pakistan there don't appear to be cycle lanes, and on your trips from hotel to cricket grounds you don't tend to see leisure centres or swimming baths. It is an outdoor culture and cricket is a part of that. When you are born it is in your DNA. Just look at the way they idolise their players. Recall the reaction when Pakistan won the World Twenty20 at Lord's in 2009 or Champions Trophy in Cardiff in 2017. Their fans swarmed all over those two capital cities, horns and whistles blaring.

The fact that those two global triumphs came on UK soil should be no surprise. Because if there is something in the surface they come alive. It is why, I believe, Pakistani cricketers get branded with words such as temperamental, volatile and enigmatic. They appear to be doing not much, almost lazing around, and then when they get a sniff it's like an explosion has occurred. They are as prolific as any team going when it comes to taking wickets in bundles and it is as if they conserve energy for when the time is right.

And Misbah-ul-Haq appeared to have been conserving his for years when he led his team to a 2-2 Test draw in 2016, a series in which he became the oldest centurion for 82 years. What an effort from a bloke who was 42 – just shows you can't keep a good old 'un down. And when he celebrated with a set of press-ups, I was willing him to double up. What would it have been next? Star jumps and burpees. He got us all going that week and I simply couldn't resist getting onto the Lord's turf and knocking 20 out of my own with Misbah as my personal trainer.

They won a lot of friends on that trip with their cheery dispositions and in a way they reminded me of Wasim's attitude 20 years earlier: always looking to enjoy, adapt to the environment and surroundings, and while playing in the right manner never allowing the focus to shift from a desire to win.

CHAPTER EIGHT

India's Twenty20 Vision

England might have given world cricket Twenty20 a decade and a half ago but India has undoubtedly become its spiritual home, and I had a great opportunity in 2018 to get back over to the Indian Premier League and work on seven matches.

The previous time I had been to cover it, some of the stuff that was occurring was a little bit dubious, shall we say. A time when you couldn't help but think, 'These matches look a bit odd.' As became clear, there was a reason for that and Chennai Super Kings and Rajasthan Royals were suspended from the tournament for a couple of years as the IPL tried to clean up its act.

One of the other noticeable changes was that the cricket side of things looked more serious. In time gone by, massive after-match parties were the norm but that has stopped as well, and the IPL experience in the 11th edition was strictly business.

As I knew that matches did not start until eight o'clock at night, and can often finish in the early hours in the event of adverse weather, the one stipulation to me accepting Star Sports' invitation to join their commentary team for a stint was that I didn't want to be haring around India covering matches every day.

When Twenty20 started it was designed to be a quick game but these days the opposite is true, with your average IPL match taking four hours. The scheduling means the commentators can be faced with coming off-air at midnight and making their way to the airport not long afterwards for a 6am flight elsewhere. At my age I simply couldn't manage that, so I was delighted to join them having agreed they would look after me in terms of travel.

The organisation for my seven-match stay was first class. India remains a chaotic place, and that is part of its charm, but against all odds everything somehow works. Aeroplanes take off on time, pick-up arrangements are met and you are never too far behind the clock despite the masses of people trying to make the same journey as you simultaneously.

Take the departure from Bengaluru airport. The exit road starts with 15 lanes but abruptly reduces into two. What a flippin' bunfight that is. Then, when the road becomes dual carriageway, just to make things a little more challenging, factor in the horse and cart heading into the oncoming traffic. Come to roundabouts and you tend to find a very important-looking police officer directing operations. 'Sod him,' seems to be the general attitude, though, because if it's chock-a-block on the left-hand side of the road, drivers will just squeeze through into the space on the right.

A journey on the roads of India is as unpredictable, and utterly gripping, as one of their IPL contests. My road experiences on this particular trip included seeing two blokes on a motorbike – one carrying an oven, the other a 40-inch television. In case you were wondering, the record number of people I saw on a two-seater motorbike was five.

My eyes almost popped out of my head one day when I saw what appeared to be a fella cycling along at breakneck speed despite pulling a cart laden with cardboard. He was going like the clappers and it was only on seeing this from behind that exactly how he managed to be travelling at around 30mph became apparent. Another bloke on a motorbike was propelling him – one hand on the accelerator and his right foot not covering the brake, where it should have been, but propped up against the back of the cart. It was like an act out of Billy Smart's Circus.

'Peter Piper Picked a Peck of Pickled Peppers'

The Indian Premier League has evolved to make the most of its brilliantly simple concept. When it started back in April 2008, it did so with the country's eight biggest cities represented, each playing the other home and away, for a total of 56 matches, plus the knockout stage of semi-final and final. Ten years later, not much has changed in terms of the scheduling, other than a slight tinkering with the latter stages.

No, the volume of fixtures is not greatly altered but the worth of each has changed astronomically. Star Sports paid £1.97 billion for the rights to screen the tournament from 2018 to 2022, and with that kind of financial commitment there is an obligation to cover your costs. They do so through adverts.

It means that any sort of delay in play – if somebody needs a drink, or a change of gloves – bang, up goes a commercial. Meanwhile, the last delivery of an over becomes business time for a commentator. You're judging how many runs are going to be scored as soon as the batsman strikes the ball so that you can work out the score to inform the viewer before the action cuts away to the commercial break. You have to be like lightning. No pontificating, as is arguably the style over here. It's '72 for three after 10' and you're out of there. Time is tight because of the need to get full adverts in between overs as part of their contractual obligations. What Star cannot afford to have is an advert being cut three-quarters of the way through, as it does not count as being shown in terms of the tally requirement for the match.

As a commentator, understanding that it's an advert-driven operation is important. The IPL is the one competition in cricket that can rival football in its earning potential and provides the kind of riches that will persuade some of the most talented youngsters around the world to take up cricket. The broadcaster gets the money back by meeting the advertising obligations. You have to get them in to pay the rent. It is the business model of a commercial channel.

At Sky things are done very differently. There are strict limits on advertising in the UK and that's why, in addition to the use of the commentary feed from IPL matches, there is a studio in Isleworth in which the likes of Nick Knight, Mark Butcher and Steve Harmison analyse the action. Being a subscription-driven rather than advert-driven channel, they are there to pick up when the Indian breaks are kicking in.

Meanwhile, it is a real exercise for the Indian production team to get it beamed onto your television set. Coming in partway through the tournament, I hadn't had the brief about the advert cues and there are so many different types to remember. You have to get them in with both precision and immaculate pronunciation. It's a completely different animal to that which I am used to, and the other guys were brilliant with me in this regard, particularly Matthew Hayden and Harsha Bhogle.

Your job as lead commentator is to get the ad-break links in, but those two in particular had a habit of quietly telling me: 'Don't worry about that, leave it, I will do it.' I was really grateful for their co-operation because it is by far the most difficult commentating I have come across. Everything you say has to be succinct. You cannot develop a point across a couple of overs because you are off screen for a minute and the thread is therefore lost.

You try saying 'CEAT Tyres Strategic Timeout' as quickly as you can. Personally, I found it too much of a mouthful. Give me a tongue twister any day of the week.

> Peter Piper picked a peck of pickled peppers.
> A peck of pickled peppers Peter Piper picked.
> If Peter Piper picked a peck of pickled peppers,
> Where's the peck of pickled peppers Peter
>   Piper picked?

Now, that I can cope with. But when I tried 'CEAT Tyres' under pressure it came out as 'Seaty Triers'.

I have certainly been critical of stopping the flow of matches with needless breaks in the past, but I now see that India is the one place where interrupting the flow with designated timeouts works, and not just from a corporate perspective.

So why do I believe it works? Well, look around the grounds or on social media and there are thousands of strategists playing the captain/coach role, telling their mates next to them or those online what their team is going to do. Or at least what they should be doing. Who should be bowling, when, whether pace or pace off is best suited for the next stretch of overs, who needs to come in to bat next, which overs will be crucial, and how many runs they should be targeting off the final five, that kind of thing.

That two-and-a-half-minute break really works for an Indian crowd. Their fans are so passionate about what's happening, and love to get involved. India's middle class of over 100 million people are engaged every evening between March and May, and that level of interactivity is one of the tournament's essential ingredients.

The most clinical part of all the strategy for me is that you are limited to four overseas players per team for any one match. There is none of the rubbish about whether a player is a Kolpak, has a British or European passport. You can play four. That's your lot.

The best players in the world want to be there, that adds to the glamour and effectively raises the standard, so part of the conundrum for the franchise coaches and the armchair amateurs is which of your four international imports will help you produce the best XI to beat the particular opposition team on a given day. The decision-making process is a bit like top-level football, in that a player might be brilliant one match but left out the next as all the selection factors are considered – conditions, team combinations and the strengths of the opposition. Occasionally, you will have to sacrifice someone because you want a particular facet in your XI.

And the coaches are spoilt for choice. To be frank, I was blown away by the standard of the cricket. You get to watch Virat Kohli and AB de Villiers bat together, for goodness' sake. That's an experience worth paying for and the skill of some of these stellar batsmen was jaw-dropping at times. Similarly, the nous of the bowlers to stop them scoring. I watched Liam Plunkett on his Delhi Daredevils debut provide a splendid exhibition of knuckle balls and slower balls out of the back of the hand, mixed up with genuine pace, to return figures of three for 17. Three matches later, he went the distance, conceding 52 runs in three overs against Chennai Super Kings, and that's the way it goes in Twenty20 cricket when you are up against the very best exponents of the game.

The one thing that struck me was the response of India's young players to being involved. If you are in an IPL XI you have to perform. There is no hiding behind your age, using inexperience as a crutch for failure. At 18, Prithvi Shaw already

Good crew – but can you name them? One of the joys of the cricket circuit is you can always catch up with old friends.

I've always been a proud Accrington lad, both as a boy and all the way through to April 2018 when Stanley was promoted to Division One. 'Please don't run on to your field,' the sign said.

Viv Richards batting for Rishton in 1987 – one of a long line of greats to play in the Lancashire League. He even hit me for a few! (Getty Images)

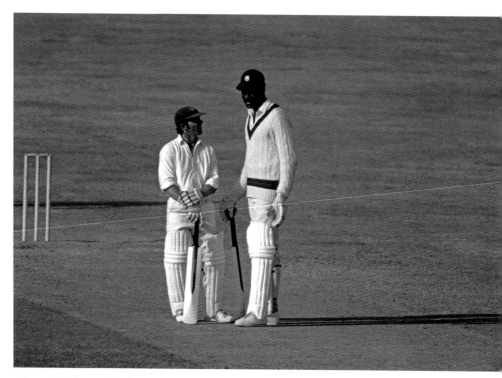

Harry Pilling and Clive Lloyd together during a 1972 match against Sussex. Harry may have been small, but he was very combative. (Getty Images)

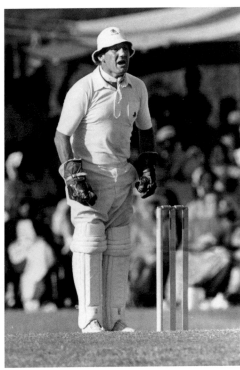

Two Yorkshire legends: Fred Trueman and (right) David 'Bluey' Bairstow. (Getty Images)

Always a brilliant atmosphere at Edgbaston – especially on T20 finals day.

With Ian Healy, Tom Moody and Michael Slater on a lobster fishing trip – but it was Mitchell Johnson who really snapped the door shut on England's 2013-14 Ashes hopes. (Getty Images)

A tour of the Caribbean is always a highlight. Reckon I'd had a few by the time I unleashed this shot.

Athers with Brian Lara – as Angus Fraser once said of him, he was 'just a bit too good'. He was always a great host.

Celebrations for 'King' Wasim Akram after an early wicket helped Lancashire on their way to the 1990 Benson & Hedges Cup.

(Getty Images)

Street cricket in Lahore.

Jack of all trades at the Wankhede Stadium in Mumbai.

That bloody camper van – Mount Maunganui.

This is more like it. Richie McCaw gets ready to show Athers and me some of the sights.

One of the great sporting duels of all time. Allan Donald this time gets one over Athers at Trent Bridge in 1998, but England would go on to win.

(Getty Images)

Graham Thorpe on the way to a match-winning century in Colombo in 2001, when he nullified the Sri Lankan attack led by Muttiah Muralitharan. (Getty Images)

A proud moment and a rare one. Left: holding up the BAFTA the Sky Sports commentary team won. Right: Nasser visits the bar. The humour and togetherness of the team help ensure that the atmosphere is always good.

The painful press conference in Cape Town after Cameron Bancroft (left) was seen altering the condition of the ball. Skipper Steve Smith looks on. (Getty Images)

Sometimes it all gets too much – but somewhere around the world there'll be another pint waiting for me.

had five first-class hundreds under his belt when he was thrust into the opening position by Delhi, then there was Shreyas Iyer, his captain, and Rishabh Pant. At Rajasthan, Sanju Samson. All outstanding young cricketers and all roughly the same age group as England's Haseeb Hameed. This is a lad who doesn't play any shots.

In contrast, these Indian lads are coming in and hitting it into the crowd, and they are not what we used to call swipers back in the day. There's no slogging. Look at them and you think, 'This kid could play Test cricket tomorrow.' They have really sound techniques and strike the ball with precision. In this regard, they are following something of a tradition. Virender Sehwag grew up trying to mirror the movements of Sachin Tendulkar on his television screen.

So why are India producing such exciting talents who could seemingly flourish in all formats of the game? My reasoning would be that while India has literally millions of players, they do not have many coaches. It means that emerging players are more often than not self-taught in one way or another. They watch and mimic things they see those at the top level doing, working out how to execute a particular skill themselves. Batting is not coached into them; they gain a feel for it by copy-cat methods. Imitation is the sincerest form of battery, I guess.

This subject comes back to an old chestnut of mine – that if I am watching an emerging English batsman, they seem quite mechanical. Compare the young 'uns over there, who are wristy, inventive, and are armed with a firm defence. Now the one bloke from England who showed during the tournament that he possesses all those attributes was Jos Buttler. It was a bold and pleasing move when England's new selector Ed Smith recalled him to Test cricket on the back of a record-equalling five consecutive IPL 50s.

He understands modern batting: he hits it into the crowd, a

whirling concoction of wrists and power, showing that foot-work is not vital. More and more coaches over there are of the belief that batsmen need a firm base. And an increasing number of players are creating that base right back against the stumps. In the modern batting stance, the knees are bent and the bat can come down at any sort of angle you like. From this position you can take on both the full ball and the short ball.

Being able to attack different-length deliveries from the same position is vital in the contemporary game because the bottom line is you have to score. Quite simply, if a player can't clear the fence, there are limited opportunities for him. I would urge all young English coaches to get out there and spend a couple of weeks witnessing how it all works, and how the world's best are preparing.

One of the matches that I covered witnessed the breaking of the IPL record for the number of sixes in a match. It was between Royal Challengers Bangalore and Chennai Super Kings. Batsmen were hitting it into the stands to order, really going some, and between them they totalled 33 – Chennai edging the count 17-16 to chase down the 206-run target with two balls to spare.

MS Dhoni played the innings of his life, hitting an unbeaten 70 off 34 balls, with seven sixes, one fewer than AB de Villiers, whose 68 at a strike rate of 226.66 came in a losing cause. These guys know how to entertain and seem to be able to turn it on under pressure.

Then, the 'universe boss' Chris Gayle turns up and decides no ground is big enough for him. As he has got older, he has become less and less interested in the fielding aspect of the game, occasionally sticking a big boot out to intercept the ball. But he still appears keen when it comes to batting, seemingly setting himself a target of how far he can hit it. He has been one of cricket's greatest showmen.

And each IPL match is a spectacle, which is why the public turn up to support it in such numbers. One of the other aspects of an IPL match is the noise that the crowd produces. You can be sat inside in a commentary box and you simply cannot hear a fellow commentator two yards away. Every match attracts a crescendo of cheers and screams. The spectator experience is ridiculously limited when you compare it to rival countries. You get a bench to sit on. Failing that you have to stand on the terraces. Food outlets and stalls are few and far between. It's not dissimilar to attending Accrington v Bacup in 1968. But it completely suits modern India.

There was a lot of negativity when the competition was launched about some people being let in for free so that television could show capacity attendances, but it has been a clever marketing ploy because over a decade it has shed the image and become the show to see. Tickets are not cheap and there are different price bands, of course, but the grounds are still bursting. A team like Bangalore will play seven matches at home in seven weeks and they keep up an average attendance of around 35,000 at the Chinnaswamy Stadium.

Then afterwards, within half an hour of the finish, they've all gone. And they leave on foot, walking off in all different directions. In England, we are used to having to fight through traffic or wait in jams to clear the ground. But not a bit of it in India. None of the rubbish that we get in England, whereby we're told at the end of a game, 'Sorry, we're not opening the gates until all the public have gone.' Without getting into full rant mode, it does my head in as most of the public are still frequenting the bar. How long do they want us to wait? Four hours? What do they think I'm going to do? Run over them all? I've been driving for 50 years!

Young people in India want to be associated with the product. They are devoted to it, rather like they are to the country's other great entertainment industry, Bollywood. They might not have a lot of money but they want to be involved – if not theorising over tactics among themselves, then taking a crowd catch to be on the screens themselves. Then there are the VIP enclosures that allow the ordinary man to get close to the celebrities, like Shah Rukh Khan and Preity Zinta.

It is not quite prime-time viewing, although ideally Star would like an earlier start. Eight o'clock at night is a bit too late for them and they have pushed for half past six. But the game getting longer and longer and longer does not seem to put the Indian public off. At a quarter to midnight there is nobody sneaking out, no one excusing themselves and saying, 'I've got a bus to catch.' It is a completely different animal to Twenty20 in the UK.

A drawn-out game would not suit us in England, and nor would it work for Australia's Big Bash. The powers that be are now saying that the Twenty20 Blast is taking too long and are working out how to quicken it up. That responsibility lies with the players and they are encouraged by the umpires to get through their overs, with the deterrent of a run penalty being used should they not do so.

Winning the IPL takes a great deal of endurance in addition to executing high-level skills of power-hitting, deft touches, spectacular catches and death bowling, and Matthew Hayden provided a great perspective on the key to success, having experienced it as a player. At the end of every tournament lots of mistakes tend to creep in because the players are knackered.

People will dismiss the fact that it's only four overs for a bowler and question how tough on the body a 20-over match actually is, but the whole package takes its toll. There is no let-up in the scheduling and that means there is huge fatigue towards the end. He made the point that he was tired after covering a full tournament as a commentator, and our job entails being sat still. The players, who make similar journeys, then train and play in between, are absolutely out on their feet by the end of the tournament.

A New Crew

Working out in India placed me in the company of two Australians: Michael Slater brought all his Channel Nine exuberance and Matthew Hayden, who I had not met before, was the most generous of colleagues. He's into yoga and cooking. Look at the size of him. A body double of Giant Haystacks into all that meditation stuff.

Hayden is someone whose reputation went before him as a player. I had always viewed him as a big bruiser and everyone I came into contact with seemed to be a bit wary of him. But he proved himself to be a real team player, not least late at night when he would invite people back to his hotel room for a nightcap. As his abode had patio doors that opened onto a nice garden, he insisted on playing host, and we would all share a glass of wine or two before bed.

It was a rather cosmopolitan crew that was pitched together to commentate on the tournament and I must say one of the number, Danny Morrison, is tailor-made for IPL. They absolutely love him out there. He's a great combination – off the wall and a bloody good broadcaster. It's great that he's found himself a niche. He is so different to anyone else. He's a commentary-box hippy: 'Hey, man, how's it going?' Peace brother. I half-expected him to give us a rendition of Scott McKenzie's 'San Francisco'.

It was also good to work with a number of women. Isa Guha, who works with us at Sky, is carving out a great career as a British broadcaster and she is making a good impression around the world with her interviews and presentations. Mel Jones, of Australia, is right up there too. Another Australian, Lisa Sthalekar, is different again, as she has a softer voice, and from an English point of view it's great to see Alison Mitchell, a very accomplished broadcaster, branching out and doing all sorts of things. Covering men's cricket on TV is pretty new to most of them, but they have quickly proved themselves in what unfortunately has been a male-dominated area for so long.

What's in a Name?

Danny Morrison remembers fondly being in the West Indies when Marcus Trescothick was captain of the England Under-19 side during a triangular tournament. As our main man strode out to the middle, the Tannoy announcer introduced him as: 'England's opening batsman, Monty Discotheque'.

But the world capital of misspelling is India. Take my most recent experience. Throughout my stay, each hotel we were booked into had the same system for guests to access the Wi-Fi. Your username was your surname and the password your room number. Frustratingly, I could never get on. Not for the want of trying either, I might point out.

I kept phoning reception to check why I was unable to log on: Do the characters all have to be lowercase? A mixture of the two? Is there a zero on the front of my room number? All the questions you might ask. All to no avail. At the first hotel they were adamant that the name would work in capitals, a mixture, lowercase, you name it. Sadly, it wouldn't. This was all very puzzling to me, and I was on the point of giving up altogether when exactly the same issues occurred at the second hotel. Once again, the guest Wi-Fi was supposed to be accessible with a legitimate name and room number. Once again, the call to the front desk to question whether I was missing anything.

'No, sir. Just your name and room number.'

Exasperated, I politely mentioned this was hopeless and that I was giving up.

'Truly sorry about that, Mr Llyod.'

Pardon?

'What did you just call me? My name is Lloyd. As in L-L-O-Y-D.'

'No, Mr Llyod. It is L-L-Y-O-D. That is what you must input for internet access.'

Turned out all my travel bookings said the same thing. So for a fortnight, I changed my name. This is Mr Llyod, for one final time, over and out.

Bat Like God (or is that Dog?)

Part of the reason cricket is so popular in India, I believe, is that there is nothing else. They're crackers about the game because they don't have rival pastimes as distractions. There is no rugby, cycling, football, swimming or golf within their historical infrastructure. The choice has always been to go to the pictures or watch the cricket. Bollywood and leather-on-wood have been integral to the vast population for half a century.

India hold such sway in cricket's future, particularly in Test cricket, and they are not top of the tree in the traditional form, as I write, without good reason. To be fair, they had a massive choice to make when they were whitewashed 4-0 in England in 2011. They could either get real about Test match cricket again or concentrate on their expanding Twenty20 tournament.

How interested were India players like Ravindra Jadeja, a

debutant in that series, who was already a millionaire from IPL? To their credit, they maintained focus on both and continue to produce cricketers for all three formats. Since losing their number one-ranked Test status to England against a backdrop of injuries seven years ago, they have given plenty of attention to developing their red-ball team. For example, at the start of the 2018 domestic season, cricketers like Cheteshwar Pujara, Varun Aaron and Ishant Sharma were just not involved in the 20-over stuff, and were therefore engaged by counties – in preparation for the Test tour later that summer.

It went to show that they have their talent spread across all three formats and the up-and-coming players have incredible attributes suited across the board. Producing young batsmen who can banjo some of the best bowlers in the world straight out of the ground augurs well for their own futures and that of the team. Batsmen in India have an appetite for huge totals. Take the news in early 2016 of 15-year-old Pranav Dhanawade, playing for KC Gandhi, who scored 1,009 from 323 deliveries with 59 sixes and 127 fours in a total of 1,465 for three. Apparently, Pranav sailed through the nervous nine hundreds!

The bar is being catapulted into the stratosphere in a country that reveres batsmen more than any other. Adulation for Sachin Tendulkar – and, to not much lesser extent, Virat Kohli – is not something you will see replicated anywhere else around the world, in any sport. This mass idolisation is to the extent that the bloke cannot lead a normal life. I am sure he wouldn't have wanted it any other way, for all the glory he has achieved, the personal goals he has accomplished and the pleasure a career at the very top has given him, but at times it must have been hard, and arguably still is – especially having to eat a bowl of noodles through a bearded disguise in your local restaurant.

In Indian cricket, more than in any of the other major nations, the batsmen become deities. This is nothing new, of course; it has been the way since Sunil Gavaskar emerged as a run-scorer supreme during my playing days. Tendulkar stole the limelight in his era, when Rahul Dravid, who spent a month of his life at the crease in Test cricket, was also a national monument. 'The Wall' showed no signs of crumbling over a decade in which he scored more than 10,000 runs from number three.

They simply don't eulogise about the blokes who have won the Test match by taking the wickets. It is all about those who have set it up. Batsmen always get the credit. Just think about how much they get for bat deals. What does a bowler get? Sore, usually. They simply never talk in the same way about the two breeds. Anil Kumble was a fabulous operator, a world-class performer among spinners, and Zaheer Khan was for a decade as good as anyone going around as a swing bowler.

When Eric Clapton was at Lord's for India's visit in 2014 rumour had it he was there on a recruitment mission for his new supergroup, having been taken by Ishant's striking resemblance to Alice Cooper. See, even I am degrading the artisans now. When in the mood, though, Ishant can be devastating as a fast bowler and his was the game-altering spell that put India 1–0 up.

The Full Monty

Yet bowlers can be so influential in subcontinental conditions, as England showed with a first Test series win in India for 28 years in 2012–13 – a tour in which Graeme Swann and Monty Panesar outspun the home twirlers.

And they did it the hard way, too. For the first Test, it was pretty clear that England had made a mistake and picked the wrong team when the slow left-armer Panesar was omitted.

Zaheer Khan, India's spearhead, bowled only two out of 40 overs in the second innings as the home team went 1-0 up.

England talked a good game heading into that series, saying their players were good players of spin, but having seen no signs of that in the opening exchanges, it was as good a turnaround victory as I have had the pleasure to witness.

Swann and Panesar lost nothing in comparison with Ravi Ashwin and Pragyan Ojha. Ashwin, the off-spinner, would go on to become the second fastest man to 200 Test wickets – reaching it in 37 Test matches, one slower than Australia's Clarrie Grimmett. But he went an eternity at one stage, searching for a breakthrough in Mumbai after Alastair Cook and Kevin Pietersen produced some of the best batting by an England pair away from home.

Pietersen's 186 was majestic and when he batted like this it made you consider that he was worth all the trouble after all. There had been a serious breakdown between him and the team just a few short months before, during the home series against South Africa. But both parties went to see a marriage guidance counsellor and after an uneasy truce at Ahmedabad, where England lost, they were back in the bedroom.

India's batsmen play spin very well but they weren't so good when they were asked to play catch-up, under scoreboard pressure with men crowding them, and after the first of the two KP and Cook shows it was 'over to you, Monty'. And he gets a massive tick for becoming the first English spinner since Hedley Verity in 1934 to take 10 wickets in a Test match in India. Between them Monty and Swann took 19 wickets in the match.

India had produced a raging turner, and were shaken to their boots by English spin. It was a similar policy when the series moved to Kolkata and it was great fun to see the 83-year-old groundsman at Eden Gardens. He'd had a sign made saying,

'Mr Mukherjee, Curator'. What a formidable character. He reminded me of a slightly bonkers groundsman we had at Accrington called Frank Nash, who was forking the pitch one day when some lads came on to play football. He tried to shoo them off and promptly threw the fork through his own foot, impaling himself on the pitch.

When in India it can be tiring work. You can get a sweat on. Unless you are Alastair Cook, of course. He had batted in excess of nine hours after England followed on in Ahmedabad, breaking the record for most hundreds by an England batsman on the subcontinent (five). He definitely added to his repertoire for his first series in charge, developing his sweep shot and looking to hit over the top. He was definitely 100 per cent inspiration, 0 per cent perspiration on that tour.

Jimmy Anderson enjoyed his best series in these conditions too, particularly in the third Test. Earlier in his career it was suggested that, unless it was seaming and swinging, he was hopeless, but at the age of 30 he stuck two fingers up at the critics with a great display of skill and experience to claim three wickets in each innings.

And the pièce de résistance of the trip came in Nagpur when the iconic Tendulkar, the people's champion, was toppled in his final appearance. The whole of India wanted him to succeed and he was simply trying to stay in on what was a testing pitch when he got a perfect delivery from Anderson that hit middle stump. That's a pretty comprehensive way to go. When he was in his pomp, England had no idea where to bowl at Sachin – it was sad to witness the demise because you want to see a champion go out on a real high.

The smile on coach Andy Flower's face at the end of the 2-1 win told of what England had achieved. To turn India over in their own backyard is as good as any Ashes win, it's the holy grail, you just don't do it. When India bamboozled

England in the first Test, they had asked for spinning pitches because they wanted a 4-0 win, but it backfired badly and England pounced. It had been a memorable series when the Andrew Flintoff-led team had come back to 1-1 but this was something else.

The size of the achievement, and how things tend to go the other way for England in spin-friendly conditions, was highlighted in Cook's last tour as captain in 2016-17. He was the captain England needed when he took over five years earlier, and put his stamp on things when he made scores of 176, 122 and 190, leading from the front with the bat and showing equally impressive handling of his two spinners, Graeme Swann and Monty Panesar.

Cook was always a careful batsman, a method batsman, and that transferred to his captaincy. For him, everything came down to a plan, and he was more often than not well planned. To sum up, he used a bit of a 'what you see is what you get' policy. But by the end he was fronting a team that was evolving rapidly under Eoin Morgan in white-ball cricket. He struggled for runs, and he was always a captain who led by example. One facet fed the other.

At that point, I wanted England to be a bit more funky, and they gave the responsibility to a man in Joe Root who does funky. He acts more on 'feel' for the game. What he senses is best for his team at that moment. Root endured a tough first 12 months himself as England captain, but the obvious rival I would compare him with is India's Virat Kohli.

When Kohli is captaining you could assign a TV camera to be fixed on him and it would keep you entertained. He's constantly thinking, doing. Both he and Root want to encourage their teams to have fun and express themselves. Unfortunately, though, India appeared to have better weaponry at their disposal when the two teams came together for the return series in 2018.

The Show Must Go On

It was a privilege to have worked on *Test Match Special* prior to joining Sky permanently in 1999, and I was glad of the experience in radio when, in October 2011, we were unable to provide live coverage of England's first one-day international against India in Hyderabad due to a 'picture blackout'.

Licence issues – effectively a breakdown in negotiations between rights-holding production company Nimbus, the Board of Control for Cricket in India and the Indian government that contributed to the latter failing to issue the paperwork giving permission to broadcast – meant Nick Knight and I had to provide phone commentary of the action.

We were on-air by 10.15am UK time, but the whole episode reminded me of the 1980s and a time that pre-dated the internet when cricket fans would legitimately dial 0898 numbers – at least I think they were 0898 – for pleasure. Cricketline used to have all the scores from around the country read by the late Ralph Dellor, and the eager would be calling on the hour every hour for the latest updates.

CHAPTER NINE

When it Comes to Egg Chasing, the Kiwis Have Got the Aussies Cracked

There are similarities between Australians and New Zealanders, as you might expect from nations so close to each other geographically and with such a similar history. The difference between them, though, is that there is a much greater humility about those who hail from the land of the White Fern. It is a stereotype, of course, but they are far more genteel people. At the heart of their national psyche is a deep-rooted respect for others.

They tend to play the game the right way – hard but fair. No wonder Darren Lehmann used the behaviour of New Zealand as a template for the Australians when he addressed his team's issues in the immediate aftermath of the ball-tampering affair in South Africa, which led to suspensions for Steve Smith, the captain, David Warner, his deputy, and Cameron Bancroft. They have a total respect for opponents and the game of cricket.

But it does not lessen their competitive hostility towards

Australia one iota. You only have to spend an hour in the company of one of my mates, Ian Smith, to get that. Smithy, or Smeffy as his compatriots call him, is your typical Kiwi, and that means the anti-Aussie gene is strong. He is professional to the core as one of the world's best sports commentators, but once dressed in his civvies he will tell you what he really thinks.

When he goes over the Tasman Sea commentating on cricket, he says, New Zealand tend to get turned over good and proper. Australia are clinical and premeditated: we are going to account for you lot over here any way we can. It all gets a bit spicy, the Aussies let them have a verbal barrage and, because of the way Brendon McCullum set up the New Zealanders to play a decade ago, there is never much coming back the other way.

New Zealand are the perfect mix of competitiveness and restraint, but it is the Australians – with the slightly higher skill factors – who ultimately come out on top. As Smith says, there is nothing he can do about that. Of course, he calls what he sees when he has the microphone. Your job as commentator is to be impartial, no matter your allegiance. Deep down, though, you always want your own country, the team you once represented, to be successful. That's natural enough.

So he has to take the comments about Australian superiority, about what his fellow countrymen like to do in the privacy of their own fields with the woolly members of their society, and how inferior New Zealanders are in general, on the chin. Until, that is, he happens to be travelling to Australia for his other line of work – as one of New Zealand's leading rugby commentators. It's quite a different experience and, in his own words: 'I flippin' love it.' Suddenly, the trip of trepidation becomes one of jubilation. 'We go over, give them a really good hiding and then come back,' he says, with a beaming smile you can't wipe off his face whenever he talks about the All Blacks taking on the

Wallabies. With relish, he will tell you: 'They haven't beaten us in Auckland for 36 years, and long may the wonderful run continue.'

It seems to be a rite of passage for an Enzedder to watch those from the land of the barbie marinated, chargrilled and skewered at Eden Park. Fifty thousand of them turn up to watch this ritual sacrificing of the green and gold. Now, I am not a rugby man myself, but there are some sporting events I could get a taste for and that's one of them.

The Great Outdoors

In New Zealand, life is all about fitness. They play rugby union and cricket, in that order. Rugby is their number one-ranking sport and defines everything else they do, while cricket is number two. And at places like Auckland they play them at the same venue at different times of year.

But they are also into all kinds of other weird and wonderful pursuits in the quest for a healthy lifestyle. Back in 2013, I spent a week in Queenstown before the first Test and discovered why it is known as the adventure capital of the world. You only have to look out your hotel room at six o'clock in the morning to see folk jogging, canoeing, kayaking, abseiling, paragliding and bungee jumping. There's stuff going on outdoors all the time. What is wrong with these kids? Have they not heard of Xbox and Domino's? By my estimate of New Zealand's evolution, those adolescent essentials should be arriving by 2038.

So while rugby rakes off all their alpha males, there are plenty of other fine athletes to be spread across other sports. There is evidence throughout New Zealand's time in international cricket that they have punched above their weight, and for a country of four and a half million people to produce such competitive outfits, particularly so in limited-overs cricket for the past couple of decades, is to their immense credit.

Sometimes, though, I would argue that having a limited pool of players is no bad thing. With my old coach's hat on, I would say that if you only have so many to pick from it concentrates the mind on who should be rising to the top.

They have definitely produced good cricketers throughout their history and during the first half of 2018, when they were ranked third in Test cricket – in addition to being fourth in each of the shorter formats – they had great depth too. For example, they had two 90mph bowlers who could not make their first-choice XI, in Lockie Ferguson and Adam Milne. Imagine having that level of luxury.

So how do they produce fast bowlers like this and prevent them from breaking down? Well, to start with they only have six provincial teams: Auckland, Northern Districts, Central Districts, Canterbury, Wellington and Otago. With that number of teams there is a real concentration of players, not talent spread thinly across many, and it follows that they are not being run into the ground by being asked to play an excessive number of matches.

New Zealand Cricket is not awash with cash, but they are extremely smart in how they use what they do have, and the identification of talent through their coaching system's development programme is arguably second to none. It's simple enough: they earmark one player from an age group, and when he or she is at the age of 14 or 15 they will have a lot of resources thrown at them for a sustained period until they reach the full international team. Identification and investment truly go hand in hand.

And they are the world leaders as far as I am concerned in making cricket an all-inclusive sport. The women's game is very strong, and I like the fact that their programme for girls mirrors that of the boys. It's certainly not lip service, either. The president of New Zealand Cricket is Debbie Hockley, one of their all-time great players, and they think less about the lines of separation when it comes to gender, perhaps unsurprising for a country that was first in the world to give women the vote back in the 19th century.

Throwing all their resources at one or two individuals is a proven process aligned with their success. Kane Williamson, Ross Taylor, Trent Boult, Tim Southee, Daniel Vettori are all examples of players they have invested in early. And it has been a long-term vision.

Daniel Vettori played his first game against the England team I coached way back in 1997. A bespectacled, schoolboy left-arm spinner, he was given his first-class debut for Northern Districts against us as a 17-year-old in Hamilton in late January, and Nasser Hussain became his first scalp. He turned 18 in the interim but he was still New Zealand's youngest Test cricketer when he made his international debut against us three weeks later. Nasser might not thank me for pointing out that he was also the first of Vettori's 362 Test wickets.

Long Live Rigor

Not that all New Zealand cricketers are of a certain type. In fact, they produce plenty of characters of difference and there aren't many more different than Mark Richardson – now a broadcast colleague in New Zealand, after spending four years as an international opening batsman at the turn of the millennium.

So, how would I describe him? Well, he's a total one-off. Before a commentary stint, I kid you not, he has been known to run a marathon. Or get up at 4am and go paddle-boarding.

It's pretty clear he's not quite right. He's almost the Kiwi version of Keith Lemon: 'Now back to me in the studio.'

But he has done well for himself within the New Zealand media, forging a reputation for controversy – he had his own sports radio programme called *The Crowd Goes Wild* before quitting to be sports presenter for *The AM Show*, which is aired each morning simultaneously on national television and radio. And it is fair to say he took things up a level when he asked the then newly appointed Labour leader Jacinda Ardern in August 2017 whether she planned to have a baby anytime soon. 'I think this is a legitimate question for New Zealand, because she could be prime minister running this country – she has our best interests at heart, so we need to know these things,' Richardson said.

Cue Ardern fronting up on the show to take him to task, arguing that, while she was okay with being asked given her position, this should not be a consideration for a country that has championed equal rights like no other. 'It is totally unacceptable in 2017 to say that women should have to answer that question in the workplace. It is the woman's decision about when they choose to have children. It should not predetermine whether or not they get the job,' she said.

It caused an almighty outrage. Within three months, Ardern was prime minister. Within three more she was announcing her first pregnancy. The man we know as Rigor certainly made a name for himself in a wider sphere with that one.

And that quest for recognition fits in with a life story that began with a dream of bowling left-arm spin for New Zealand. For that is how he started out on his professional career, until he got the yips and was forced to transform himself into an opening batsman. Starting out as a number 10, he moved up the order place by place and earned his nickname once the journey from bottom to top had been completed.

It's Rigor, as in rigor mortis. As a player there was nothing more apt. His batting did give off the impression that death had set in. There was certainly no life to it, to the extent that he made Geoff Boycott look like Chris Gayle. He had a couple of shots – the straight drive, the forward defensive – plus 27 variations on the leave. But they were sufficient to earn him a New Zealand debut at the age of 29. And, speaking from experience, you can be pleased with a Test average above 40. Rigor averaged 44.77 over 38 matches, which constitutes a fine record.

Personally, I wouldn't have been putting my hand into my pocket to watch him play, but there are a couple of YouTube delights involving him that are well worth seeing. During a Test match in Mohali, Richardson gets down into the ideal position to sweep Anil Kumble's leg-spin and makes the perfect connection to help the ball 70 yards to fine leg, yet doesn't get a run for his effort as he simultaneously lets out a humongous scream, as though he has been shot, and collapses in a heap on the pitch, triggering huge guffaws from the Indian team.

He had been in for a while, to be fair, with New Zealand 232 for one, and they were probably quite keen for him to suffer. With Richardson unable to get up, writhing around in agony with cramp, good old David Shepherd wanders down and counts him out like a boxer.

Then, there is his bodged practice stroke during a home Test match versus India in Wellington where he bunted the ball through mid-off off the bowling of Ajit Agarkar and re-enacted the checked drive as he reached the non-striker's end – to comic effect. The bat flies out of his grasp and lands 15 yards away, where mid-on would have been stationed. Another yelp from our hero. Only this time it is triggered by concern for the safety of others, and instead of turning to run a second he makes after the flying willow. Luckily, the ball dribbles into the rope, otherwise he would have sacrificed more international runs.

It reminded me of the celebration of Bud Hill for his hundred off 100 overs for Derbyshire against us one year. Let's face it, when you have batted for that long you've had quite some time to think about it. He ran through for the all-important single and raised his arms aloft to coincide with coming into his ground at the non-striker's end. The fielder throws the ball in, it hits the foot holes and flies up and hits him straight him in the mouth.

To be fair, funeral directors tended to move quicker than Richardson and he was notorious for his involvement in run-outs. Most notably, when he totally stuffed a young Brendon McCullum on his one-day international debut in Sydney. A fresh-faced McCullum nudged to the leg-side off Jason Gillespie and set off for a single. But with Rigor hard set at the other end, Brett Lee had all the time in the world to run in and remove the bails. 'I didn't think he was going to be any good,' he says, offering his own defence 15 years later.

During his playing days, whenever he went into an international series he would make a point of challenging one of the opposition to a race. It would take place after the last ball was bowled, and was the kind of thing you might expect to happen after two villages had played each other at an annual local gala. 'Our man's faster than yours.' That kind of thing.

The fact of the matter is, though, that Rigor has never been much faster than his name suggests at any given discipline. But he simply never gives in, one of those annoying creatures you can't get rid of whenever you are in direct competition. Now, I don't mean this in a nasty way, but if one of those loons with a red button at their fingertips ever decided that the option to press was nigh and the world ended, there would only be the cockroaches left. Or, more accurately, the cockroaches and Rigor.

I am not sure why I am apologising about doing him a disservice because he would see such a reflection as a badge of honour. Here is a man who prides himself on being totally unpopular. When we work together he is never happier than when he is sat on his own, and he would never think of coming out for a drink once the shift has been completed. It is the rarest of beasts when he does break from his routine, and even experiencing his delivery of this information is a painful process. 'I will come out, t-o-n-i-g-h-t,' he says, his voice going into slow motion by the end of the sentence, and therefore synchronising perfectly with the groans and sighs from the rest of the room.

His pitch reports are like the Gettysburg Address. The requirement for such reports is to keep things brief. You want to get all the salient points over to the viewer as succinctly as possible. 'It's overcast, those clouds alone might persuade whoever wins the toss to bowl, but with the bit of dampness under foot and with the grass left on you would be pretty sure that's the way to go. Expect win toss and bowl here.' That sort of thing. But no, a Richardson report lasts 10 minutes, goes round the houses, presenting the case for one thing, then the other, and by the time he gets to 'so in conclusion . . .' you have lost the will to live.

On commentary he is as mad as a box of frogs and says random things designed to cause a reaction. One observation in particular over the winter of 2017-18 got under people's skin. My old mate Mike Selvey, once of *Test Match Special* and the former cricket correspondent of *The Guardian*, was apoplectic. We were sat three in a line: me, Ian Smith and Rigor. There was a bit of a lull in proceedings and the chap to our right suddenly popped up with a sigh of 'I hate the media'. To say it stung me and Smith was an understatement.

'Right. Would you like to elaborate on that at all?'

'No, I just hate the media.'

The media of which, with a permanent position on a current

affairs programme, and being sat in the commentary booth, he was very much a part.

Later, when we got off-air, we naturally quizzed him on what he was thinking.

'Bit left-field that, Rigor.'

'I just wanted a reaction.'

He got one of them, all right.

'I'd not said anything for ages and I bet they're all piling in on Twitter now.'

'You're dead right there, mate.'

'Oh great.'

'What a shallow comment,' was the reaction of Selvey.

All water off the duck's proverbial to him, though. If someone told him he was the biggest shit on the planet he would celebrate like he'd been awarded a Nobel Prize. That's just the sort of reaction he wants to provoke. It takes all sorts, I suppose, and he is never happier than when he is rubbing others up the wrong way.

When we are sat at the back of the box, we turn our attention to the kind of games you might have got up to in the common room at school or in the clubhouse after one of your own matches. We pick our greatest XIs of all time. Then move on to the other end of the spectrum and select the Greatest Team of Shits that has graced cricket.

That always seems to foster the same laddish debate: what's the difference between a shit, a twat and a c***? Which one could you be? It's not such a bad thing to be a shit, you can live with being a twat but you can't be one of the c's. You wouldn't want to be in that XI. But I have to report that some of the players – who for legal reasons must not be named here – get selected across the board. I will leave you to decide on that.

Smithy had me in hysterics over our brews when he made his first pick for the most unloved team imaginable. With the use of his eyebrows, and a twist of his head, he declared: 'Look no further for the opening batter and captain.' His gaze descending upon the bloke wearing the cans and talking those in their living rooms through the action. Would Rigor have been upset with that? Upset? Nah, he'd have been flaming delighted.

Lambing's No Way to Prepare

Before Stephen Fleming and Brendon McCullum were in short trousers, New Zealand were led by another highly respected leader. Jeremy Coney is a wonderful man and was a very astute cricketer who took to captaincy in the most natural manner. He hails from Wellington and, as an all-rounder, bowled the most gentle medium pacers imaginable. One of those bowlers best described as possessing a total 'lack of nip'. International wicketkeepers couldn't risk standing back to him for fear of nicks not carrying through. As a bowler he really didn't have any cunning variations to turn to if a batsman decided to get after him, as Kapil Dev did in a tri-series contest in Brisbane in December 1980. India's innings was going nowhere at 136 for six. Until Kapil lined up Coney, that is.

They reckoned the first six he struck off him was as big as anything ever deposited into the Clem Jones Stand at the pre-developed Gabba. Then he matched it, opening his shoulders to launch another towering hit straight down the ground. Coney, typical of the way that his countrymen have played the game down the years, simply stood and applauded the batsman's 50, as did Warren Lees behind the stumps. Then, to show that even at the top level there should be elements of fun, respect for your opponent and interaction with the crowd, he removed a handkerchief from his pocket and waved it at Kapil as if it was a white flag.

It occurred to me when there was a bit of a gust up in Wellington one day that no fast bowler I knew would have fancied slogging his guts out at this kind of venue, and recalled that Paul Allott, one of my best mates, used to bemoan the fact that he would have to run uphill into the wind when he played as one of the overseas players. 'So who took the new ball at the other end?' I wondered out loud when the subject came up between Coney and me.

To which Coney responded: 'Well me, of course. It was captain's pick.'

'Walt' Allott would have been bustling away, trying to get it through against all odds in the face of the most unhelpful elements possible, and there at the other end being given an assisted start would have been Coney with his gentle dobbers. Priceless ...

He's got funny bones, has Coney. One of those blokes who makes you laugh without trying. Take our stroll back to the middle after England were dismissed for 58 in the 2018 floodlit Test match in Auckland, when he said: 'I enjoyed your pitch report this morning. It was very entertaining. I like that, entertaining the public.'

He then paused, before adding: 'But what about the opening batsman, Alastair Cook? What preparation has he had? I'll tell you ... He's been lambing,' referring to the fact that Cook had been working on his wife Alice's family farm before arriving in New Zealand.

With that he strolled off, leaving me in tears of laughter. He is an unbelievably clever man and gives off an impression of being the absent-minded professor. Make no mistake, though. He's got all his tables and chairs at home, and in exactly the right place. He's a brilliant broadcaster. The best seem to have very reassuring, soothing voices, and I would have no hesitation putting Coney in that category.

Camper Still

One day over lunch, my wife Diana and I turned our thoughts to the future and she proposed, 'When we retire, why don't we drive through Europe in a camper van?' I am not sure where that sense of adventure came from, but as she had put it out there we just ran with it.

As it seemed a bit of a large step for two novices, I cut her a deal of a trial run, hiring one at Scotch Corner and heading up to a farm at Bamburgh for four days. You probably know the kind of place – everything is catered for and all the mod cons can be used via plugging into the electric and water supplies. Emptying the toilet – the equivalent of removing a cassette – was a little bit more challenging, but it all seemed to start pretty well. However, Diana first suggested she wanted to go home after about an hour and, although we kept going for three days, it wasn't for us. For a start, we always seemed to be parked on a slant and I kept rolling out of bed.

Undeterred, however, I mentioned to Rob Noonan, our Scouse producer, that it would be fun to go round New Zealand in one on the 2017-18 tour. In some major cricket-playing countries, flying is the only option given the logistics, but here is a place that is all about the open road.

Collecting our charabanc involved an hour's drive out of Auckland. And the collection point really was in the middle of nowhere. Arriving at a dirt track, we had to slow down to about three miles an hour, the surface was so bad. At a little homestead along the way, two ferocious dogs jumped out ready to attack us, but we did eventually get to the bloke who had offered Rob 'the fastest camper van in New Zealand'.

It didn't take much of a test drive to put this claim into doubt. Installed in the passenger seat next to Ian Ward, I was not filled with confidence when Rob, who was tailing us in the car behind, called to say, 'Your brake lights aren't working.' To which Wardy responds: 'That'd be right because the brakes aren't working either.'

In fact, on closer inspection not much was: there were no lights, the clutch had burnt out, the gear lever was jammed and the windscreen wipers didn't appear to be attached. In fact, every vehicle we were offered appeared to be a death trap. Until Rob secured one fit for purpose a couple of days later.

So we headed to Mount Maunganui in this special edition contraption for the second one-day international between New Zealand and England. I was thinking of a big Winnebago and doing it all properly, travelling around, living the rustic life, and everything was fine when we were driving along having a singsong. Parking up and emerging from the living quarters with *Fast Show*-esque lines like: 'Today, I will mostly be eating ham and cheese toasties.' It was a bit more challenging, though, when we camped up on the lakeside site.

Nasser Hussain and I decided to go the whole hog and slept in this thing, Nasser keen to do so in order that he could go for his early morning run on the beach. Unfortunately, though, our location proved to be a bit of a problem. We were parked next to the steps from where people began their ascent up the mountain. Wrongly, we thought this would make us safe at night-time. But no such luck – the intrepid explorers just donned miners' helmets and ploughed on. With my head being about five metres from the rusty gate, it meant I didn't get a wink of sleep thanks to a combination of its creaks and bangs and the flashes of light from the head torches. Next morning I discovered I'd been bitten from top to toe, including the most unmentionable of places in between.

We also got across to the west coast of the north island to a spot called Raglan, where the local dudes go to surf. It's not something I have done much of; the one exception springing to mind was when I went body-boarding on Bondi beach with my youngest sons, Steven and Ben, in the late 1990s. I went out to catch one of the waves – hang 10, cowabunga dude and all that – when I hit one of them, or rather it hit me, and turned me over like I was in a washing machine. Unfortunately, I landed on the beach, losing both my board and my dignity. There I was, the England coach, sat in the Bondi surf, bollock naked, with my trunks coming up towards me on a wave, forcing me to crawl along like a crab on my arse cheeks and slip them back on. I was just pleased to avoid charges of indecent exposure.

It was pleasing to say that the atmosphere around the international matches on the 2017-18 tour of New Zealand was a lot more demure. It really is a throwback to old-style touring, with its relaxed vibe and traditional cricket grounds. Being on the tour is a real holiday experience, and that is no coincidence as it is exactly what New Zealand Cricket are aiming for.

We were hosted one day by the NZC chief executive David White, who explained that they need England cricket tours of their shores like we wouldn't believe. They welcome our supporters because they don't have the massive sponsorships other countries do and so they need footfall to generate income. Being a northern hemisphere team, without a domestic season that clashes directly with those of the southern hemisphere, we take so many spectators abroad, and that provides a healthy source of revenue for an organisation that doesn't have the financial clout from sponsorships that other nations have.

England and other 'have' countries need to be aware of this and look after some of the 'have-nots' in ways like this. Part of New Zealand Cricket's marketing strategy is to persuade everybody what a great place it is to visit, to make the whole package very desirable. The climate, the folk, the lifestyle. Watch some cricket, visit some historical sites, botanical gardens, get out and do some cycling, canoeing, climbing, go horse racing and wine tasting. Personally, I would like to see the ECB getting tour groups arranged to pull in travelling fans, using current and former players as figureheads. International cricket needs to be strong for the game to remain attractive to a wider audience, and that means funding infrastructures around the world via whatever means possible.

They have certainly made touring New Zealand a pleasant experience, using traditional-looking cricket grounds with grass banks like Maunganui, Dunedin, Hamilton and Christchurch. The picturesque backdrops certainly enhance the experience and, with capacities typically between 6,000 and 9,000, the atmosphere is great. The crowd is on top of the action and it also looks fabulous on television when the ground is full, whereas when 15,000 turn up at one-day internationals at much bigger stadia like Auckland's Eden Park or the Cake Tin at Wellington, folk complain that they look empty. New Zealand Cricket believe they have found their niche.

Late-Night Jury Out

The jury is still out on day-night Test cricket. Speaking as a senior citizen, pink-ball matches like the one we had at Eden Park in early 2018 completely mess up my body clock.

Don't get me wrong, I can handle a night out in Auckland just fine but preferably one drinking Dogfather, a Tui brew that comes in at 6.5 per cent – albeit very slowly to avoid thinking I was Wolverine's twin brother by the end of my second pint. And I could chill out in Mo's Bar in Auckland into the early hours, as I did with Mike Selvey and David Saker, then *Guardian* cricket correspondent and England bowling coach respectively, five years ago. In 2018, I was back there distributing the complimentary oysters I'd been sent by a local supplier — a bit like the fish man used to at local pubs up and down Britain. That seems like a far more sensible pastime in Auckland past eight o'clock at night.

It was revealing that when I popped in to do a Q&A with the Barmy Army before play, it got an overwhelming thumbs-down from 170 people. And, from what we've seen, there's no evidence that people are flying into the ground for the last session. In fact, they were streaming out for the Ashes equivalent in Adelaide four months earlier.

As it was, the contest was virtually over before it began and what I would say of England being blown away for 58 with the pink ball is that sometimes the perfect storm can hit for a bowling side. That was certainly the case for New Zealand: bowling conditions were favourable and the batsmen kept obliging by getting out. Sometimes the bowlers put it in the right place and you nick 'em.

It is almost inexplicable how it happens and I was on the receiving end of such an occurrence as captain of Lancashire back in 1977. We were bowled out for 33 by Northamptonshire at Wantage Road and no one could give you an explanation as to why it happened. Sometimes a match takes an unexpected turn. Just ask Henry Blofeld. Back in 1983, Blowers, my dear old thing, wrote up his *Guardian* match report of Essex v Surrey early and departed Chelmsford having sent a note to the sub-editors to fill in the gaps of a sentence that referred to Essex being _ for _ at the close. Inserting the numbers 14 and 10 just didn't seem right somehow . . .

What the Auckland capitulation did bring attention to was England's woeful preparation. Two knockabout two-day matches in Hamilton were not representative of meaningful cricket, but that's all they could possibly manage because of the saturated scheduling. They'd just finished a Twenty20 tri-series and a one-day series of five matches. There's just not enough time to fit everything in on condensed modern tours.

It also came at a time when England were struggling away from home and therefore could have done with the best acclimatisation possible. It was clearly a longer-term issue that Joe Root inherited. Between December 2012 and April 2018 they played 33 Tests overseas and won only four of them, losing 19. Andrew Strauss and company have to be careful. It is a situation that needs addressing.

Not that there is a lot else to get you down in this fabulous land, and there are some lovely perks of the job at times. Yes, it is always a disappointment to call a match in which England are thrashed. No matter what people might suggest to the contrary, and as objective as we remain, it is only natural to want England to be successful, particularly if you have once worn the shirt yourself. But when downtime involves jumping in a helicopter with Mike Atherton and looking at the sights of Canterbury, with our pilot none other than All Blacks legend Richie McCaw, who's complaining?

There is so much to do outside the cricket. On another day, I was taken out by sponsors Dilmah on a fishing expedition to Waiheke Island to catch snapper, chat about the cricket and have a cuppa. Having recently invested in a 26-foot boat myself back on the River Ouse, it was a thrill to drive one more than twice the size and, at 35 knots, that went five times faster.

I wasn't sure about bungee jumping when we were in Queenstown, though. I might have told you that at my time of life it is a pastime best enjoyed from the viewing platform. But then this lady turns up and says, 'I'll have a go at that.' Turns out Ronnie, from Sydney, was 73. She got strapped in and jumped straight off without a pause for thought. As she re-emerged to a standing ovation, she triumphantly exclaimed: 'At least I didn't p*** myself.' Spoken like a true Aussie.

Mac the Knife – the Sharpest Captain Around

It was at the 2015 World Cup that Brendon McCullum peaked as an international captain. His New Zealand were all over England like a cheap suit in that tournament and he was showing himself to be an astute leader without comparison at that time. He never did funky fields. He just knew where to put the fielders for every batsman. And when he had done that and bundled England out for 123 he went after them as if he had a train to catch. He made statements by playing decisively and winning in 74 balls of the chase.

That was McCullum all over: always on the front foot. And he built a legacy by engineering a team with a decent attack, a solid opening pair and a good engine room in Kane Williamson, Ross Taylor and himself. Whenever his team needed reminding of their modus operandi, he would take it upon himself to do so with acts such as crashing the first ball he received in the Headingley Test of 2015 over extra cover for six.

McCullum's attitude has also been credited for influencing the terrific counterattack from Joe Root and Ben Stokes at Lord's that tour. England found that attack was their best approach too, post-2015 World Cup. And, like New Zealand, they applied it to all formats. I have discussed the compelling cricket New Zealand play with their coach Mike Hesson and he made an illuminating point. As his side are quite used to playing two-match series, they have more limited opportunity to make their mark with a win, so their batsmen try to score in excess of four runs an over to buy the time for their bowlers to take 20 wickets.

A good example of this policy was when they whacked 460 for nine at that kind of gallop in Dunedin in 2013. It opened up a huge lead on first innings, only for England to find the pitch as flat as a London pint second time around. Even Steven Finn, as nightwatchman, got to 50, for goodness' sake.

McCullum also got those playing under him fully committed physically and emotionally to the rigours of Test cricket. Take fast bowler Neil Wagner, who in 2018 proved such a menace with the short ball despite not being express pace.

This game is all about opportunity, and five years earlier Doug Bracewell would have been opening the bowling in the first Test, but he stepped on some glass at a social function or – as they call it in New Zealand – a rave. In came Wagner for his fourth Test appearance, ripped out three early doors and four in the first innings. Including that match, he would go on to play in 33 of New Zealand's next 47 matches. He leaves nothing on the pitch and has found a niche with that mid-innings delivery into the armpit of a batsman.

They are a resourceful nation, the Kiwis. I recall on one visit to Dunedin, students carrying their own sofas to the ground so they had somewhere to sit and then set them on fire at the end of the day to keep warm! And their cricketers make the most of their abilities. Think of Peter Fulton, who scored his maiden hundred at the age of 34 and then followed up with another in the second innings of a dullfest in Auckland in 2013. Or Bruce Martin, a left-arm spinner at 32, who was hardly a Murali or a Warne but somehow pacified England's batting. He didn't have the tools to last, but for his short time at the top he produced one bowling spell when he conceded a dozen runs in 14 overs to provide his captain with control.

New Zealand also have a history of finding people who know how to put a good team together. The godfather of this now is Derbyshire's John Wright, who is fascinating on what makes a good 50-over or Twenty20 XI. During the 2015 World Cup I was invited out to his farm 20 minutes outside Christchurch. He's got 70 cows and a sit-on tractor! And time to mull things over. He certainly proved good at it with Mumbai Indians in the Indian Premier League, and his return to county cricket in 2017 coincided with Derbyshire's first T20 quarter-finals appearance in a dozen years.

The Godfather of Pace Bowling

Like all the best players of our great game, Richard Hadlee was blinkered. He knew exactly where he was going and no one was going to get in his way. He was also the subject of one of the great lines from my old *Test Match Special* colleague FS Trueman. When Hadlee went past 400 Test wickets, our Fred announced: 'Well, no wonder he's got that many. He's been bowling at both ends. Have you seen the rest of them? They're hopeless.'

Accusations of New Zealand being a one-man team were nothing new, of course, but Hadlee had unbelievable pride in his performance. He was no-nonsense, kept every one of his batting contemporaries around the world honest, and he was a fine lower-order player himself. If anything he might have been kept back too low.

But boy did he understand bowling, and I actually see shades of him in Jimmy Anderson. From being a tear-arse, get it down as fast as you can merchant, he evolved into an artist, knowing exactly what that spherical object in his hand could do and how to make it do it. The first time I saw the young Anderson bowl, in a televised match for Lancashire, I turned to the on-duty Sky producer and asked if the speed gun was working properly. He assured me it was. It said he was bowling at 90mph. Back then he used to just bowl as fast as he could. Since that time, Jimmy has become a cultured operator – and has answered every question posed of him. Anderson can only bowl in English conditions, it was said. It has to swing for him to prosper, it was said. Now that he has obliterated Sir Ian Botham's English

Test wicket record and has the capacity to get close to 600, not much is being said at all.

Hadlee is a good template for pace bowlers, after cutting his run down to a minimal length later in his career, with no loss of pace. That is something Anderson did successfully, of course, and in New Zealand during the winter of 2017-18 we saw similar from Ben Stokes. Ambling in off about 10 paces he seemed to bowl quicker than he had ever done.

For Stokes, the reason for change was not so much age and a change of tack but a combination of other factors. For one thing he was coming back from an injury. And in his previous hustle-and-bustle approach to the crease, he jumped in towards the umpire as he got near delivery stride. The change to a reduced run-up was also designed to focus the mind on running in a straight line. Fewer steps, concentrate on the task in hand. In a straight line over a short distance, he had to be more deliberate in his movements, and so he was looking for 10 paces of rhythm rather than bounding in over twice the length and losing focus on his journey. The results seemed to suggest there will be positive results in future. The ball was coming out of his hand quicker than when he was off his full run.

I have been through this kind of process with bowlers over the years as a coach and the analogy is with a golfer adapting his swing. Leading golfers can report similar anecdotal experiences: they always say, 'Don't try to burst the ball when you hit it, you are looking for rhythm. The club will do the rest.' Stokes's solid action will make the ball get down the other end quicker.

If he can get it through at speeds in excess of 88mph then it will not only make him an asset to the team but provide him with longevity in the all-rounder's role. Think of Jacques Kallis and how he adapted his game over the years. He didn't take a lot out of himself but he was very effective with the ball. This measured approach can potentially take the strain off one's body and extend a career. Just as it did for Hadlee, who retired at the age of 39 with a Test bowling average of 22.29 and a strike rate of a wicket every 50.8 balls.

CHAPTER TEN

Bumble: International Captain

Derrick Robins was a wicketkeeper who played just two first-class matches for Warwickshire in 1947. Later, starting with a cement mixer in a field, he turned his firm Banbury Buildings into a major public company and enjoyed a successful career in business, constructing outbuildings, garages and sheds. In 1960, he became chairman of Coventry City, hired Jimmy Hill as manager and helped transform them from a football club without direction to one that would remain in the English top flight for 34 consecutive seasons. But he retained an involvement on the board at Warwickshire and also became one of English cricket's most significant patrons, allowing players like me to earn a winter wage playing abroad.

Having taken over the Eastbourne Festival in the late 1960s – organising fixtures and, indeed, appearing himself against touring teams, despite being in his fifties and with 22 years between his second and third first-class appearances – he clearly found pleasure in these kinds of representative matches and began looking further afield to do so.

So when the South African administrator Jack Cheetham asked him to start organising tours to South Africa, it provided opportunities in the off-season for English county professionals to supplement their earnings. In terms of remuneration, the Indian Premier League it was not, but I had been on the Ashes tour 12 months earlier and this was a chance to add once again to my Lancashire income. Earlier in my career, I had worked in a brewery to do so. This was nothing comparable to £1.4 million contracts. No, a place on the Robins tour paid £40 a week. But it was work with sun on your back rather than frost on your fingertips.

When these tours began in 1972-73, the touring party selected was comprised of English players only. By the time I got involved in 1975-76, we had players coming from all around the world. There were one or two established county professionals combined with some emerging players and others who were on the periphery of their national teams. Myself, David Steele, Frank Hayes, Peter Lee and Fred Titmus had all played for England in the previous decade, and then there were up-and-coming lads like Nottinghamshire's Derek Randall and Philip Slocombe, a 22-year-old batsman who played for Somerset, three from Yorkshire – Phil Carrick, Geoff Cope and David Bairstow – plus Geoff Howarth and Gary Troup, both of whom made their international debuts for New Zealand that year. The Australian element included Trevor Chappell along with John Douglas, a quick bowler from Victoria who also played top-level Australian Rules football, and Dav Whatmore, who was to become better known for his coaching exploits with Sri Lanka 20 years later. Robins's tours broke the anti-apartheid boycott but touring teams were multi-racial. John Shepherd, of Kent, went in successive years, and Sri Lankan-born Dav was on the tour for which I was named captain. There were other elements of the trip that didn't sit comfortably with me, though. For a start, it was all a bit too old-colonial for my liking, and if truth be told I didn't hit it off with Robins. When we got off the plane, I was greeted with: 'Welcome, captain, this is your Mercedes. You'll be driven around in this. The rest of the boys will be in the combi.'

'No, no. I'll be in with them, thanks.'

I wasn't interested in having my own driver. Things didn't get off on the right foot. He must have been living in the dark ages if he thought that was how things were going to go. No names, no pack drill, but I could provide a page full of people who would have taken up the offer. As I say, no names – although it's safe to say most have lots of initials. This smacked of the gentlemen and players era, and that was one I believed had been left behind long before.

Although we were rewarded financially it was in essence a social tour, providing us with the chance to play good cricket in the off-season. And as such it took us to some fabulous places, and some interesting cricket venues. I didn't want to be travelling around on my tod in a Merc.

It was akin to the old-style international tours, in that you played a series of matches against the provincial sides plus what was the equivalent of a one-day international against the full South Africa team under the guise of being an Invitational XI.

This is the trip on which I got to know David 'Bluey' Bairstow better. We played a couple of games at Cape Town, where his son Jonny scored that brilliant Test hundred in 2016. Newlands is one of the more picturesque grounds in the world but, no matter where you played, Bluey had the same infectious attitude and would stand out not only because of this but also his attire. Behind the stumps, he would boom out encouragement from over the top of these huge pads. There were no wicket-keeping pads in those days, of course, and I am not sure whether he would have worn them if they had been around. It wouldn't have fitted the image. Huge pads, huge gloves. That was him.

Bluey just called everything as he saw it. As the bowler was getting ready to run up, he would bellow things like, 'Look at them folk walking up there, on top of the hill.' That hill in question being Table Mountain, of course. This was indicative of the relaxed nature of the cricket we played, despite the fact that good performances against strong South African opposition might get noticed by national selectors. After all, before being excluded from international competition, they had crushed Australia 4-0 six years earlier to earn unofficial world champion status.

An example of the relaxed attitude came immediately after lunch one day when I set the field to Troup, a bustling left-armer. The opposition batsman nicked the ball down to third man, and I was pretty relaxed as I thought it was just a single. However, next moment I realised the umpire was signalling four. I counted up the fielders and realised we had only 10 men out there. Where was third man? David Steele, the man in question, was sat in the stands. 'Won't be long, youth,' he said. 'I've not seen this bloke for years. Just having a quick catch-up.' This was a proper three-day game. Give me strength!

It was inevitable that the cricket tour was played against a political backdrop, but I grew up in an era in which you much more readily accepted things. We were told what to do and were compliant. We didn't necessarily challenge the order of things, even though there was enough of everyday life to stir the emotions. In fact, at that stage in my life it pains me to say that I didn't really grasp the severity or significance of Basil D'Oliveira's story.

When we travelled round, we didn't question that black people weren't allowed to play cricket with white people. We played a token match in Soweto on a matting pitch against a local side captained by Peter Chingoka, the chap who went on to become the chief executive of Zimbabwe Cricket. Looking back, despite the tokenism, it was pleasing to play that kind of fixture because as cricketers we were all pretty ignorant of what was going on in terms of apartheid.

All we knew was travelling from ground to ground, from bus to bus, plane to plane, being shepherded towards where the nets were or dropped off at hotel receptions, with our cricket coffins in tow, going about our daily routines, playing the game we loved and the one that provided us with our income. Sadly, we did not give a second thought to the social inequality and utterly inhumane nature of the problems South Africa had as a nation.

By the end of the tour it is fair to say my eyes had been opened as to how wrong certain aspects of South African life were. The world was a different place back then and we didn't get the flow of information through news channels that we do as we approach the third decade of the 21st century. We only knew what we experienced, and the segregation and the treatment of black people as second-class citizens left a bitter taste.

The enjoyable part of being on a tour like this was the coming together of all different nationalities to share a cricketing experience. There were pranks, camaraderie and fun. Among the group was Trevor Chappell, who at that time seemed completely, utterly mad to me. He would be up to mischief and not good mischief, either, pulling stunts like leaving the bath running and heading out for the day, returning to the chaos later on.

'Is it the Iron Bird?'

Cricket is also full of politics, though, and as captain I had to get involved in sorting out an internal problem within the team. The issue stemmed from the fact that our fast bowler Mike Hendrick was not overly enamoured with Robins. He therefore effectively downed tools. When picked for one game, he informed me: 'I don't think I'll be able to play in this one because I think I'll get injured.'

I sought clarification: 'Are you injured, Hendo?'

The answer came back: 'No, I'm not injured. But I think I might be very soon if I play.'

I was beginning to catch his drift when he continued: 'My boot's sore.'

'Your foot, or your boot?' I probed.

Hendo had a terrific sense of humour and his boot being sore was code to tell me he didn't want to be out there on the field. To be fair, it was quite amusing to see him rubbing Vaseline into the leather to try to ease the pain for his faithful size 13s. Of course, you would always want an international-class seamer on your team, but I was grateful for being kept onside. As captain, I wouldn't want to be taking a player out onto the field with me who would not be putting in a shift.

However, while it was all very well getting things cleared with me, there was another level for him to crack and that was the tour management. Above me were the legendary Ken Barrington and Don Bennett, his assistant on the Robins tour, who was coach of Middlesex for years and years, a period coinciding with the emergence of guys like Mike Gatting, John Emburey, Angus Fraser, Mark Ramprakash and Phil Tufnell. On the bench on the balcony of the home dressing room at Lord's is a commemorative plaque in his honour, containing a quote on how the game should be played. They were two dyed-in-the-wool cricket men who shared a belief in pride in the shirt and discipline. In their wisdom, they decided that if Hendrick was not playing, he had to go home and it was down to me to break the news.

'Hendo, we need to have a chat.'

It was a rather unique experience for me to tell someone that they were being sent home, and even now when we see each other we have a laugh about the episode. Before anything else is said between us, Hendo will enquire: 'Is it the iron bird?' That is how we ended the conversation that day. When I confirmed it was, his typically laconic response was, 'Thank God for that!'

Rubbing Shoulders with the Best

South Africa had some crack players at that time and so the standard of the matches was very high. I'd played against the full South Africa team in a tour match before their ostracism in 1965, and the star-studded opposition at Old Trafford led by Eddie Barlow included Graeme Pollock, Peter Pollock, Tiger Lance, Ali Bacher and Colin Bland. They were a bloody good side. I took four wickets and top-scored in our second innings with 42, but I was out-bowled by Harry Bromfield, who with his little pencil moustache bore a passing resemblance to Adolf Hitler and bowled tidy off-spin. He took a five-for as we were skittled for just 117 chasing 284 to win.

On this particular tour, we won two and lost two of the provincial matches. One of the wins was when we played Eastern Province on a real wet 'un at Port Elizabeth, persuading me to open the bowling with Lee and Titmus. Lee was unplayable on pitches that were like that, and its sticky-dog nature, reminiscent of ones we got in county cricket, convinced me to go with the off-spinner at the other end. It was one of my better calls. The ball bit in the surface, we bowled out an Eastern Province XI (including Phil Edmonds as overseas player) for 68, and won by 10 wickets midway through the second day.

With an early finish like that it was customary on those kinds of tours to play a one-day game on what would have been the third and final day of the first-class match. Ken Barrington played and, as if to emphasise what a class player he had been in his heyday, he was still the best on either side, years into his retirement. He couldn't run between the wickets but we were all agog at his finesse with bat in hand. No post-war England batsman has averaged more than Ken's 58.67; everyone knew of his record, but it still could not suppress their admiration for his talent. While he was batting, the dressing room shared a collective 'wow'.

It was very similar to an experience I had in 1998 when, during my time as England coach, we won the Champions Trophy in Sharjah. We trained at the Gymkhana Club in Lahore, and arranged a practice match there against a local team. Our guys were absolutely shellshocked by the quality of one particular opponent.

'Bloody hell, this guy can play.'

It was none other than Majid Khan. Useless between the wickets. But that was hardly a handicap given the touch he possessed. It was 15 years since he had played his last Test match but such was his class that he seemed to have twice as much time playing the ball as anybody else.

The one trait that made Ken Barrington stand out from others was how he was able to change tempo. Having been dropped by England in his dashing days in the mid-1950s, he was a much more careful kind of batsman on his return to the Test team four years later. However, despite his restraint he retained a wonderful eye, and so everything changed whenever he got towards his hundred. He liked to charge through the 90s, often hitting a four and a six in quick succession to get to three figures.

You've probably played with similar guys yourself in club cricket. You know the ones. None of this pussyfooting around with singles. Just wham, bam, 100, thanks very much. Ken was a lovely bloke, popular with all, and it was a real shock when he died while on duty as England manager on the tour of the Caribbean in 1981.

Raising the Steaks

It was in South Africa in January 2016 that I had the pleasure of witnessing one of England's great innings, when Ben Stokes evoked memories of his maiden Test century. The difference between this one and that one versus Australia in 2013-14? The one versus the South Africans was 10 times better.

The key to both efforts was the surface. Where was the first one? In Perth, on exactly the same type of pitch as at Newlands. To give it a rating, it would have been a Hot Chocolate – as in 'Everyone's a Winner, Baby'. It offered pace and bounce and even some turn later. In other words, a classic Test surface.

And because it allowed the bowlers to get the new ball through, it offered the chance for stroke play. Stokes's style is scintillating, and to hit 30 fours and 11 sixes without losing control of his shape when striking the ball was phenomenal. Some players you would say possess pedigree, they look pretty and nice, well, Ben doesn't. Although he has a very solid technique, he is an absolute mongrel who tears bowling attacks to bits. But you cannot take your eyes off him when he is in full flow.

To be there to call Jonny Bairstow's own maiden hundred was equally special and I could hear Bluey's voice on the same ground 40 years earlier as he did so. You could really see the emotion there.

When conditions are right Newlands can be a fast-scoring ground, and when the sun is out it is one of the great venues, with the backdrop of Table Mountain. In one way it's a bit like Headingley, where you look up at the sky to see if the ball is going to swing. Over there they say if you can smell the hops from the brewery it will swing. Well, we didn't smell them that week. The only movement was by those sat in the stands taking evasive action.

This was also the series in which we saw South Africa's fast-bowling baton pass from a great in Dale Steyn to a new go-to man in Kagiso Rabada. The worry is that they do not manage him properly. Just listen to Michael Holding on this, who says: 'If a young fella like him, not properly developed, is run into the ground you will only get four or five years out of him.' At 20, he showed he had a good physique, decent action and the skills to challenge Steyn's 419 Test wickets at 22.32 runs apiece.

Both these men are untypical of South African fast bowlers I would say, being lithe and whippy. They clearly don't eat at the world-famous, celebrated Butcher Shop & Grill in Sandton, Johannesburg, which, you are probably not surprised to hear, specialises in red meat. They have steaks from 'ladies' size' right up to ones that look like the animal in question has simply had its horns shorn off, its backside wiped and been thrown on the table. I've never seen such huge pieces of meat coming out of a kitchen in my life. I was off the ladies' tee and couldn't play to my handicap. No wonder there are so many big blokes stomping about over there.

It's a smart place is Sandton, where international teams tend to stay when playing at the Wanderers or up the road at Centurion. The kind of place where you can get your shoes shined – as Michael Atherton did out the front of our hotel. Sure enough, it turns out that the pair he's been wearing since graduating from university actually are black. It's the best hundred rand he spent all tour.

Talking of Atherton and hundreds, it is said that his greatest innings was the defiant 185 against the South Africans in 1995–96 when he and Jack Russell beat the odds to salvage a draw at the Wanderers, Johannesburg. But the best I saw from close quarters came when he finished two runs shy. His unbeaten 98 was a study in the physical effort required against a typically ferocious pace bowling attack.

When people recall the win at Trent Bridge in 1998, they tend to focus on the pivotal moment early in the chase of 247 when Allan Donald appealed unsuccessfully for Atherton's dismissal caught behind. Donald believed the ball had brushed glove, Steve Dunne, the neutral umpire, did not and, while Atherton remained his impassive self, this incident only served to raise an already pumped-up Donald to greater heights of passion. To withstand one of the most hostile barrages I have ever witnessed and take the team to a series-levelling victory was to highlight his greatest strength: mental fortitude.

The subsequent win over South Africa at Headingley represented my proudest moment as England coach, and I will never forget that last morning when we needed two wickets to win, South Africa required 34 runs and Yorkshire threw open the gates. We got Matthew Wood, the 12th man, to give the team talk and, pointing to the opposition training 100 yards away, he said, in a broad Huddersfield accent: 'You see that lot over there? Let's spoil their f***ing day.' It did the trick.

South African teams tend to be a tough nut to crack and the one we faced 20 years ago had a battery of five fast bowlers to contend with, including Donald and Shaun Pollock at the peak of their powers. Makhaya Ntini, Jacques Kallis and Brian McMillan weren't too shabby either. To beat them on their own soil, as the England teams of 2004-05 and 2015-16 managed, was outstanding; and since readmission to international cricket in 1992 they have travelled as well as any nation, which is why Joe Root was so pleased with the 3-1 victory in 2017, his maiden series as captain.

South Africans tend to grind opponents down because they are very methodical in their play. They are well suited to the long game, and never more so than at The Oval in 2012 when they started the series in the most clinical manner possible. England would have been mildly satisfied, having won the toss and put 385 on the board, and then seen Alviro Petersen dismissed by Jimmy Anderson in the third over.

Trouble was that only one further wicket fell in the next 186! AB de Villiers, Jacques Rudolph and JP Duminy were still to come off the bench when Graeme Smith called time on an unbroken 377-run stand between Hashim Amla and Jacques Kallis. Conceding a total of 637 for two declared is fatiguing. It is also dispiriting at the start of a three-match series and England – a team ranked number one in the world at the time – never recovered, losing both the series and their top-dog status that August. Others such as the Pakistanis and Sri Lankans dazzle you with their brilliance but that has never been the South African style.

CHAPTER ELEVEN

Dare to Be Different

Don't be fooled by the smiling little men from Sri Lanka. They'll happily take your pants down and smack your backside – a skill they were taught by none other than Arjuna Ranatunga, the captain who led them to the status of world champions in 1996.

For three decades they have shown that they are the masters of upsetting the old world order with their collection of idiosyncratic skills. Arguably, there has not been a country quite like them for developing cricketers of difference. The greatest resource any of cricket's major nations can have is natural talent, and Sri Lanka's has been harvested within the cities of Colombo and Kandy, from the strong school system that exists within the country and indeed from the beach matches that dot the coastline.

My personal experience of their brilliance came in what was a shocking match for me as England coach. Back in 1998, we had just finished a series against South Africa and we were shattered. It is a series that sucked out every last drop of sweat. Unfortunately, the powers that be tagged on a one-off Test match against Sri Lanka and as an extension of their generosity offered up a Colombo-style dust bowl to play on. Muttiah

Muralitharan got 16 wickets, Sanath Jayasuriya got a double hundred and I got a reprimand.

Only later did I come to appreciate what a genius Murali was, but in the heat of defeat at The Oval I did not choose my words carefully enough. To say of his bowling action 'if that's legal we should be teaching it' was inappropriate. What I would say, however, is that with me what you see is what you get. As an England team we thought it looked odd, and I was trying to get that point across when directly asked about his action in a television interview.

Technology has highlighted what a freak of nature he was. I have never seen anyone able to put their fingers on their wrist before. The mobility of his joint was just logic-defying and, when you watched him deliver a ball at 2,000 frames a second, you could see that his elbow was damn near straight and it's just his wrist that is all over the place. His shoulder seemed to disjoint when he let go of the ball.

Of course, the emergence of such a one-off meant that others tried to emulate him. Something that was nigh-on impossible and so occasionally has caused issues – such as when Sachithra Senanayake became a victim of a haphazard and slightly unfair system for bowlers with suspect actions. My preference would be for players to be placed on notice and monitored in match situations instead of being sent to the laboratory. Tell them they're being watched and get them to bowl in short-sleeved shirts so the umpires can see exactly what they need to.

They have produced some classical batsmen in Kumar Sangakkara and Mahela Jayawardene and bowlers in Chaminda Vaas and Rangana Herath, but the Sri Lankans rejoice in the promotion of the unorthodox. Examples being Murali, and his 800 Test and 534 ODI victims, and Lasith Malinga, whose round-arm bowling action wouldn't have got him past under-13 nets in England in the mid-1990s. While England have always followed traditional-looking players, however, it has arguably been to their detriment.

Take when the two countries met in 2014. It was extraordinary to me that, after Jos Buttler had graced Lord's with a quite magnificent 121 in an ultimately forlorn chase of 301, the then England captain Alastair Cook should dampen it all down by saying that he was not ready for Test cricket. I would have had no hesitation in throwing Buttler into the first Test at the same ground the following week had Matt Prior not been fit. This was yet another example of the sort of 'Englishness' I've seen time and time again, where we concentrate on what someone cannot do rather than what they can.

Occasionally, we expend more energy on the negative aspects rather than the positives. And that is where we ought to have learned lessons from the Sri Lankans. Think also of the limpet-like West Indies batsman Shiv Chanderpaul – it was as if he was attached to the crease by superglue. His style is unique and certainly not from the MCC coaching manual. It worked for him and took him to the number one ranking among batsmen in the world.

It Ain't Half Hot, Mum

When Sri Lanka play at home they have humidity on their side, a factor which has made English successes there all the more special. The best of these victories, I would argue, came in 2000-01 when Graham Thorpe got them over the line on his last legs, fighting off cramp at the SSC in Colombo to hit unbeaten scores of 113 and 32. No other England player managed 35 runs in a low-scoring match.

It was the one time that I can recall an international team negating Murali. His 14 wickets at 30.07 runs each was not bad, but the most vital statistic was his strike rate. He took a wicket every 101 deliveries – the only time in the last 16 years of his career that he possessed a three-figure strike rate in a home Test series.

In those hot, sweaty conditions on dry pitches, the Sri Lankans had a tendency to swarm all over opponents who couldn't have found them more alien – the spinners on, men crowding the bat, every ball an examination of technique. That's about as hard as it gets for an English team abroad. That's Test cricket, eh? It does what it says on the tin. It tests you and there is no let-up.

The same is true when the Sri Lankans have toured the UK. You have to be ready to go whatever the temperature, and Sri Lanka didn't look like they really wanted to be out in the field at times on their 2014 tour. They brought hand warmers back into fashion and donned woolly hats under their caps.

Or take the 2011 tour when England declared in inhospitable conditions on the fifth afternoon in Cardiff and, despite having only 96 runs as an advantage, ran through the Sri Lankans like a dose of salts for an innings win. It was a bit damp; it needed a bit of a dig-in from Tillakaratne Dilshan's team and it wasn't forthcoming.

Arrack Attack

When in Sri Lanka it is Mark Lynch, our director at Sky Sports, who leads the charge. When he calls an all-dayer, it is rather like he has unearthed some of the world's dingiest bars, and the tipple of choice when on Sri Lankan soil is not beer but arrack. If you haven't tried it, it's like meths. Remember that childhood smell of turpentine? Sounds enticing, eh?

If the establishment is as grotty as imaginable then we go, and as it is our downtime we are dressed accordingly. Michael

Atherton is usually in this crew, as are two others from the production team, James Lawson and Alex Hakes, whose husband is an ex-Gurkha. These days he works in insurance. The kind of insurance he provides is that people like prime ministers don't get killed. You might also call him a close protection officer. He's a pretty uncompromising chap in his day job, let's put it that way. Alex is always pretty vivacious when she is out, and whenever she gets chatted up she has a staple line to ward off said interest for the chap's own good, usually along the lines of, 'Ooh, my husband would kill you with a plastic spoon.'

It is almost a challenge to downgrade on the last place that we go to, but the one variation on this trend came when Tillakaratne Dilshan invited us out of the blue for dinner at his boutique hotel in downtown Colombo. Its surroundings are so tranquil that you cannot hear a thing. With all the tuk-tuks, cars and buses, bumper to bumper around it, you cannot believe this beautiful oasis exists. It is a magnificent place with half a dozen bedrooms, plunge pools and a fine restaurant downstairs. It was wonderfully hospitable of him to invite us all down and he even gave us a gift as we left. Yes, you've guessed it, a bottle of arrack each. Not the stuff that would take the paint off your walls but its top-end equivalent. Think Château Margaux and you are on the right lines. The crème de la menthe, as Del Boy would say. I've still got mine in the drinks cabinet at home. Untouched.

Toll Roads and Toilets

Travel in Sri Lanka can test the patience. The road infrastructure of the country is still not great, so the journey from Colombo to Kandy is one of the slowest anywhere in the modern world. It is something like 100 miles in distance but it takes you around five hours – and that's on a good day!

One year we were staying at the same hotels as the England players and I decided to have some fun at either end of the arduous trip. I had seen them all lining up for the team coach in the morning and so when we arrived in the hills before them I couldn't resist stirring things.

'What a journey,' said James Anderson, or words to that effect.

'Didn't you come on the motorway?' I replied. 'Did you not just pay for the toll road? It only took us an hour and a half. It's a godsend is that.'

He was aghast.

'I know what's happened,' I continued. 'It'll be Phil Neale. He will have considered the two options and decided that you lot would prefer to take in the cultural route.'

With that, Jimmy stormed off. I think he said something about seeing Phil, the England operations manager for 20 years. I hope I didn't cause any trouble ... And before you ask, of course there was no toll road.

Road isn't the only way to get from A to B, though, and on England's one-day tour in 2014, my wife Diana insisted we catch the train from Colombo to Kandy. We got sorted in advance by purchasing tickets on the Internet. Even though we secured a first-class compartment, I told her I wasn't so sure about it. Mainly because it had cost me all of about 30p. Now, I know from experience that when something looks too good to be true it usually is. A first-class compartment for 30p? Well, you've never seen anything like it. It was full of flies and midges, and didn't seem to be any different to economy class, being chock-full of hundreds and hundreds of people. Perhaps they guaranteed a higher species of diptera?

Inevitably on a five-hour journey, Vipers decides she wants to go to the loo. This means I have to go on a recce. 'It's back there,' the reluctant hero says, pointing the way. Soon afterwards, no more than a matter of seconds later in fact, she was back.

'There is no toilet there,' my better half tells me. 'Only a hole.'

'Yes, I know. But that hole is the toilet. You've just got to do your best.'

'But there's no door either.'

'I know. You've just got to do your best.'

If looks could have killed. My only defence was a bit of plain speaking.

'Well, it was you who wanted to come on this contraption.'

We managed to get by with me standing guard at the door. It got better too. Or worse, if truth be told. Minutes later, we are settled back in the carriage when the train comes to an abrupt halt. As I mentioned, it's stinking hot. Do you think there was any air conditioning on board? Well, I will give you a hint. There's no need to phone a friend. We had to wait another five hours while a second train was despatched from Colombo to shunt us up into the hills. Jimmy might have called it karma.

We then decided to get a driver for the return journey, which naturally enough featured another Vipers comfort break. What is it with women wanting to go to the toilet? There aren't any public conveniences like on Silver Street in York, where you can pay your 40p and carry out any business you see fit. But while I am on the subject, charging 40p and not giving change from a 50p coin is a total rip-off, York City Council. Anyway the driver stopped and we knocked on the door of a house. In she went, into this home of total strangers, to use the lav. Kept her going for an hour did that. They're wired differently to us are women, aren't they?

Record Breakers

When it comes to cricket's records, Sri Lanka appear to have an addiction. The highest Test score of 952 for six against India in 1997 belongs to them; one-day international cricket's top total, of 443 for nine, was theirs until 2016; they have dismissed opponents for the three lowest ODI scores, of 35, 36 and 38, and the Netherlands for a Twenty20 international low of 39.

They also specialise in the long name. Take Chanaka Welegedara, the fast bowler with six initials. UWMBCA on a scorecard makes him look like a one-man social club. In case you are interested, the record for a first-class cricketer in this country is seven: John Elicius Benedict Bernard Placid Quirk Carrington Dwyer. But globally? Yes, that'll be a Sri Lankan. ARRAPWRRKB ('a good score in Scrabble, you can call me Rajitha') Amunugama.

CHAPTER TWELVE

What a To-Du

I nearly died in Bangladesh during England's 2009-10 tour. A bit dramatic, I know. But if something's worth doing, it's worth doing well, and so during time off from the cricket we booked to do some trekking in the Himalayan foothills. It was quite an adventure, involving helicopters, rogue planes and dengue fever. The last of these confined me to bed for a fortnight and meant I missed covering two Test matches. I am sure Mark Butcher thanked me at some point for his career break.

The big adventure began with a flight from Dhaka to Kathmandu. Fellow trekker Bryan Henderson, then a producer of Sky's cricket coverage, and I boarded a propeller aircraft – along with a dozen Japanese tourists – that went to take in the views at the top of Everest. We got to know some of our fellow fliers intimately as they clambered all over us to get the best pictures possible.

We then had a couple of days trekking down below, staying in tiny huts along the way, taking in the wilderness, just the two of us. It was a remarkable couple of days in the outback. Some way in we were passed by a fella with two milk churns hanging either side of a pole. Where on earth had he come from and, more to the point, where was he going? We were absolutely miles from anywhere, on a single track in the bush. Further on, we still haven't seen a soul. Then this bus turns up with what seemed like a couple of hundred people hanging off the sides. That's Nepal for you.

On the return journey we had an almighty drama because we needed to get back ahead of the first Test match and the flight was cancelled. Amid our panic, an airport official piped up at the 11th hour to tell us there was an unofficial flight available – whatever that meant – departing from the far runway.

It was all a bit haphazard and I had never seen an aircraft like the one we approached. It appeared to be from a vintage collection. A dozen other people were being herded around the tarmac and, as we approached, they were being told: 'Yes, you can get on.' Not a bag between them, mind, which all seemed very odd. Upon boarding we were advised that there would be no food or drink served. But it got us back to Dhaka and while we were let off one way our fellow passengers went another. Who they were other than local residents of Kathmandu, who knows? The mind boggles.

We got back in one piece, that was the main thing, although I needn't have bothered as it turned out. For the next fortnight I was tucked up in bed shivering and sweating.

Double-Booked

Back in 1998, when I was England coach, we were despatched to Bangladesh for the inaugural Champions Trophy, which had been set up by the International Cricket Council to raise funds for non-Test-playing nations. It was an unusual situation for us as it clashed with the Ashes that winter, meaning we had to send two separate teams. While a group under the tour manager

Graham Gooch went to Australia, I took the one-day specialists to Bangladesh. Or Atlantis as it became known. The place was totally under water.

It is fair to say that our preparation wasn't great. We played a warm-up game against the Bangladeshis and, as our kit was still in transit, we turned out in training gear, including shorts. It was unbelievably hot out there. We didn't acclimatise well but there was no time to, really.

As I say, we had other things on our minds, but it was a commitment we had to fulfil through the ICC, as disjointed as it made our winter plans. It was a similar situation to that in early 2018 when Australia sent their Test players over to South Africa for pre-series preparation while they were still involved in a home one-day series against England. We were threatened with sanctions should we not turn up.

The heat and humidity are very demanding and you need time to acclimatise and get used to the conditions. It's not somewhere you can fly in and get on with things. Not that I would argue that the climate is something that provides Bangladesh with any kind of advantage when they play at home. You lose weight and you need to rehydrate during matches, and let's remember that it's the same for both sides.

Rather like the rest of cricket's Asian stop-offs, getting about is a challenge as the place is teeming with people. The roads are absolutely jammed with motor vehicles, coming at you from all angles. On this trip, our team bus packed up but, thankfully, our bus driver was a tremendously resourceful chap. He clambered below the ginormous steering wheel, started fiddling about, lit a match and then whoosh, the engine was back on again. And his choice of musical accompaniment was a cracker, too. He appeared to possess one cassette, and on this one cassette was one song – 'One Way Ticket' by Boney M. It was rather apt, really, as we appeared stuck there against our will, and so it became the team's tour song. It was played all the way on repeat, on the journey out and the journey back, our man singing every word too, leaving us in tears.

We were knocked out by the eventual winners South Africa, but the real eye-opener on that trip was the desperate state some of the population were in. The sadness is that Bangladesh represents reprehensibly cheap labour, and so if you have anything stitched, whether it be clothing or leather goods, there's a good chance it's been done there. In a morning you can see lines hundreds of yards long of ladies going into these sweat boxes to be paid a pittance.

For some men and young males the hard graft takes place in the Chittagong ship-breaking yard, a place that does exactly what it promises, dismantling the world's ships including some of the biggest liners. The compound is a no-access area, guarded by blokes with guns, which all looks a bit sinister, and it is an unbelievably labour-intensive process to break up these enormous container vessels – which have a life cycle of about 25 years – so that the parts can be recycled. Where does everything go? Well, the oil unfortunately appears to be released into the water but the paraphernalia, such as the ships' compasses, bells and clocks, is sold at market stalls on the sides of the roads.

The House of Sin

When I returned in 2003-04, Bangladesh were established as a Test nation and we had an absolute hoot. The first of the two venues we stayed in was Dhaka, and we were put up in a nice hotel. It was the usual thing.

'Have you got a bar?'

'Yes, along the corridor, past a couple of shops and on your left-hand side.'

All cushty. Although when we got down there, a fella on the door was demanding money to go in, which we considered very odd because you don't generally pay to go into a hotel bar. But who were we to argue as guests? We paid our money and in we went. Welcome to what was to become known as the 'House of Sin'. It wasn't so much that scantily clad ladies frequented the place as very well-clad ladies. They had lots of clothes on, and would come along, cavort in front of you, then ask for cash for the privilege. It seemed to be the place where all the locals descended, and lots of money changed hands. Of course, we had to support the local economy by attending the House of Sin nightly – just out of curiosity, and for medicinal purposes, you'll understand. Before it got shut down, that is.

But the real drama was saved for Chittagong and the luxurious Hotel Agrabad. Now, it was anything but luxurious, only the name by which it came to be known, and so when England got there they decided that in between games they would return to Dhaka to practise. For the journalists this was a big problem as they had naturally booked rooms in the relevant city. At short notice this meant going back to Dhaka.

One of the great characters of that time among the press pack was Graham Otway, of the *Daily Mail*, who decided to keep his room on in Chittagong and flit back and forth, leaving all but his essential kit. Then when the team came back, he followed suit. All went swimmingly until he got back to find a bloke fast asleep in his bed. Not a man to remain calm under provocation, Otters played hell about it and charged down to reception where he discovered a chap splendidly dressed in local regalia. He was wearing a red crown and a long jacket and for some reason Otway thought he was a policeman, so he insisted he accompany him to the reception desk to perform an arrest on the duty manager who had sub-let his room. At which point the well-dressed doorman had to make clear he was a member of the concierge not a constable.

It was also at this hotel that Paul Allott taught Bob Willis and me how to play bridge. The Blackwood convention, as explained by Walt, featured a large bottle of whisky and it's fair to say that the first few bids were bold as a result. We were playing for imaginary Bangladeshi currency. In the end I was about 1,500 taka down, which I was pleased to learn amounted to – imaginary or otherwise – about £12.

Outside, however, on our evening trips to the Silver Spoon Chinese restaurant which served its soup in dustbin lids, we had to negotiate pitch-black streets before reaching the stereotypical velvet carpet that led through a warehouse and upstairs to the establishment. These streets, sadly, were full of little children running out of alleyways, tugging at your jacket, wanting money, something we were only too pleased to provide at first. Until we saw them run away to hand it to a man. As a result we later handed out food parcels rather than cash.

Spin to Win

Some parts of the cricketing globe are desperate places, unfortunately, Bangladesh prime among them, but people get on with life. They are a hardy lot. It is a country that is only at sea level in lots of places and I have been there when it's been completely submerged in water. Yet they meet their challenges stoically. Cricket is a massive outlet in terms of relieving the monotony, an outlet for their people to be proud and an escape from everyday struggles. It provides them with an identity.

As an international team they probably haven't made up the ground on the other sides as quickly as Sri Lanka did after being granted Test status in the early 1980s, but offer playing conditions that suit them and they are a handful, as England discovered in both Test and one-day cricket in the autumn of 2016 when they edged a tight one-day series 2-1 and lost for the first time to Bangladesh in the longer format of the game to draw 1-1.

There aren't the fields to play on as there are in India and Pakistan and those fields that do exist are either used to grow crops or are flooded. In the cities it is one concrete structure after another, further limiting the space for playing outdoors. It makes participation very difficult, although I would argue that they are a very resourceful nation and they always appear to find some way, developing a competitive team, building around some wonderful players in Tamim Iqbal, Shakib Al Hasan, Mushfiqur Rahim and Mahmudullah.

And what has made them more competitive is the ignorance, justifiably arrogance at times, of non-Asian teams playing in their conditions. One of my issues with England away from home over the past decade or two has been their habit of 'thinking English' and carrying on with their favoured make-up of bowling attack. Just because they are accustomed to playing three seamers, a one-size-fits-all policy should not be applied on their travels. They need to think how India have tried things, such as opening the bowling with their off-spinner, and only including one pace bowler in their XI at times. Bangladesh threw the new ball to two spinners in Mehidy Hasan and Shakib from the start of the 2016-17 series.

Matches in Bangladesh therefore tend to feature heavy crowding around the bat, lots of deliveries skidding into batsmen's pads, and umpires under pressure to make judgements on what has been struck – be it an appeal for an edge or a leg before.

On the subcontinent, with the heat, the spinners and men round the bat, making on-field calls can prove to be the toughest of jobs, and it wouldn't surprise me to learn of tactical whiteboards in dressing rooms with instructions to 'test the umpire'. It is a mental and physical challenge for the officials and, during the series in question, we witnessed an umpire with a great depth of experience in Asia pressurised into a couple of rare mistakes – thankfully, that is what the Decision Review System is there for. The exertion of standing in the sun for six and a half hours concentrating on the front foot, then looking up to see what's going on at the business end, can be draining, and you need to stay hydrated to maximise concentration.

And the bounce – or general lack of it – makes a contest in Bangladesh all the more challenging. Umpires get net practice in alongside the players from both teams during the build-up to matches so they can assess the bowlers' actions, lines and lengths. Above all, though, they will be gauging the bounce, which tends to be similar on the practice pitches to the one in the middle. If you are umpiring at the WACA in Perth, you know that a batsman practically has to be hit on the shin to be given out lbw. But DRS has taught us that, contrary to previously perceived wisdom, few full deliveries from the slow bowlers tend to clear the top of the stumps.

PART THREE

Hopes for the Future

CHAPTER THIRTEEN

One for the Shelf

Winning a Bafta was a real thrill. It's a lovely thing to say: 'I've got a Bafta.' Okay, technically Sky Sports won it for their coverage of the 2015 Ashes and I was one of the recipients on the awards night. But where would they be without me, eh?

In case you are still with us, and considering offering me a new contract, Mr Bryan Henderson, I want to make clear I am only joking. We were all very proud of what we achieved and it was a huge team effort. When it comes to working in British film and television, there really is no accolade bigger than one from the industry experts recognising you've reached the heights to which you aspire.

There is no denying that covering an Ashes series, like playing in one, carries with it more kudos than just about anything else we will cover over a four-year cycle. You get up for it. You want to be there. Every morning you have a spring in your step. But there is also no denying that it is hard work covering a series like that. It is 25 days of cricket in the space of seven weeks and that makes it physically demanding, not least because we work 12-hour days. Not many people work 12-hour shifts and look as good as I do at the end, you know.

At Sky, we like to think we are at the forefront of technology, delivering a product that is both enjoyable and reliable – unlike the Wi-Fi on Mr Branson's trains when I pop down to London on the rattler. Ironically, on the day of the 2017 Baftas it was bang-on.

We like to think that we are pushing the use of technology constantly, and one thing going for cricket in this regard is that it has the framework to implement it to add to the viewing experience. We have that one important commodity not so readily available in other sports: time. Football, in particular, does not have that luxury. It's generally faster and not stop-start, so they struggle to use gadgetry and on-screen graphics while in play.

But cricket – rather like American football, another sport that has explored the technology market – has regimented breaks in play, allowing real-time tactical discussion. To dip in and out of live pictures and replays with the use of different angles, different cameras, gizmos such as Hawk-Eye, Hot Spot and Snicko, or statistics and graphics.

I love the way we try to bring the game into the living rooms of folk all around the country, and getting that connection with them in whatever way we can takes me back to Accrington and the sharing of the game we all love. So, from a personal perspective, it was a real thrill to be voted sports commentator of the year at the 2018 Sports Journalist Association awards. To be considered to be making that connection is what it's all about and follows the advice my father David senior gave me. 'Be natural,' he told me, and he meant for me to apply that in everything I turned my hand to.

I feel that word from my dad to be natural applies to commentary perfectly. I have always reasoned that a cricket match lasts all day and that seven hours is a long time to be miserable. Sometimes the situation warrants serious analysis, sometimes you need to entertain a bit, and there is a knack to finding when it is right to switch on and when to have a laugh. And I like to have a laugh.

My association with Sky has actually spanned more than a quarter of a century, although it was not until 1999 when my tenure as England coach ended that I became a permanent fixture. And as a company it has shown incredible dedication to cover the England cricket team. Just think about some of the numbers involved: the 200th Test involving England alone covered by Sky took place in 2014. Since that inaugural match back in 1989-90, I've drunk 2,974 pints of bitter. More surprising among our stats, perhaps, was that Nasser Hussain has smiled twice in that time, Mikey Holding has backed three winners on the gee-gees and Mike Atherton has worn as many as eight pairs of socks.

We Didn't Start the Fire

Humour plays such an important part in what we do at Sky. Let's face it, if you are not enjoying what you do then what's the point, right? In the summer of 2015, we got in on London singer-songwriter Elio Pace rewriting Billy Joel's 'We Didn't Start the Fire' and used it as our Ashes promo. Every member of the commentary team took part in voiceovers, with Elio and his band playing cricket's modern version of an old classic.

> Donald Bradman, Peter May, at The Oval, final day,
> Little Urn, Bob's perm, WG Grace,
> Walter Hammond, Mitchell Johnson, at the Gabba,
>   Big Decision,
> Chris Broad, Pons-ford, Riiiiiiichie Benaud,
> Larwood's Bodyline, Athers slips on 99,

Laker, Jones's dive, Gower flying in the sky,
Baggy Greens, swing/seam, Warnie's ball in '93,
Ricky Ponting, Pratty gets him, Freddie makes the
   bails fly!

Chorus
We didn't start the fire,
It was always burning,
Since the world's been turning,
We didn't start the fire,
No we didn't light it,
But we tried to fight it
10-11 whitewash, Nasser . . . and that toss,
Tubby Taylor, Sher-minator, Brigadier-bloc,
Swansongs, follow-ons, Headingley '81,
Mark Waugh, Steve Waugh, Harmy's shocking first ball,
Brett Lee, on his knees, Aussies got a winning team,
Davy Warner, third man, Andy Flower's En-ger-land,
Jon Snow, final Test, Manchester, yes, Chef!
Thommo, Lillee, fierce pace, Bumble smacked in
   that place.

What a tune. I loved what our Elio had done. Or at least I did until his pay-off line . . .

Only the Best

Those of you familiar with the Sky Sports masterclasses will know we try to get the experts in to demonstrate a particular set of skills. To show what set them apart from all their rivals and got them to the top of their sport. And for our coverage to go beyond the broadcasting of the matches themselves.

For keeping wicket to spin bowling, who better than Ian Healy and our own Australian leggie Shane Warne? We did one such masterclass before play one morning during the Edgbaston Ashes Test of 2015 and, for any young wicketkeeper who missed it, it was sensational viewing. Healy was a master at work and showed how much fun keeping can be. But the way Warne bowled to him must have had England's batsmen glad he was no longer available. He spun it like you wouldn't believe.

For batting, take your pick. There have been any number of stars to come in and show our viewers what has made them the players they became. Ian Ward, in his own laconic way, teases every little trade secret out of the individual in question in such a natural manner. Take Kevin Pietersen, for example, when in the twilight of his career he shared what made him such an X-factor cricketer.

Nasser Hussain's passion for the game is still obvious too, and his dissection of the white-ball king AB de Villiers's tactical outlook at SuperSport Park in early 2016 was totally gripping. De Villiers broke down the combination of supreme skill, invention and destructive hitting power that made him one of the most sought-after Twenty20 players of his generation, high-lighting the methods he has used in practice and the thinking behind them.

Like the best players throughout history, de Villiers devised his own bespoke games of skill to hone his touch and tech-nique. Think of the best of the lot, Sir Donald Bradman, whose unorthodox batting evolved from hitting a golf ball against a wall with a single stump, a process that he believes improved his eyesight.

De Villiers's own story goes that his grandfather would sit outside the back of the house on a chair up against the wall reading his newspaper and a young AB would hit tennis balls alternately either side of him, getting as close as possible without causing a disturbance. It sharpened his hand-eye co-ordination and taught him how to control his placement under pressure. His grandad, engrossed in what he was reading, never flinched, apparently.

It was fascinating to hear him reveal how he viewed the rhythm of his hands in his pre-swing as being the key to his success. Traditional coaching manuals would have been extolling the virtues of foot movement when he grew up in the quiet northern town of Warmbad, but although AB has had to work on his overall technique, the power – as Paddy McGuinness is so fond of telling those wannabe Lotharios looking for a cheap weekend on the island of Fernando's of a Saturday evening – is in his hands.

And when he walks out to bat, unless the situation dictates that he has to be gung-ho from the get-go, he is trying to get those hands through the ball in the most conventional way possible. When he first walked out to the middle he was looking to produce traditional straight-bat shots down the ground, no matter the form of the game. It just goes to show that even the greatest tinkerers, or those able to muscle sixes like they're swatting flies, are working from the same base.

When at the crease, AB views himself standing in a box and does not want to be reaching out to balls. There is always time to premeditate later in the innings, he told Nasser, but when he does it early he gets into bad positions and is prone to soft dismissals. Even when it doesn't look that way, he is committed to the basics of batting. Watching him check-drive through the off side, flat-batting full deliveries with precision, relying on hands not feet, rather like Virender Sehwag used to, was fascinating. And he likened his use of hitting down on the sweep to that of Pakistan's Younis Khan.

Nasser seemed in awe. He certainly did better as the interviewer in that scenario than when we did a slip practice masterclass ahead of the 2015 Ashes. He appeared alongside Ricky Ponting and Mike Atherton, with guidance from then England fielding coach Chris Taylor and the long-serving Phil Neale. After shelling a couple of efforts there was talk behind the scenes that we might need to be sending Nasser to Spain ourselves for a bit of El Catching.

Ding, Dong, Hitting Murali on High

Just like the next guy I always fancied myself that little bit more as a batsman once I'd packed in, and I guess that's what kept persuading me to come back out of retirement for Accrington over the years. Every now and again there would be chat around the club of just being a decent player short when it came to the first-team squad, or how there were not quite enough to pick from in the height of summer.

I love the club and would do all I could to help it survive. One of my comebacks was based on not much more than being a publicity figurehead. As a reminder to a town that still boasts in excess of 35,000 residents that there is a cricket club – offering opportunities to play, socialise and contribute to the commu- nity – on its doorstep. Cricket clubs used to be the heartbeat of towns and villages, and in some areas they remain so. In gen- eral, though, reminders of their existence are required as well as huge efforts on the parts of the few to keep them running successfully. So for one reason or another I kept coming back and having another go.

Back in 2011, Grappenhall Cricket Club, where my former Lancashire team-mate Neil Fairbrother played, hosted an England v Rest of the World contest to provide much-needed funds for the club. You get asked to play in these kinds of games quite a lot over the summer, and work and family commitments dictate that you can't accept all the invitations. But this was one I was pleased to have said 'yes' to.

Wasim Akram was opening the bowling and he told me before we walked out that he had never been as fit as he was at that point in his life. As it happened, despite nearly being a pensioner, so was I. And, with my varifocals on, I was ready to take on two of the world's best-ever bowlers. Wasim from one end and Muttiah Muralitharan from the other – just imagine that kind of challenge when they were in their pomp.

To say I loved it was an understatement. In this kind of situation, when a load of old pals get together, men being men and all that, you can't help telling them exactly what you're going to do to them. As a batsman in my professional playing days I would have been much more careful, eschewing elements of risk to occupy the crease. That's how most people played back then, certainly within the English domestic game. Generally, batting carried with it an element of restraint.

If only I could have had a go during the devil-may-care era of Twenty20. What a feeling of liberation it is to be able to get out there and have a whack. In some dressing rooms I frequented, you might not go back and take your place next to your kitbag if you sliced one 50 feet in the air. You'd be found at the bus stop instead. But bold as brass when facing up to Murali, I turned to Wasim at slip and Fairbrother at gully and told them: 'He's going out the ground, here.'

Not many people had done that to that little magician, ever, but I was eager to get out of my crease and launch. A soft-shoe shuffle got me to the pitch of the ball, and whoosh, the bat came through via a nice big swing to launch the ball high over long-on. The way cars had parked just yards from the boundary edge, I am not sure any of the spectators were expecting sixes to be hit all match, let alone off international cricket's most prolific ever bowler. So everyone cringed as they saw this towering strike charting a course beyond the rope … and straight into the windscreen of a Mercedes.

It felt flippin' great – taking on a bowler of his ilk and winning, not causing a crack in the glass, you understand – so I warned Was and Harv, my two old mates from my coaching days at Lancashire: 'I bloody told you he were going. Watch this, he's going again!' And he did, only this time it was less of a free-flowing swing of the bat and a bit more of a drag that sent those in the hospitality tents scrambling for cover.

Consecutive sixes off Murali! Two in two balls. My ratio would have been something like two in two seasons when I was on the professional circuit. As I say, if only I'd had such confidence when I was younger. Nasser, bless him, reckoned it was his favourite moment of that summer, reminding me that when I was England coach I would instruct them never to sweep, to use their feet to the spinners, and hit straight. They used to say, 'Okay, coach, whatever you say' – and then ignore me.

The Men in White Coats

One of the masterclasses we put on in 2012 was not so much of a masterclass at all. It was a demonstration in the MCC's indoor school at Lord's to show what a difficult job umpiring is, and just how good the ones operating at the top level are.

These days virtually every single decision made by an umpire is mulled over and then prodded and poked with the use of technology. Imagine doing a day job in which just about every action you perform is placed under the microscope.

Nasser and I were taking part in an umpiring experiment, set up by Fraser Stewart, the master of the laws of the game at the MCC. Using a bowling machine and one of the MCC young cricketers as a dummy batsman, we had to judge whether or not a host of deliveries that struck the batsman's pad should be judged out or not. Our decisions were then checked with the use of Hawk-Eye technology, and I'm ashamed to say that despite having much more experience of officiating than Nasser – and my own glasses – he was excellent while I got a couple wrong. I could have sworn that one ball pitched outside leg.

It just showed what a demanding job officiating can be, and how unfair it is when modern players challenge the umpire's authority. Although the level of scrutiny is not the same, it is a similar scenario even in county matches when players question an official's decision. Let's not pretend that cricketers of my time didn't mutter under their breath or even exchange a cross word in frustration. Of course they did. But it was nothing like the histrionics of the modern day.

I should know, as I umpired myself for three seasons in the late 1980s. One of the episodes that stands out for me came when Northamptonshire were involved in a contest on a sporting track at Derby. Michael Holding was making inroads at one end and I was stood at the other, the one at which Ole Mortensen, a Hagar the Horrible of fast bowling, was tearing in.

Allan Lamb played at a Jaffa outside off-stump and the ball fizzed through to Bernie Maher, the wicketkeeper, the thud into his gloves triggering a raucous appeal-cum-celebration from the bowler who didn't bother to turn to address me. Nope, he just carried on to the slip cordon to indulge in a sequence of high-fives with his team-mates. When he realised Lamb was not going anywhere, Denmark's greatest gift to the international community since the loudspeaker bellowed: 'How's that?'

Cupping my hands to make my own megaphone response, I shouted back: 'Not out.'

Not fluent in Danish profanities I cannot tell you what he said on his stomp back towards me, but he did give rather special attention to the Dennis Taylor-style glasses I used to wear when umpiring as we came face to face. Lifting them from my head, he questioned whether I could see through them okay.

'Aye,' I said. 'You try 'em.'

He did. Bowled the next delivery in them, in fact. By the time he returned them all the nonsense had been forgotten and we played on. No animosity, no ill feeling. Exactly the way it should be.

It's All About the Pitch

I have always believed that cricket should be about having fun like that, although I am not sure what would happen if anyone were to repeat a trick used on me by Essex's great swing bowler John Lever back in the day when he ran up and bowled a complete Jaffa. Well, it was complete for a short time – until it hit the bat and exploded everywhere. No, there would probably be a post-match inquiry in this day and age if someone exchanged the new ball for an orange in a first-class match.

But sport should be about fun and whenever I have been offered the chance to have a laugh with the viewers I have taken it. Most notably during my mock pitch reports for Sky's old Saturday morning show *Cricket AM*. The tongue-in-cheek offerings, linking to Simon Thomas in the studio, included having a detailed look at the famous Lord's slope for Pakistan's visit in 2006. 'It's almost like batting on the side of a mountain,' I said. 'And if we get a closer look at this pitch we will see that it's got a very white sheen to it and all the grass has been taken off. It's almost like a block of ice.' Cue a bit of downhill slalom. Only took 53 takes, did that. The things you will do in the name of comedy, huh?

Exaggerating the characteristics of a ground was always great fun and sometimes you really couldn't tell the difference between the location and the venue you were taking off. Think of the squelchy farmer's field that sucked in the full set of keys. No one would have questioned that being Headingley. Or the faux Wantage Road: 'It has a reputation of being a spinners' paradise and Northamptonshire are very well set in that department. I think the groundsman has left this top surface just a little bit loose and on a closer inspection – yes, have a look at that, I think he's put a top dressing of sand on this and that brings spinners right into play.' No one would have been any the wiser had the pictures cut away. Unfortunately, though, the camera was still rolling as I tucked into my ice cream and Arthur threw me 50p to have a go on the donkey.

Just occasionally a bit of innuendo doesn't go amiss live on-air either – particularly if all you are doing is saying what you are seeing, such as in the summer of 2007 when Sky introduced Hot Spot to its batch of technological tools. Looking for an edge off England's left-arm spinner Monty Panesar, the two infra-red cameras used in the process appeared to have highlighted some friction elsewhere and I couldn't resist: 'Looks like the umpire's got a little hot spot as well.'

Know Your Place

Those lovely people in production let me loose on the toss for the Edgbaston Test between England and Pakistan in 2016, and it was all going swimmingly until my last question to Alastair Cook, when I thought a herd of elephants was running in behind me. It turned out to be Stuart Broad on his practice run-up. He insisted he didn't know we were there but it put the captain right off his train of thought. Not to mention mine.

Not sure Sky will ever let me do the toss again, not for that incident, but for head-butting the match referee. I can assure you that no physical contact was made with Richie Richardson. But that's what it seemed like if you looked at the picture posted of me and Richie by Ian Ward on social media.

Star Spotting

We don't mind a competition or two in the Sky box during matches. One of them when in London, particularly at Lord's but also at The Oval, is celebrity bingo. Sir John Major, Hugh Jackman, Stephen Fry, Sir Mick Jagger, Sir Michael Parkinson, Sir Trevor McDonald, Alice Cooper, Russell Crowe, Lily Allen, Brian May and Harry Potter have all been known to pop in. If it's decent weather and a good standard of opposition you can be in for a full house on your card.

You can even carry it on into the evening. I was out for dinner in Primrose Hill one night when who should sit down at the table next to me but *Strictly Come Dancing* judge Bruno Tonioli. I couldn't resist it, so I shouted out, 'Sevennnnnn!' Len Goodman should have been there, really, for it to have the right impact, and perhaps I should actually have shouted, 'Six!' Not that Bruno cared a jot – he only had eyes for Grace, his miniature schnauzer.

We were told that Mick Hucknall of Simply Red fame was going to be at Lord's for the 2015 Ashes Test, only for him to call off ill at the last minute. It was a shame, because as a fellow northerner he might have backed me up on my crusade against the food prices at the ground. More than a tenner for a steak sandwich? You would have to wedge the whole cow between two baps for me to pay that price. His absence did get us all reminiscing about his most famous hits, though. Who can forget some of British pop music's all-time classics? 'Holding Back the

Beers' is a personal favourite. Then there's 'Ev'ry Time We Say Leg-Bye', and Nasser's 'Too Tight to Mention' . . .

We get onto the subject of music quite a lot, and once when the presence or otherwise of the Barmy Army's Billy the Trumpet came up, we got talking about famous trumpeters and I mentioned Chris Barber. Suddenly the phone goes. Bloke called Clapton. He reckons Barber played the trombone. They tell me Clapton's got a bit of musical pedigree, so who am I to argue?

Cricket-related songs always get us going. From old ones like 'Bat Out of Hell' by Meat Loaf and 'Born to Run' by Bruce Springsteen. When India are in town, the winner has got to be 'You're [Shikhar] Dhawan That I Want' from *Grease*, with 'Unforgettable' by Nat King Kohli a close second. The Yorkshire Tea brass band are always worth a listen on Test match days and their pièce de résistance is a version of the Eurythmics' 'Sweet Dreams (Are Made of Cheese)' together with the line, 'Everybody's looking for Stilton'.

I love a bit of banter on these kinds of puns and Twitter went into meltdown on the final morning of the Adelaide Test in the 2017-18 Ashes as people offered cricket-themed carols. 'Ding Dong Murali on High'. 'Once in Rahul Dravid's City'. 'Hark the Harold Larwood Swings'. 'O Little Town of Brett-Lee-Hem'. How about 'Frosty the Stoneman' and 'Santa Claus is Cummins to Town'? And my personal favourite: 'Good King Wenceslas Looked Out' . . . but he's asked for a review anyway.

A Fool and His Money

They say a fool and his money are easily parted. Well, I can tell you categorically that my Sky and *Daily Mail* colleague Nasser

Hussain is no fool. In 2016, ahead of the Pakistan series, we had a lovely pre-Test dinner in Portman Square with the rest of the Sky crew, and afterwards Nasser kindly asked if anyone would like to share his taxi. What a wonderful gesture, I thought, until he revealed that he had inadvertently left the hotel without any money. I should have known.

His generosity really knows no starts. With all the comings and goings on the pitch now during play, we had a sweepstake one day about when the next stoppage would be. Nasser won £10 – of which £2 was immediately used to settle a three-year debt with a cameraman. Parting with that would have hurt.

One thing you cannot criticise Nasser for is his sartorial appearance. He is always immaculately turned out. So his bad start to the day during the Edgbaston Test that summer stands out. He managed to empty his hotel breakfast, including milk churn, all over his suit. Nobody likes to see that sort of thing – except, of course, when it involves Nasser. He didn't have another suit with him so he had to declare Phil Collins rules – No Jacket Required.

And you can tell how often he stands his rounds when you consider his reaction during a game I was not covering. I was sitting at home watching a Twenty20 game on TV with a beer in my hand when suddenly one of the commentators popped up and said: 'David Lloyd would know that but he's probably not watching.' So I texted in and said: 'Of course I'm watching and I've got Mr Timothy Taylor with me.' To which Nasser broadcast: 'That must be his neighbour.'

Fred Stacks it

Twenty20 finals day at Edgbaston is always a big day out in the calendar for English domestic cricket and the atmosphere just keeps getting better and better. 'Sweet Caroline' has become a bit of a T20 crowd anthem, closely followed by 'Hey Jude'.

It sparked Rob Key into a suggestion that the commentators should be more interactive in this regard, proposing a sing-off at the 2017 event. Next thing you know it's me and Freddie Flintoff up in front of the gloriously rowdy Eric Hollies Stand. Fancy asking two shy guys like us to get up and perform in front of a 25,000 crowd.

I wasn't sure how many people would know the words to Johnny Cash's 'Folsom Prison Blues'. Meanwhile, Flintoff was taking professional singing lessons and owned his own Elvis suit. Some bright spark at Sky had the idea of taking me off to a kara-oke booth at Tiger Tiger in Leeds and dressing me as Johnny Cash to belt out the song for a finals-day coverage promo.

Freddie has a habit of stealing centre stage at Edgbaston. In 2005, he produced one of the all-time great cricketing per-formances during England's memorable two-run victory over Australia. While he may have sent Aussie wickets tumbling on that occasion, he was the only one uprooted this time as he drew attention to himself for entirely different reasons.

Dressed head to toe in vintage Elvis regalia, complete with white outfit and gold necklaces, our Fred grabbed a selfie stick to film himself conducting the crowd. But as he stared into the camera, which took over the coverage on Sky Sports, he failed to keep an eye on where he was going, falling over a speaker and losing his wig. Ever the showman, he refused to let his head-over-heels moment affect his performance.

Typically, he saw the funny side and showed his composure despite the bemusement of all. It also gave me another go at blurting out 'Sweet Caroline'. It was the highlight of a long but extremely enjoyable day. Not that our Nasser would have had much positive to say when he found his car wouldn't start. He had only left his fog lights on! Jump leads didn't work and, to

ONE FOR THE SHELF

make matters worse, the battery was locked in the boot, which wouldn't open. He had Mr AA to thank for getting him home by half past four next morning.

Midsomer in Midwinter

England's batsmen went down like villagers in Midsomer during the 2013-14 Ashes. Anyone seen that programme? It's run for about 20 series. Why on earth would you move there? It must have the lowest life expectancy on the planet.

And Sky appeared to have grotesque plans for my demise on that tour. As I said, there are some pretty poisonous creatures in Australia, and some dangerous animals too. The producers are always very keen for us to get among it in between Tests, while I am reluctant – funnily enough – to be subjected to anything that's got a nasty bite. For example, I refused to vox-pop the people in Brisbane, and also turned down the chance to go out work-shadowing a snake catcher in South Australia . . .

Next, I was invited to go diving with great white sharks near the Neptune Islands (with the protection of an aluminium cage, fortunately) before being asked whether I could be filmed holding one of those funnel-web spiders. Sharks, snakes, arachnids – I got the distinct impression they wanted to get shot of me.

At one point even the oysters were scaring me. Down at Port Lincoln, where we headed off for the shark dip, I saw a single one for sale for $100 (which is about £55). I was told that was a real delicacy. Most oysters are four years old when you eat them. This one was seven. But was enormous, like a fillet steak, so I made my excuses and left.

People often ask what we do on Christmas Day when we're on a tour like the Ashes. Funnily enough, we have a Christmas meal, organised by our production manager, Roger. As you can imagine it tends to be a seafood bonanza, and the Australian attitude towards it offers great succour to a whingeing Pom. They put on magnificent spreads, but it's always tarnished by a distinct lack of Christmas pudding and no bread sauce for the turkey.

Walking it all off during the festive period is always a hoot, too. Wandering around the suburbs of Sydney, I came across three intriguingly named shops. The first one was called Holy Sheet, which sold bedding, then there was Legs and Breasts which, unfortunately, was a takeaway chicken joint, and the third was called The Stool Company. I was not so taken by what they might have sold.

Winter Work

It's not a bad life dodging the winter chill every year and heading for sunshine overseas. It serves a dual purpose, if I am honest. Lots of unpleasant jobs pile up from October to March and, let's be fair, you can't fix things if you are not there. It's why I invested in some drain rods for Diana. She's a dab hand now.

Autumn is an opportune season to catch up with house repairs and get on top of the falling leaves, not forgetting to clear the gutters. The shed roof also needs re-felting every four years and I hate the thought of getting in her way, or stealing her thunder. It's nice to be able to give her something to keep her occupied.

Unfortunately, however, we can be caught out due to no fault of our own. For example, when BT Sport gazumped Sky Sports for the 2017-18 Ashes – breaking a cycle of 27 years of overseas England tours being screened by Sky. It meant having to stick one's hand up and sort stuff out. Bugger!

With inclement weather about in England, there are all kinds of things that can go wrong. What about the winter in which the boiler packed up at Hussain Towers? As we sat in the Isleworth studios, poor old Nasser was inundated with Twitter advice saying his condenser pipe had frozen and it needed a kettle of hot water poured on it to release the ice and kick-start the boiler. All well and good, but when the £100 call-out fee was mentioned, Nasser turned white as a sheet, said he would take time to consider whether any further action was required and advised Mrs Hussain to put on another jacket or go for a brisk walk.

Sunny Delights

Due to a last-minute levy being applied for Sky Sports to enter the grounds, our commentary for England's historic away win in India in 2012-13 was carried out from our home in west London. It meant staying in a local hotel and led to a bit of a senior moment from yours truly. I was convinced I'd set my alarm for 2.30am but, during one of my frequent bathroom calls in the night, I glanced at the clock and noticed it was 3am and I was due on-air in half an hour. I then realised I had indeed set it for the correct time – but half past two in the afternoon rather than half past two in the morning.

I found my sleeping patterns were all over the place, having to get up in the early hours, and I was hit by a double whammy one night when there was a wedding reception in the hotel, followed by the fire alarm going off.

It was certainly different commentating from the studio here in the UK rather than at the ground. You struggle to 'feel the game', and it's a different discipline because you cannot convey some aspects as you usually would, such as the atmosphere. We still managed one or two lighter moments, though, talking about our favourite lollipops, and when the great Sunil Gavaskar came on Indian TV for the 'Ask Sunny' segment, I chimed in with: 'Where's Cher?' I got Yuvraj anyone?

I have worked alongside Sunny for ESPN, Sky's broadcast partners in India, and I can reveal that not only is he one of the great batsmen but also India's champion biscuit eater. He demolishes packets of them. What I have yet to get confirmed is whether, like my old mate Jack Simmons, he used to slip them into his pockets while fielding. I kid you not that we used to find crumbs in the slip cordon from when Flat Jack felt peckish.

When you reach a certain level in India you can do what you want. Take MS Dhoni who, when Zaheer Khan went down injured in a Test match against England in 2011, took his pads off and had a bowl in shades of league cricket. It's been done before, of course. In my day AC Smith of Warwickshire, the captain, secretary, chief cook and bottle washer, would often take his pads off and turn his arm over. Well, you can when you're the boss, can't you?

Grub Up

Being at work for the equivalent of three meals means food plays a big part in our daily chat, and Test matches at Lord's are always special for the culinary delights they purvey. The kitchen in the media centre provides wonderful scones but also a debate about which way round to eat one. As far as I am concerned, following extensive input from viewers in Devon and Cornwall, it's official. So next time you are out having afternoon tea, or happen to be in attendance at St John's Wood, remember it is jam at the bottom and cream on top.

Then again, my lot do make some controversial choices. Take the time we had rib of beef for lunch, and I conducted a survey on the big issue: should you have mustard or horseradish with it? It's horseradish every time for me, but my panel of Sir Ian (Beefy) Botham – who should know best – Philip Tufnell and Nasser Hussain all went for both of them on theirs. Controversial.

And in between meals there are lots of snacks, and therefore opportunities to prank your colleagues. For example, who'd have thought Shane Warne, a man of the world, and the greatest spinner the game has seen, with all those Test wickets, would be Botham-ed so easily. Beefy likes to leave a packet of his favourite pork scratchings in the Sky commentary box, laced with a liberal sprinkling of chilli powder. Warney grabs a handful, and soon his eyes are watering and his voice has gone.

Beefy does get caught out himself occasionally, though. Not least when we had a little wager with our New Zealand colleagues back in 2012-13 – five dollars each on how many runs will be scored in the day, or how many extras, that sort of thing. The fourth day's poser happened to be how many runs would be scored in boundaries and Sir Ian was straight in with 169 – you do the maths!

He tends to think of things in a slightly different way to everyone else, does our Buffness. Like back in 2012 when I had to don my hat and gloves to act as his chauffeur. The reason? It was his mother-in-law's 80th birthday party. Sir Beefy measures distance by how much he can drink and told me the journey would be a 'two-bottle job'. That's bottles of wine, by the way, in case you were wondering, and his assessment was clinical. It did take 45 minutes.

The Ticklers

Some days provide greater humour than others, and when a mate suffers it can be great fun. When two mates suffer, all the better!

Take a day at The Oval back in 2011 when a couple of former England captains were on the receiving end of some serious ribbing. First, the award-winning journalist Mike Atherton got a bit tongue-tied on-air when he referred to India's left-arm bowler 'RP Swing'. Then, after doing his best to identify Singh, his phone went off when he was on-air. He claimed it was his alarm clock. Schoolboy error.

Then there was poor old Alec Stewart, who was denied entrance by a steward who didn't realise the Gaffer has one of the gates at the ground named after him and practically owns the place. It's not so funny when it happens to you, though, as I found out a few weeks later when I was manhandled by the jobsworths in the Old Trafford members' bar before England's Twenty20 win over India. I was there browsing the old photos, some of which, as a former captain and player for 19 years, I was in. But I kept being told I was wearing the wrong accreditation. A stalemate ensued when I advised them, as a life member of the club, I wasn't moving. Being forcibly removed was not a pleasant experience, and I was sad that it showed Lancashire in such a bad light. Even sadder when my mates saw me entering the local Waitrose and one of them bellowed: 'You shouldn't be in here. Get out!'

It's the simple things that get me giggling. Take England's tour of South Africa in 2015-16 when the administrators found it difficult to come up with a mascot smaller than James Taylor. The young lad he was paired with in Durban was three inches bigger . . .

Or when, just after lunch in the England v Pakistan Test at The Oval in 2016, Azhar Ali hot-footed into the groundsman's shed for a comfort break. I am not sure how comforting it would be to carry out your business in front of an audience of eight members of the Surrey ground staff. But as he took less than four minutes, he clearly just got on with things. At one point, I wondered whether this was one of Azhar's rituals. Some blokes have habits they like to keep, their little tics that have been part of their success. Perhaps a crap after a long lunch break is one of his.

We all know that Jonathan Trott had his crease-marking rituals, and what about South Africa's Morne Morkel? He never receives the ball until he's walked back to the top of his mark, at which point he scratches it with his boot, then he walks in a little anti-clockwise circle before starting his run to the crease. It must all be very disorientating, which might be why he ended up in Bill Gordon's hut rather than up the stairs to the dressing room when he was dismissed the previous year. He had to turn round sheepishly and creep back up the steps. Perhaps Azhar hadn't noticed and thought he was still in there.

Or when Tom Hampton, a young shaver who was one of England's 12th men in the Lord's Test versus India back in 2011, was out before play taking high catches. He somehow managed to demolish a bucket of whitewash on the outfield and was covered from top to toe in a scene reminiscent of *It's a Knockout*.

Talking of game shows, you occasionally have to make your own fun. A while back I acquired a keyring which plays Jim Bowen's best catchphrases. I remember one fella going on *Bullseye* and Jim asking him how he was. 'I've not had the best of years,' came the reply from the contestant. 'My wife has left me and I've lost my job.' Jim's response? 'Super, smashing, great.' Unfortunately, the catchphrase is no longer in circulation following Jim's passing in early 2018. Nor is the keyring. Or at least it's not allowed to circulate anywhere near the commentary box. It was good for a few matches, but then word came from on high to lose the thing before I was court-martialled.

Start the Car

One day it will be time for me to deliver my own catchphrase for the final time on-air. It has been a great ride and it can be tiring. Some say commentary ages you prematurely. Just ask Nasser.

When the former Test sponsors Investec laid on a quiz night in 2016, the picture round featured close-ups of various body parts. There was a smiling mouth, and everyone put Michael Vaughan, when it turned out to be yours truly. Then there was a forehead full of wrinkles. To a man, they all said Henry Blofeld. In fact, it was our very own Hussain. He's been working too hard.

Or perhaps it's just that we all need to take a leaf out of the spinners' union pamphlet. Phil Tufnell earned his nickname for his penchant for catnapping during his playing days, and Graeme Swann has carried it from the dressing room to the commentary box. Back in 2014, he nipped into the Sky box from the adjacent *Test Match Special* one and scooped up the cuddly zebras Investec used to hand out as mementos. When I took him to task on what he was up to, he confirmed: 'I just need a pillow.'

But I will not be getting on the blower to my agent Neil Fairbrother hoping to follow others from cricket into reality TV. You can forget *Strictly Come Dancing*, with its sequins, flowery blouses, false tans and all. Leave that to the likes of Vaughan, Darren Gough, Mark Ramprakash and Tuffers.

But I can propose a better programme. What about *Strictly Come Drinking*? Travelling all over the place in the search of the best pint – up to Scotland to sample the best whisky. Where is it distilled? How do they make it? Over to Ireland to sample some Guinness. Down to Somerset to find out what constitutes a good cider. They throw everything in, you know. Wasps, bees, beetles, rats, it all contributes to forming this hallucination liquid. That's why all those on scrumpy tend to have two heads.

Where is the smallest pub? Which boozer is the most remote? Who is the longest-serving landlord or landlady? What length is the longest bar? Let's get up to the highest. Who is the oldest regular in the country? We should protect pubs as social havens and seeing the wonder in their unique aspects might just save what is one of our most important industries.

CHAPTER FOURTEEN

Clean it Up

One of my major worries as I move towards the end of my working life in cricket is the image now projected at the top level. I sometimes have to consider whether the modern player really does have a deep love for its history and whether, like me, they have analysed its importance, its richness and its unifying properties.

The lads who are playing at the moment put on a great product. There is some terrific international action around. But they are just the custodians of the game in this era. We've all had a go; others will take part in the future. With the privilege comes a responsibility to see that the right spirit and standards are retained, not drag the game down with behaviour that's not becoming of the sport. It's a hard ball and, when it hits you, it hurts. Cricket involves long days and can be physically demanding, particularly for fast bowlers. There are going to be flash points and anger but players should be disciplined enough to manage that themselves.

In early 2018, the International Cricket Council chief executive Dave Richardson conceded that the governing body had been complacent on bad behaviour. Well, all I can say is that the admission was long overdue. To be honest, I'd been banging on about this subject for two or three years without getting past first base. My concern developed not just regarding the indiscipline of players at the highest level but the millions of youngsters around the world subjected to it. Mark my words, when kids see actions taking place in big matches on television it is natural for them to try to re-enact them in their grass-roots games.

Unfortunately, the ICC were complicit in some of this process. Had they been hitting players harder it might not have got to such a crisis point, because for me the time to say enough was enough on poor conduct by players had already expired when the Australian trio of Steve Smith, David Warner and Cameron Bancroft received their bans for ball-tampering in March 2018. And let me be clear here. Although their punishments were officially triggered by the actions of trying to alter the condition of the match ball in the third Test defeat to South Africa in Cape Town, they were actually in response to a much broader set of offences. Namely, the team's collective indiscipline over a lengthy stretch of time.

As someone who has been around cricket for a career spanning more than 50 years – as a player; then an umpire; a coach from grass roots all the way up to international level; and a columnist and broadcaster for three decades – it's sad for me to say, but quite simply I have never witnessed behaviour, on and off the field, as bad as it is now.

Players need to stop and think about what they look like because what they are getting up to is deplorable and looks infantile to the outside world. The way they are trading insults while competing in the middle shows a total lack of respect for each other, the officials and, most of all, for the game. I just cringe. Snarling obscenities in each other's faces, rushing into others' personal space, marking their territory like feral animals. What are they doing? These guys are the custodians of our sport and have a responsibility to pass international cricket onto their successors in at least as good a state as they found it. Yet they seem to have shouldered arms at such a prospect.

Barely a week went by in the opening quarter of 2018 without one incident or another bringing cricket into the spotlight for the wrong reasons, and as a long-term advocate of yellow and red cards at all levels of the game, I believe we would have been better served bringing them in rather than talking of creating a culture of respect. That's what should have been done if cricket was truly serious about cleaning up its act. Since when did posturing towards an opponent become the norm? Since when did physical contact between opponents become a regular occurrence? Trading insults like stroppy teenagers? Give me a break.

It may seem as though I am focusing specifically on the Test series between South Africa and Australia in the early part of 2018 here. It is not my intention to do so, or to single out any particular player, but it is clear to me that what happened in Durban and carried on in Port Elizabeth was the tipping point. To have players insulting each other's family members, bringing up personal issues such as sexuality and appearance, and doing so via direct references in the media. Are you for real? It makes me want to tell some of these guys that their mummies are calling and it's time to pop off indoors for their tea.

All this stupid tough-guy chat about what you can and can't say. In fact, what baffles me most is all this talk about a line that players will or will not cross. What is this line? The particular line in question: was it invented by the players? Is it the Maginot line? From memory, despite being constructed from concrete, the Germans got around that one easily enough. The Plimsoll line? You could end up in deep water using that one. I hope it wasn't the whitewashed one used in Brisbane when Moeen Ali was given out stumped in the second Test of the 2017-18

Ashes. It certainly looked thicker in some places than others. No consistency there at all. Or do the Aussies simply whip their sandpaper out of their pockets, scrub it clean and move it somewhere else as and when it suits them?

It's all very confusing to me, but the conclusion I have drawn is that nobody except them seemed to know where this line was placed. This line is certainly not anywhere to be found in the laws of cricket. The laws make it perfectly clear that responsibility for any team lies with its captain. So from now on, with Smith's 12-month absence a deterrent to other captains on the world scene, we need to start cleaning up further. To my mind, the process has only just begun.

Make no mistake, umpires are in the wrong too. Because they hear obscenities, nasty comments and the like and don't report it. Neither is it helpful when a match referee is trying to earn his corn, and then faces legal challenges for taking firm action. Take the case of Kagiso Rabada, who had his two-match ban for touching shoulders with Smith – after dismissing the Australian batsman – overturned. Jeff Crowe, the match referee in question, was trying to nip all this stupidity in the bud with a strong message. Only for the lawyers to win the day.

I am not sure we want every reprimand for a player resulting in a legal challenge. For one thing, it's time-consuming. It's also a costly business. If a lawyer coughs, it can cost you £100. Put a firm's name on the top of a letter and it will set you back a few hundred more.

Tarnished Image

Then, of course, the powder keg went up. Steve Smith, David Warner and Cameron Bancroft, three leading Australian cricketers, featuring on the front of newspapers and in the headlines of news bulletins in each and every continent after their bungled attempts to alter the condition of the match ball in the Newlands Test match. What was staggering was the number of current and ex-players around the world who were saying 'it's about time' when Australia were taken to task by their own board. That should have been a huge sadness to everyone purporting to be a fan of international cricket.

If you are a great team like Australia aspire to be, and have been over the decades, surely you want to be seen in the best possible light? Yet the bottom line was that absolutely everybody in the game had come to view them as complete fools. No one from the world community appeared to be stepping up to help them to their feet when they had been knocked down.

The abuse and ridicule of opponents had been there for all to see, and the surprise to me was not the severity of their bans but the fact that it took as long as it did for Cricket Australia to act. They must have seen what was happening, and could have acted internally to improve their own environment and avoid such public embarrassment.

Towards the end of the dramatic sandpapergate week that played out in Cape Town, Johannesburg, Perth and Sydney, I read a telling piece by the former England batsman James Taylor in the London *Evening Standard*, in which he chronicled the despicable mocking that had become the calling card of the Australian team, and the level one of the ringleaders in particular had reached. Taylor recalled his second-ball dismissal to Mitchell Starc in an ODI in Sydney in January 2015 when, as he turned to trudge off, he was confronted by David Warner running at him and shouting obscenities in his face. England were nought for two at the time, halfway through the game's opening over. The Australians should have been acknowledging the fine work of Starc in claiming two early wickets, not rejoicing in the demise of an opponent. They had normalised the process of rejoicing in others' misery rather than their own joy.

Australia had been on the slide for some time. After hitting one of their lowest ebbs when Mickey Arthur was sacked in 2013, they turned things around by reverting to a win-at-all-costs attitude. I know Darren Lehmann pretty well. He was a belligerent player and an engaging character, who was quick to have a beer and a fag after a day's play. But through that grubby period in South Africa in March 2018 he came to understand that the events unfolded because of a culture that he, as the team's coach, partly created.

It was certainly not how Australia started under him. I recall his first Test in charge and the Australians bore all the hallmarks of Lehmann as a player. They just wouldn't lie down at Trent Bridge, and instead of receiving the expected thrashing of a team in disarray they lost by a mere 14 runs. They had looked dead and buried with only four wickets left standing, on a pitch that wasn't conducive to stroke play. They could just have eked it out. But they were belligerent and played proper cricket shots to take the game to England head-on, and when you play that way it is natural to earn admirers.

I loved the way that both sides embraced the concept of the Ashes that week. They went hammer and tongs at each other for five days – and, trust me, I could hear the stump mic; the chatter was fruity but not personal and vindictive – then went and shook hands at the end of it all, and said: 'See you in a few days at Lord's.' It's how the game should be played.

But they lost that attitude somewhere along the journey back up the Test cricket rankings and by Cape Town everybody in the cricket world would have recognised how poor they looked. Cricket Australia's sanctions sent a massive message to boards around the world to get their own houses in order. Over time Australia can get rid of all this business with a new set of values.

When an elite Australian sportsman retires he is usually considered a champion for the rest of his life. How many of this team will be thought of as champions when they pack up? At the moment the answer is not many. They have work to do.

Of course, it all started with the premeditated scratching of the ball with a piece of sandpaper by Cameron Bancroft – under instruction from Warner, as the trio all admitted under questioning later. Condemnation came quickly and hit like an avalanche. However, there were a minority of people on social media coming to their defence, suggesting it was simply a small part of a much bigger problem. That the use of chewing gum, mints, Brylcreem and suncream to alter a ball's condition was prevalent.

To me, however, those kinds of products are used only to help shine the ball. To improve its sheen. Not to promote its deterioration. Enhancing the polishing process is the equivalent of driving at 32 in a 30mph zone, in my book. They're not damaging the condition of it. There's a big difference in levels of 'tampering', I believe. And if the umpires are concerned about the excessive use of such products by a team in the field they can have a quiet word. Remember, it is also within their jurisdiction to order the ball to be changed and impose a five-run penalty.

In such an instance, I am not sure the offenders would start trying to hide what they had done like Bancroft did by shoving the sandpaper strip down his trousers. The shifty way he tried to dispose of the contraband item, and subsequent denials it even existed, highlighted the difference to me.

Steve Smith talked about the 'leadership group' deciding to tamper with the ball in an isolated incident at lunchtime on that fateful day at Newlands but, in any walk of life, it is the main man who carries the can, not some minion like Bancroft told to do the dirty deed. And so he had to take the hit for allowing it to happen on his watch.

I still struggle to believe that the whole Australian team and coaching set-up did not know of the plan being hatched. But Cricket Australia carried out what they said was a thorough investigation and said they could find no evidence to suggest the knowledge extended beyond the three to be reprimanded.

Personally, I don't have any sympathy for the players involved. It was sad to see two great players in Smith and Warner removed from Test cricket when the most traditional form of the game needs all the stardust it can muster to help with its marketing in an age increasingly obsessed by the white-ball game. But the time had been coming. It had been an accident waiting to happen.

Yes, there was an emotional tug provided by the teary press conferences given by Smith, Bancroft and, latterly, Warner, after they landed back on Australian soil, and another when Australia coach Darren Lehmann announced he would stand down after initially intimating he would stay on. Yet I do not believe the bans of nine months for Bancroft and 12 months for the former captain and vice-captain of the team were too severe. A year-long ban for Smith and Warner ruled them out of the 2018 summer tour to England, but left them eligible to return in time for the one of greater significance in 2019 – the one that includes an Ashes series and the World Cup.

Undoubtedly, seeing men broken like that on television would have affected some differently to others. And in accepting their punishments rather than appealing, they sent out a strong message that they had done wrong to those who look up to them. They should be commended for that.

But, as I viewed that very first press conference on the third evening at Newlands, when Smith pinned responsibility for the plot to cheat on the 'leadership group' and Bancroft claimed his comical blundering had involved 'yellow sticky tape', I couldn't help thinking that this was somehow payback for previous actions over the winter. I've been in this game a long time and I would tell everyone the same thing: don't mess with Mother Cricket, because she has a habit of coming back to bite you on the bum.

Sat flanking each other in a uniform manner of which Ant and Dec would have approved, their appearance in front of the cameras evoked memories of an incident at the start of the winter. Remember Smith and Bancroft sitting in Brisbane having a good old chuckle at the expense of Jonny Bairstow and his unusual head-butt greeting? They seemed to enjoy making life as difficult as possible for him and I am sure they would have seen life differently just a few short months later.

Turn it Up

Stump microphones have been an issue, with some players wanting them turned off. Why? What have they got to hide? Well, the answer is simple. Lots of stuff. They are taking it upon themselves to insult opponents' family members and debate things like sexuality, race and personal appearance.

If someone is prepared to get down in the gutter like that, hit them back in the shape of removal from the field and an official report of what has been said. Let's have some transparency about what cricketers are saying in their place of work – unless, of course, the player on the receiving end of the abuse feels strongly that they do not wish it to be in the public domain – because I think that revealing it would make them cringe.

Although the microphones are there to provide some of the on-field atmosphere – to literally transport the viewer or listener into the middle – one of the responsibilities as a broadcaster is to ensure that bad language is not transmitted live. It means we have the benefit at Sky Sports of muting it.

I must tell you that during the 2013-14 Ashes some of the things that came out of Warner's mouth in particular were just nasty. I would have liked to take him back to 1980 and listen to what he had to say to Viv Richards, Gordon Greenidge and Dessie Haynes. Coming right behind them was Michael Holding, Andy Roberts, Joel Garner and Malcolm Marshall. Banter is great – I listened to enough of it when I played in Australia in 1974-75 – but coarseness is unacceptable. As my old mate Wes Hall used to say: 'In Australia, nobody sledged me. Or Charlie Griffith.' And Steve Waugh was known to say to his own team-mates: 'If that's the best you can do then you are best shutting up. It's not worth bothering.'

Something to make clear here, though, is that contrary to the belief of many, the punishment of expletives on the pitch has nothing to do with the presence of stump microphones. It's whether any foul and abusive language is audible to the umpire. Yes, we are obliged to apologise if any swearing is heard on-air, but Sky are not the reason players are punished.

It's a nonsense, of course, to punish anyone for swearing in frustration at themselves when a boundary is scored or a catch is dropped. And the anomaly comes if the umpires do not understand the language being spoken out there. We all know of one Test team who are major offenders and get away with this. But if you go too far with clear obscenities you run the risk.

Let Them See Red

Historically, there have been instances of players who I would have sent off for poor behaviour. For example, when my old pal Dennis Lillee and Javed Miandad started going at each other in Perth in 1981. It all looked rather comical because of a cowardly kick up the bum by Lillee followed by a swish of the bat from his adversary, but there was a serious side to their altercation following initial contact while Javed was running between the wickets. And the result would have been simple enough if I could have had my way: both would have walked.

Another mate of mine, Michael Holding, never swears, wouldn't say boo to a goose in fact, but he would have seen red for kicking the stumps out of the ground in New Zealand in 1980 when his appeal for a caught behind against John Parker was turned down. Mike Gatting would have been dismissed when he finger-jabbed Shakoor Rana in Pakistan in 1987-88. You simply cannot do that to a match official. Michael Clarke's warning to James Anderson to 'get ready for a broken arm' during the 2013-14 Ashes should not be condoned either. See you later, alligator.

Where you have to be sensible, though, is for incidents like Marlon Samuels's salute to Ben Stokes in the Caribbean in early 2015. Sure, Samuels walks the line when it comes to disciplinary issues and rubbing opponents up the wrong way. But there was no swearing or obscenities, his gesture was not rude, so I would have no problem with that. Some might not find it amusing, some might. And, of course, some people are just downright funny. Take when Shane Watson stayed at Lumley Castle in Chester-le-Street and thought he saw a ghost. Darren Gough cottoned on to this and kept pulling ghost faces at him in his run-up and screaming, 'Wooooooo!' Now that's proper sledging.

While trouble was brewing for Australia in South Africa, England were on a tour of New Zealand and the one-day series there was as keenly contested as any I have seen in some time. There was no quarter given, it was all on the line, the score-line fluctuated one way and then the other, and words were spoken on the field. But the behaviour of both sides had been exemplary. There is room for the odd 'you lucky so and so' or a muttering of frustration under the breath bemoaning one's luck. It showed there was no need to make things personal. Why can't it always be this way? It's time for administrators to clamp down. Time for captains and coaches to set the right example. Time for umpires to get tougher. We need respect before it's too late.

I watch league cricket in Yorkshire and Lancashire and you can see the influence top players are having on the grass roots. There's no respect for the umpires. At that level they officiate for the love of the game, but they are being driven away. Why stand there to be insulted for six hours? They are there to officiate, not work like nightclub bouncers or social workers, policing anti-social acts.

It never used to be like that and it is a huge worry that the MCC reckon that five organised games were abandoned in the 2017 season because of violence. It should be said that there are very few serious incidents in international cricket, but bad conduct has a ripple effect down to club and league cricket. There is no way we should accept players at grass-roots level abusing each other or the umpires, but there's clear evidence that this is happening.

Nasser Hussain, my colleague at both Sky Sports and the *Daily Mail*, has two young sons who play the game and he reports back from umpiring at school level that bad behaviour is rife. It is a concern that young cricketers are trying to think of the next sledge because they've seen and listened to their heroes coming up with them on TV.

People say to me, 'You played in the seventies, it must have been bad.' Well, the players were tough, hell they were, but there was nothing like what goes on in the current climate. Sure, you clicked with some folk better than others, you might not take to one or two opponents, but in general a mutual respect governed on-field conduct.

Ian Chappell was one of the greatest captains ever. His

Australian team played tough cricket – when their fast bowlers, like Lillee and Jeff Thomson, were unleashing their full artillery it felt like you were on a different kind of national service – but at the end of the day they invited you in for a drink. They showed respect for the opposition. I'm still good friends with a number of the Aussies I played against. And if they said anything on the field it was good fun. It was banter. No more than general wise-cracking. Not foul-mouthed inanities. So much of what is going on today is vindictive, insulting poison.

In theory, following recent amendments to the laws by the MCC, umpires have the power to do exactly as I recommend and send players off – but the process is still too long and drawn out in my opinion. Actual cards must be shown by the officials. That way the people who pay their money to get into the grounds and those at home will know exactly what's going on.

Under the new law 42, introduced in October 2017 and used as a template for the changes in domestic cricket in England from 2018 onwards, misconduct is divided into four levels and any transgression can lead to a five-run penalty. The most serious level of offence, a level four, such as threatening to assault an umpire, making inappropriate and deliberate physical contact with an umpire, physically assaulting a player or any other person or committing any other act of violence, can result in officials halting play and the captain from the offending player's side being summoned to be notified of the transgressor's expulsion from the remainder of the match.

From that moment forth the team plays with 10. If the offending player is a fielder, no substitute shall be allowed for him. If a bowler in mid-over, the remaining deliveries must be sent down by someone else. In the case of batting, any ongoing innings is concluded immediately and recorded as retired, as is any subsequent innings in the match for the individual in question. Under the protocol the umpires communicate with the scorers to notify a level-four offence has taken place. And the match referee is notified that the International Cricket Council's code of conduct has been broken.

But my concern regards communication with the paying public and fans of the sport. They should know exactly what the offence is there and then, and that is why I believe the showing of cards is appropriate. Why keep people guessing? Let's get it out in the open.

Cricket is not like boxing where you can stand toe-to-toe and say, 'Okay, we'll sort it out in the ring.' It's a non-contact sport at the minute – but it won't be for long unless things change. That is why the powers that be have made provision to nip in the bud confrontations that could become physical. My message to the ICC? Get tougher still. If you impose the toughest sanctions possible, those sanctions will never have to be implemented. Or never more than once.

There should be a set of rules that players have to abide by or pay the consequences. If you feel you want to engage the opposition batsman, you should not move from your position when you do so. And if you give a dismissed player a 'send-off' you should be banned for two matches, simple as that. There's no place for the cheap, boorish, classless act of abusing someone as they make their way back to the pavilion.

If a player does something really bad – and that includes behaviour on a stairwell on the way to the dressing rooms – then show him a red and remove him from the game. And let such offences carry multiple-match suspensions. That will stop people verbally abusing and jostling each other, I am sure.

During the 1990s, when he was captain of Warwickshire and I was coach of Lancashire, I had a full and frank discussion with Dermot Reeve after play in the committee room at Old Trafford. The difference of opinion arose because, as the bowler was running up, Warwickshire fielders were moving their positions so that the batter couldn't see where they were. I thought it was against the spirit of the game. Dermot argued it was fine.

It's fair to say that things got a bit heated between us. But we sorted it out. That is the only time in my career that I can recall things getting that way. Dermot has had his two penn'orth on the issue since but that doesn't bother me. I am still fine with him. The point here is that it happened away from the public eye and we moved on.

I am not advocating an on-field vow of silence here, but think of Alastair Cook, a bloke you never hear on the stump microphones. He would probably be having a quiet chat with anyone who would listen about tractors and sheep shearing. Sledging? He'd only be doing that when there was snow on the ground.

Jimmy Anderson and Glenn McGrath are two of the loveliest blokes you could meet away from the field. Both fairly quiet and softly spoken. But when they got on the field they needed that bit of anger. They lived on the edge when it came to aggression. They were in a fight with their opponent and fighting is not for the passive. I have no problem with all that. Let the umpires work with the players. If the chuntering goes too far or gets abusive then allow them to step in. If you get the umpires interested, you ought to know it's time to calm down.

Bowlers and umpires should work together. An umpire understands that players are going to get wound up and frustrated. They know the game, too. They are there to advise and arbitrate fair play. Their last resort is to go to the captain. Let's face it, we all like an easy life. Do you really think that an umpire wants to be filling forms in and reporting to the match referee? Then attend after-match hearings. Of course they don't. It is so easy to control.

The wonderfully gifted Kagiso Rabada has accepted that he needs to curb his emotions better on the field and I believe bans help in this regard. I am not listening to other players about the locations of lines; I am listening to Rabada on this, who to his credit acknowledged: 'I have to stop.' And so he should. What a tremendous talent, what a fabulous bowler, who because of his own misdemeanours deprived his team of their best chance to compete during the summer of 2017.

No one wants to see exciting talents like the South African fast bowler on the sidelines. But that's where he found himself for one Test match after he was charged by the ICC for using 'inappropriate language' towards England batsman Ben Stokes during the first Test at Lord's. His crime? Screaming, 'Yes, yes, f*** off!' after dismissing Stokes on the first day of the game.

'Rabada was found guilty of . . . using language, actions or gestures which disparage or which could provoke an aggressive reaction from a batsman upon his/her dismissal during an international match,' said an ICC spokesperson. The incident earned Rabada a fourth demerit point within 24 months, meaning he had to miss the second match of the series at Trent Bridge. But instead of an accumulation, if he was shown a yellow card and removed from the game for a 10-over spell, say, as was recently introduced in English domestic cricket, it would get people interested in his behaviour a lot quicker. Not least his captain. You simply wouldn't want to have a bowler, with his dander up, forced from the field mid-over as a new batsman walks to the crease. In that scenario your team is ceding the momentum you have just engineered with a fine piece of bowling.

Red cards for abuse of an official would curtail incidents like the one in 2011 when Australian umpire Daryl Harper received a torrent from MS Dhoni and Harbhajan Singh, which led to him refusing to stand in India's final Test against West Indies. Not sure India would have risked that had they had the threat of playing with nine for the rest of the match hanging over them. It's draconian and dramatic, but it would be like a nuclear deterrent. It would make players show respect immediately.

The ICC's most recent commission in spring 2018, it said, was to conduct a wide-ranging review into player behaviour, the spirit in which the game is played, and establish a 'spirit of cricket' code based on a culture of respect. 'There has been significant debate over the last few weeks around behaviour of players and the leniency or otherwise in some cases of the associated punishments. The match officials work within the framework of the current ICC Code of Conduct and sanctions are applied according to that. To go outside of this current framework would be to disregard the rules,' the ICC said in a statement.

'This is an opportune moment, therefore, to shape what the game looks like in the 21st century and take a much broader look at the issues currently facing the sport and consider how we define what a spirit or respect code looks like today.

'The spirit of the game, contained in the preamble of The Laws of Cricket, is something unique to our sport and the review will consider how we can proactively make players, and indeed everyone involved in the game, more accountable for the role they have in upholding the Spirit of Cricket.'

Don't Get Caught Out

With the wealth on offer as a top cricketer these days comes obligation, and I am not sure it has been fully grasped. For me it's fine as a commentator at 70 years of age to do what I want within reason. For example, if people want to be taking photos of me with their mobile phones when I am out then let them get on with it. I won't be dancing with my undies on my head (again). Despite the requests. If I was accused of being in a bar after midnight I would congratulate myself because, despite having my moments, I generally don't seem to be able to get past about 11pm these days.

But if you are a young lad playing Test match cricket, you need to be aware there's the potential for somebody in a bar to snap you or for video footage to emerge from an inappropriate incident. Because people think there will be a bob or two in it.

I hate the word 'professionalism' because it suggests my generation didn't have it, but the modern cricketer is very well paid now. And for their remuneration they have an obligation to be at certain levels in terms of fitness for 300 of 365 days a year. In the sixties and seventies, life as a professional cricketer was a good career, but you were never going to get rich. So you enjoyed yourselves, had a good time and a few beers.

These guys are fitter and stronger, and to continue to earn the money they do you have to be in peak condition and aware of what you are doing in your extra-curricular activities. Someone like Kevin Pietersen grasped that, I am sure. Now I bet that Kevin knew how to enjoy himself. But my observations would always have been that he had great discipline in the build-up to and during games. Afterwards he would go for a couple of beers to either enjoy the team's success or get rid of the failure. Then there was a cut-off point where he built up to the next game and hit his training hard.

I am not saying he was a goody two-shoes, but he never left himself vulnerable as Jonny Bairstow did on the Ashes tour. The teams of England and Western Australia were in the same bar in Perth celebrating, having a yarn and generally letting their hair down post-matches. What happened with Cameron Bancroft should never have come to light, in my opinion, as I am not sure there was much to it. Jonny may reasonably be described as a bit eccentric. And it might seem odd to some folk that you would greet another bloke with a butting of foreheads. But there was no malice to his actions.

Bancroft played a blinder in the press conference, playing the fool and acting up. He's obviously never been to Scotland. If you get head-butted up in Glasgow, you are out of it, mate. Your nose might need returning to its usual location with surgical assistance. Oh, and you don't buy the bloke who did it to you a drink.

CHAPTER FIFTEEN

The Game Moves On

Twenty-first century cricket is a highly competitive, extremely well-remunerated sport across the world, but one thing that should not be lost sight of is that it remains a social game at heart. Still in essence the one that I began formulating opinions on in the bar at Accrington Cricket Club in the opening year of the 1960s.

As I have made clear in the previous chapter, I am passionate in my desire for improved on-field conduct towards each other from our role model players. That is not to say I don't want the game to be contested fiercely, for cricketers to strive to be winners, or that I do not back their quest to be paid commensurately for being the very best. Furthermore, I accept that the professional trappings added since the millennium tend to be at odds with the generous spirit towards opponents that has been a part of this game's fabric since Victoria sat on the throne.

Even in county cricket, performances are scrutinised like never before – just about every ball of every competition is recorded in some way for analysis. And in international matches, individual techniques and results are there to be picked apart in such a variety of ways courtesy of technology, with each and every one televised live by one broadcaster or another. And so under-pressure players, accustomed to accepting fates on the words of umpires or oppositions when dismissed earlier in their careers, are now less trusting and more willing to allow a third-party judge to intervene.

There is an etiquette that remains at the heart of a match: the toss of a coin dictating which team will bat first and which will bowl, the ringing of a bell by the officials to notify the teams that play will start in five minutes, the clapping of batsmen's fifties and hundreds by those who are trying to dismiss them, fielding teams waiting for their two opponents to leave the field of play first at intervals. Imagine Cristiano Ronaldo applauding a Lionel Messi goal in a showdown in the Champions League or World Cup.

Yet cricket is a rather unique marriage of the quaint and the cutting edge because all this emphasis on sportsmanship and good manners comes against a backdrop of a more litigious world. Just as in life, major events on a sports field are put under the microscope contemporaneously, to an extent that suspicion and doubt are never far away. Cricket now seeks conclusive proof on decisions and occasionally that means a player who would have walked on the say-so of an umpire or fielder is increasingly disposed to stand their ground.

I am a traditionalist in that I would always like the power to remain in the hands of the umpires – and believe the way the Decision Review System is implemented generally upholds this, highlighting how much they get right – but one of the negative aspects is that it encourages players to challenge authority. Thanks to the implementation of some technology, the umpire's word is no longer final. I am at the coal face and see this more and more. The MCC have an obligation to protect an umpire's authority.

DRS

Now that DRS is uniformly with us, by virtue of India belat-
edly accepting it in the autumn of 2016, international cricket is
getting more correct decisions than ever before. Another aspect
to this is that umpires are more confident in giving marginal
lbws, and that is because deliveries cricket watchers had trained
their eyes to believe were sailing over the top of the stumps are
often hitting.

On occasions arguments have raged in our Sky Sports commentary box about certain incidents - such as Shane Watson's
lbw being a 'poor decision' during the first Ashes Test of 2015.
Previously, umpires of Marais Erasmus's class would not even
have considered it: front foot, big stride and the delivery from a
bowler capable of sharp bounce in Stuart Broad striking the pad
above the knee roll. Nowadays, though, it's precision cricket.
Forget all that previous convention. Watson only got to challenge once more in his career – and did so unsuccessfully – as
he succumbed leg before for the 29th time in 59 Tests, to Mark
Wood in the second innings at Cardiff.

Another prime example of new thinking came in August
2017 when Alastair Cook was closing in on what would have
been his 31st Test match hundred, against South Africa. Morne
Morkel is not tall, he's gigantic, and was going round the wicket
when Cook was hit on the flap of his pad a dozen runs shy of
three figures. Again, there's no way old-timers would have
given it (Dickie Bird would have been saying not out before the
appeal had begun), but a bail-trimmer can now go the bowler's
way – and the umpire's.

I am fine with that – the game is moving on. But an episode in the same match at The Oval did bring up one cause
for concern. Cook survived a massive lbw appeal from Chris
Morris that in real time looked to be missing leg stump. In

fact, it was hitting leg, but Hawk-Eye picked up a faint edge. Or did it? And this is where we need definitive guidelines for the reading of instruments like Snicko, because as I understood it an edge gives a definite spike, not a murmur – and this looked more like a murmur. In an age when a high percentage of dismissals are adjudicated with artificial aids, the DRS protocol should be crystal clear. In this instance it was not.

One way the authorities have generally improved things in this regard has been by engaging with viewers and crowds by getting the third umpire on a microphone. This innovation was certainly a great bonus to TV coverage, to be able to understand the process while he reviews a decision. And why shouldn't fans get to know what is being looked at and why? In years to come 2017 will be known as the Elvis summer because of the number of times Rod Tucker requested a bit of rock and roll in England matches.

For too long there had been a lack of transparency in what an umpire was thinking when viewing evidence, and in some cases we were getting a lack of consistency in decisions through no fault of their own. Take England's 2012-13 tour of India, for example, when there was no official use of DRS and there was even the absence of the affiliated technology by the local broadcaster Star Sports. There was no Hawk-Eye or Hot Spot for the aficionado, and their application of Snicko was rather like watching a penguin walk up a beach for the first time.

While the Board of Control for Cricket in India vetoed the tech for use in Test matches involving India until two years ago, reviews in other series such as Pakistan v England in 2015-16 were high risk because TEN Sports, the host broadcaster, did not have all the tools for the DRS. It was crazy that Hot Spot and Snicko were available for some Test series but not others because of cost and a reliance on the TV companies to foot the bill.

Ian Ward and I attempted to demystify DRS on SuperSport in 2015-16 because, for the casual follower, it was so difficult to explain that the game could have different rules in different parts of the world. There was full DRS in some series, mini-DRS or no DRS at all, and the personal and collective results were still being input into Test cricket's annals. It was like saying there should be no scrums in southern hemisphere rugby and no line-outs in the northern hemisphere. Thankfully, from 2019 and the start of the World Test Championship, DRS will be uniform and everyone will be playing under the same rules.

Foreshortening

Undoubtedly, the increased role of technology is the biggest advance in cricket over the past decade. In one regard, however, it causes a problem, and a big problem – I am talking about adjudicating on low catches with the use of slow-motion camera shots.

Sending decisions upstairs in such cases, I believe, is giving a consistent decision, but not necessarily the right one. A good example came in the Durban Test in 2015-16 when AB de Villiers, the prized wicket among the South African XI, offered a low chance that was claimed by Ben Stokes at gully. Stokes said he wasn't sure it had carried and, with my experience, that would mean as an umpire I would not be either. Every single cricketer in the commentary boxes, both English and South African, felt de Villiers was out, but it's never conclusive when it goes upstairs because of the foreshortened images. And of course whenever there's a doubt, the TV umpire tends to go with the batsman.

Two Tests earlier for England that particular winter had shown similar evidence. Both were slip catches by Younis Khan in Pakistan's victory in Dubai: one given out, the other given not out. The camera angle in Joe Root's dismissal in the second innings clearly showed his fingers underneath the ball. With Jonny Bairstow in the first innings, the pictures seemed indecisive, but the gut feeling of cricketers would be that he caught it. As someone who has worked a long time in live television broadcasts, I would have to say that the camera does lie, unfortunately, because of the foreshortening of the lens – in layman's terms, some angles provide less depth than might be expected.

Sharp practice by fielders is difficult because of the multitude of cameras. The ones that genuinely are not out – those few that are shown to bounce short – are with the fielder diving forward, not looking at the ball. In good faith he thinks he's caught it, and there is no problem with that. But I would vouch that 95 per cent of these low catches are out. Just out. If it looks out at first viewing in normal speed then the fingers tend to be under the ball in my experience. Personally, I don't buy this claptrap that a 'blade of grass might have been sticking through the fingers'. That's irrelevant. The ball is not in direct contact with the grass; there are fingers in between.

In these situations, the bloke who's hit it and watched the guy catch it knows it's out but they also know they might get away with it, and I would argue it has contributed to batsmen expecting to be reprieved if they can get the decision passed upstairs, as was the case for Steve Smith during a one-day international between Australia and England in Sydney in January 2018.

When I was playing, if involved in this kind of incident you would turn to the catcher and say, 'Have you caught that?' He would say 'yes', or he would say 'no'. Sometimes he would say, 'I am not sure.' Jos Buttler declared that his low grab was clean but Smith was clearly not accepting, displaying dissent by mouthing 'no way' while walking off and later calling for the abolishment of 'soft signals' by the umpires.

Chris Gaffaney indicated that although he wanted the decision checked, his belief was that Smith was out. Contrary to the view of the then Australia captain, however, I am a fan of this system. The umpires are the nearest to the action. Between them they have four eyes, will in all probability have got some kind of view of it and are at an angle to make a judgement. When they send the decision upstairs they are only looking for the third umpire to unearth anything that will help completely overturn what they've seen.

New Zealander Gaffaney and people like Kumar Dharmasena, his partner on this occasion, are out there working for a living. They are experts in their field and would like to say definitely 'that's out'. They do not, in the knowledge that no one is infallible and that if they have the technology to check they should use it. If they didn't it would not prevent broadcasters zooming in with the same camera angles and slo-mo shots to scrutinise after the event. So the soft signal is the safeguard.

To those like Smith who argue that if officials are checking upstairs then they are not sure – and therefore any call should be taken out of their hands – I would counter that the best course of action would be to go the other way and empower the umpire. What I wouldn't want is for the officials in the middle to offer a soft signal unless they were certain. It should never be guesswork, and if the view of both men is obscured in any way then there should be a signal available that allows them to pass responsibility over to the television umpire.

'Do Unto Others As You Would Have Them Do Unto You'

Without going all biblical on you, this, I believe, is a decent way of playing cricket. Of course, there are times when teams just make the wrong calls. Paul Collingwood's international captaincy will be remembered for delivering a first global trophy for England, but as he has acknowledged himself a failure to call back Grant Elliott following a run-out incorporating a collision with the bowler Ryan Sidebottom at The Oval in a one-day international in 2008 will always be on his conscience. It takes a lot to ruffle Daniel Vettori's feathers and I have never seen him so angry. The closing of the away dressing-room door on Collingwood post-match was symbolic.

Occasionally, we witness a real conflict between the laws of the game and its spirit. I must have been in a minority of one up in the Sky commentary box, where everyone else said they had no problem with the run-out when Ian Bell was dismissed on the stroke of tea during the Trent Bridge Test between England and India in 2011.

The majority believed Bell was a lucky man, that his act of assuming the ball had gone for four was pure doziness. We could see from the press box that Praveen Kumar had saved a boundary, and there was no evidence to suggest either umpire had called 'over' before Abhinav Mukund took the bails off. It was the last delivery before tea, and Bell appeared to read from the body language that the ball had indeed touched the rope before being hurled back.

But I'm older and maybe a bit more compassionate. I always played it tough, but I played fair too, and what India did just didn't look right to me. Having said that, it was absolute class for India and Mahendra Singh Dhoni to change their minds and reinstate him after he was initially confirmed out. It led to the unusual situation of an ICC chief executive issuing a statement congratulating cordiality mid-Test. 'Absolute credit must go to Team India, the England team and the match officials – Ranjan Madugalle, Asad Rauf and Marais Erasmus, as well as the off-field umpires Billy Bowden and Tim Robinson – for the superb way that they all handled a tricky situation,' said Haroon Lorgat.

Occasionally, things occur around the world that are within the laws of the game but remain contentious nevertheless. Such as Jonathan Trott seizing on a Ravindra Jadeja delivery that had slipped out of the bowler's hand and dribbled off the pitch to the leg-side, smacking it for four, during a Test match in Nagpur in December 2012. It was not the right thing to do, it was against the spirit of the game, and although India generally appeared to laugh it off, some were clearly angered. I did it once, having a bit of a giggle, but I regretted it straight away. The laws state Trott was in his rights but the best thing would have been for the umpire to call dead ball.

If he needed a bit of guidance on the moral fibre of his decision it was provided later in the innings when Ravichandran Ashwin threatened a 'Mankad' dismissal with Trott out of his ground at the bowler's end. He did not go through with it, as if to prove a point.

To be honest, I don't have an issue with this kind of dismissal. Things can get a bit spicy in matches between England and Sri Lanka, as was the case at Edgbaston in the summer of 2014 when Jos Buttler was run out in this way during a one-day international. There was no 'Spirit of Cricket' issue there for me. Sachithra Senanayake, the mystery spin bowler, had clearly warned Buttler about backing up too far – and according to the laws he doesn't have to do that. It doesn't matter that he wasn't charging down the pitch, being out of his ground was sufficient for an appeal to be made and the batsman to be dismissed.

Of course, it was an unsavoury scene and everybody involved in the game would have wondered what they might have done. What you need in such a situation is a strong captain who is able to step back and take the heat out of it. If it had been me in Angelo Mathews's shoes, I might have gone up to the batsman and said: 'Look, you've been warned and you've done it again. You have put me in a really difficult situation here because you are out. I might just give you one more chance but if you do it again I'm sending you packing.'

He could have bought himself time by having a look round the field at two of his seniors, two great modern-day players in Kumar Sangakkara and Mahela Jayawardene, and taken a moment to ponder this kind of action. But he was not obliged to and I don't blame Mathews for not doing so. Technically, if a bowler removes the bails and the batsman is out of his ground he's out. That's the simplest interpretation. But I also have sympathy for the batsman if – unlike Buttler – it has come without a prior warning of, 'You're backing up too far and if you do it again I am within my rights to knock the bails off.' That should be said in front of the umpire.

But the wider thing to look at is whether the batsman is really stealing a march two yards down, or is he slightly absent-minded and has dragged out marginally over the line? I would always insist the batsman stays within his ground. It's so easy to do. You shouldn't be stealing an advantage and so the bowler is well within his rights to bring you back. Some batters are absent-minded but there are others who take the mickey. That's when the law comes into play and, let's face it, only comes into play really in one-day cricket.

Most such instances disappear from memory not long after the post-match commotion dies down. In major events, however, flashpoints like these stay with you. Take the Under-19 World Cup in Zimbabwe in 2016. Three runs were required heading into the final over when West Indies fast bowler Keemo Paul ran up and removed the bails as tail-ender Richard Ngarava's bat dragged out by millimetres.

Clearly, these were young men not well versed in the etiquette of the game. There really ought to have been an offer made. I played in matches in which the bowler has warned a batsman, but do not recall anyone going through with it. The warning had been enough. It might be that attitudes change when a bigger prize is at stake. Winning the tightest of contests on that decision sparked West Indies into life and soon afterwards they were crowned surprise champions.

Thankfully, incidents in which one team becomes incensed tend to be so isolated. Ben Stokes was furious when he was given out obstructing the field at a crucial juncture of a one-day international versus Australia at Lord's in September 2015, branding his opponents' decision 'embarrassing'. But Australia clearly saw it from a different perspective. A fast bowler like Mitchell Starc will instinctively look to throw the ball if he thinks that the batsman is out of his ground.

Starc did, Stokes was and fell foul of the letter of the law: 'Either batsman is out obstructing the field if he wilfully obstructs or distracts the field by word or action; furthermore it shall be regarded as obstruction if while the ball is in play, either batsman wilfully or without the consent of the fielder strikes the ball with his bat or person.'

In slow motion it appeared as though he clearly handled the ball, preventing it from hitting the stumps. In real time, he was getting out of the way. My only point here is that the captain has the power to step in, withdraw the appeal, and say, 'Forget it, let's get on with the game.' Steve Smith chose not to, allowed the umpires to make their judgements and accepted his dismissal. That doesn't worry me at all. Again, the test for players here is how you would feel if the roles were reversed.

Faking it

As a sport we appeared to be jumping on the bandwagon with Mr Donald Trump when it came to one particular rule change in 2017-18. Fake news has officially infiltrated cricket. No one knows whether what they're seeing is actually happening or not anymore and the ICC have had enough. You can no longer pretend you've stopped the ball when you haven't, you see. Fake fielding is simply not cricket. Ask Marnus Labuschagne, who dived when a drive had gone five yards beyond him in order to dissuade the opposing batsman to take a run and was punished with a five-run penalty.

Thanks for returning some normality to fielding, Donald. In yesteryear, fast bowlers would be flagging the ball through to the boundary, willing it to get there so they didn't have to bend down in an attempt to intercept. Or if it was really necessary they might stick out one of their plates and hope for the best. They certainly wouldn't be busting a gut to hurl themselves full length. Now there are cricketers who are convincing on the pseudo stop. The ICC were clearly concerned enough that conning of opponents was taking place to take such action.

These days fielders are chasing everything down, diving, refusing to give catches up and even back-flipping beyond the rope to try to pat the ball back from beyond the boundary to save anything they can for their team. Watch top-level practice nowadays and tandem catching is a drill that is worked on by just about everyone in an XI. One man will jump and arch backwards to take the ball above his head while the other hares from a position 30 metres away in readiness for it being relayed somewhere in the vicinity of the perimeter.

This is not a skill that just happens by chance; it can entail hours and hours of practice. Take Adam Lyth and Aaron

Finch when they were team-mates at Yorkshire. They pulled it off not once but twice in one season. These sorts of things have taken cricket to a new level, because securing a dismissal in this way can totally change the course of a contest, as devastating a blow as a magic delivery or a six hit out of the ground.

Fielders can influence a match like never before, and the devotion and attention to detail, I would argue, is a positive by-product of a win-at-all-costs mentality, something that suits the increasing influence of Twenty20 and the riches it provides for winners. I cannot tell you the number of times on commentary when I have thought, 'Oh, that's a six.' Then a fielder comes into view and leaps. In a flash, there are two of them converging upon each other and they have sufficient agility and spatial awareness to combine and complete the catch.

Twenty-over cricket is now big business around the world and winning, as it always has, tends to increase a player's personal value. They are now commodities on an open market for multiple global tournaments and franchises, and if they can bring that level of fielding expertise in addition to their primary skill it makes them even more valuable.

It's all a far cry from my playing days. When was the last time you saw an old-school dolly catch dropped? Some people wake up in cold sweats in the middle of the night thinking they have got an exam that day, concerned that they haven't revised properly. My mate's 43 and he still thinks he's doing his A-levels. I took 334 catches in first-class cricket and didn't shell too many. But I still have a recurring dream about one I fluffed in the 1970s.

I was fielding on the square at Old Trafford and this bloke from Gloucestershire called Wycliffe Phillips had an almighty swipe at this particular delivery. The ball went skyward off the splice and travelled no distance at all. There was no need for me to move a muscle at mid-wicket, I had time to wipe my brow, replace my cap and compose myself and yet I never touched it. It went right between my hands and my body and landed on the floor at my feet. I picked it up, threw it back to the bowler and there wasn't a murmur. Not even a heckle from the pit of hate. There was no 'butterfingers'. No 'give him a bucket'. It was such a knob-ender even they realised it wasn't worth it.

No-Balls

Mankads, obstructing the field and episodes of fake fielding are rare, but one thing we are finding the world over is a proliferation of wickets being taken by no-balls missed by the on-field umpires. How often do you see bowlers guilty of earning a breakthrough with a delivery only to be denied when the third umpire checks the front-foot landing.

I can only say, as one of the advisers to the ICC on the subject of umpires, that they are being asked to stand further back by the bowlers, which they do out of courtesy. The laws say they really should stand where they can see what's going on and accommodating such requests means they can't see the front line from where they stand.

I have umpired. There are some bowlers who, as a matter of course when their front foot lands, have their body in the way. If you go back 50 years pretty much everybody used to have a sideways action so that the front foot came across in full view of the umpire. But in more prevalent chest-on modern actions, the body tends to be in the way of the front foot.

Umpires do draw lines where the back foot lands too so that, if it passes beyond that mark, he will know that in all probability the bowler has gone beyond the front one as well. They're looking all the time but they also have to use other methods of detecting them and they have to be sure.

It is laughable that we are talking about a painted, white-washed line. In two hours it's obliterated. What do we do then? We draw a line with a bail where we think it might be. Guesswork. Primitive. Odd, isn't it, that we can put a man on the moon, but at cricket matches we're still messing about with a bucket of whitewash and a brush. There must be a way, using sensors like in tennis, for there to be a clear sound if there's a no-ball.

Odds and Sods

A good pub debate is always: how many dismissals are there in cricket? Take a bonus point if you can name them. It used to be 10. Until the MCC scrapped the rarest of them all – handled the ball – in October 2017, incorporating it under obstructing the field and leaving my mate Michael Vaughan as the last such victim in Test cricket, in Bengaluru in 2001.

Players tend to influence rule changes, particularly if something untoward is happening with regularity. Take the 'Steve Finn' no-ball rule that came into force in 2013. It had become an issue the year before when Graeme Smith, of South Africa, made a complaint about being distracted by Finn's habit of dislodging the bails at the non-striker's end by knocking his right knee into the stumps. Until that point it wasn't an issue and, as a former umpire, for me dead ball had always seemed the appropriate call.

One change the other way that I do not like is that the ball is now deemed dead if a team reviews a leg-before decision in a one-day international. That's all very well, but it can be craftily implemented as a tactic towards the death of an innings and that can't be right. If a team has a review in the bank, there is nothing to stop them appealing for leg before if the ball flicks a boot or thigh pad and trickles off to the fine-leg boundary. They're not looking for a dismissal in that situation. They're looking to save four valuable runs and it's all within the rules. Not so sure it should be.

The game has to move with the times, but one thing that has not changed since WG Grace was in short trousers is the role of the toss. Despite a proposal to follow the suit of the English County Championship and scrap it in the spring of 2018 – to dilute the effects of home advantage – the ICC's cricket committee recommended its retention. I am not sure how much influence it has, to be honest. I might argue that the team better equipped for the particular conditions tends to prevail.

Take England's 2012-13 tour of India – Alastair Cook proved himself a world-class batsman for all conditions but a terrible tosser! Five times he called heads and five times it landed tails. Maybe he needs to take a leaf out of the book of the former Nottinghamshire captain Brian Bolus, who used to practise the toss on a green towel in the dressing room. Then again, he was a touch eccentric.

Get On with It

Forget sharp practice. If you want to get me on a rant over a pint of Timothy Taylor's Landlord ask me about over rates. All this work on a code of conduct. Well, slow play would result in a yellow in Bumble's code, too.

Time-wasting as a law of the game is non-existent, I am afraid. At a time when it is in everybody's interests to keep some pace to the spectacle in the face of a growing threat of Twenty20 eating into cricket's next-generation audience, Tests just meander along. Fifteen overs an hour really shouldn't be any sort of problem at all but nobody in authority seems bothered if we get 12 or 13. Take the 2015 Test v New Zealand at Lord's. Play went on until 7.30pm on the Saturday evening – admittedly with an hour's rain dictating so – and six overs were lost. Half the crowd had gone home by then. And New Zealand are by no means the worst offenders.

The amount of work these lads in certain roles have to get through in a day puts incredible strain on their bodies. It is not uncommon for players to wear GPS devices to track exactly how far they have run over the course of seven hours. Fast bowlers are monitored so that their training programmes are amended accordingly. It's important not to overwork the big men after an intensive match, and that is one of the major advances in technology over recent years.

But it's not them that I am so worried about. It's the 12th men, who are at breaking point from what I can see. They are lifting and carrying non-stop. No wonder Graeme Swann used to say he was too lazy to do twelfths. He would have been cream-crackered. He'd have fancied bowling a dozen overs off the reel. It would have been less demanding physically, that's for sure. The constant changing of gloves, bats and helmets and having drinks brought on within five minutes of a drinks break means they are being worked harder than a bleep test – get on with the game, lads! Just when you think the batsman in the middle is all sorted, back comes squad-man with some pills; then it's time for the bananas; towels; a *Reader's Digest*. But what really gets my goat is that if a team gets a wicket – drinks come on, obviously – the 12th man comes on to join in the celebration. They're high-fiving, fist-bumping, dabbing, flossing. Only after the new batsman takes guard does the captain set the field. Just get ready!

Test matches are supposed to feature 90 overs a day and I blame match referees for not enforcing better timekeeping on the players. Allowances are made too easily. 'Oh, you've got a minute there. Another minute for the changeover. The sight screen had to be shifted. Whoozit slid into the rope, and it needed putting back.' There seem to be endless reasons not to bowl a full complement of overs.

When the ICC launched their discipline crackdown they should have become firmer on this area too, as once again the people who are suffering are the paying public. Exactly the group cricket should be looking to keep sweet at a time when spectator interest levels are being analysed like never before.

Currently, there is no deterrent to breeze through a day four overs short – and when I say four overs short, that is including the extra half-hour's grace tagged onto the end of the day's schedule. The tempo of the game once they get going is great. Teams no longer look to play for a draw. The influence of the shorter forms on Test matches is there for all to see, but even in 50-over and Twenty20 cricket the flow is lost with all the inter-ruptions. Sometimes slowing the game down can be viewed as a tactical consideration, altering the momentum of a contest that is fast running away from your team.

And it is not just the batsmen. How about the fast bowlers who, after a five-over spell, shamble off the field. What are they doing? Are they off for a fag behind the dormitory? Or putting their feet up and reading the paper while a young shaver comes on to do a shift?

Some are like kids in the back of the car on a long journey.

'Are we nearly there yet?'

'No.'

'But I need the toilet.'

'We've only been going half an hour.'

Players are supposed to ask the umpire for permission to leave the field, and they do. All they need to say, though, is, 'I've got a problem with my heel.' But you would halt liberal exploitation of this – and the slowing of proceedings – if when a player exited you could not have a substitute for any reason for two overs. That would stop it. A captain wouldn't want to play with 10.

The players stroll around. When they get playing it's fabulous. The ethos is to score your runs as fast as possible and get bowling. You have to take 20 wickets to win the game. But they still lack urgency.

And more equipment comes onto the field than ever before. I said to Andrew Strauss on commentary one day during his stint with Sky Sports that the only member of the fielding side allowed to wear protective gear should be the wicketkeeper. 'Well, that's just an old bloke talking,' was his response.

No, I think every batsman should have the right to disperse the field and allowing a fielder to wear armour in addition to the obligatory helmet for close fielders (those playing for England at least) counters this. I am speaking as someone who stood at short leg for 19 years. As well as being cumbersome – recall Mark Stoneman fielding in the Ashes with pads on and dropping a crucial chance in the deep at Adelaide, or a young Cheteshwar Pujara, standing at first slip with shin pads and a chest guard on, looking like the Michelin man's stunt double and shelling England's anchor Alastair Cook in 2012–13. And it also encourages them to change on the field, causing more disruption.

If the public weren't so bothered about losing overs throughout a day, then so be it. Let the game change. Don't worry about trying to get a uniform 90 overs in. However, if you look at the evidence on social media that is not the case. They do mind.

These people are paying good money. And I am crusading on their behalf to quicken it up.

When I was captain of Lancashire we had to go at 18 overs an hour. We moaned about it, of course, but we did it because it was mandatory. Forty years ago there was a different format to a team. There were two quicks, a medium pacer and two spinners. That provided a balance and helped you catch up when you got behind on over rates. Once your fast men had their spells, you could bring it back with your spinners. It stands to reason that a spin bowler with a shorter length of run-up will bowl six deliveries in a shorter space of time than a bloke who, when stood at the top of his mark, is in a neighbouring postcode.

Let's keep Test cricket at a guaranteed 90 overs each day, but empower match officials to clamp down even more than they do now on slow over rates. If a captain can't get his bowlers moving along at 15 overs an hour, he's banned for a Test – no questions asked. At the moment, captains get a warning and a fine before they are banned, but for me it's one strike and you're out.

I also received a letter from none other than Ricky Tomlinson, aka TV's Jim Royle, who is a massive cricket fan. Ricky was asking why new batsmen always have to mark their guards at the crease so elaborately, adding to the time lost. His answer? 'Surely three neat holes drilled into the pitch and filled with soil which is dyed is a better solution.' Even sent me a diagram. To which I couldn't resist replying: 'Jim, dyed soil my arse . . .'

But I couldn't fault his commitment to speeding things up. Bad light is a bore too and can prove a mystery to fans when state-of-the-art floodlights are on and play is still suspended. The umpires work to regulations which state the floodlights should only supplement not overtake the natural light. But it's something the ICC should look at again, I believe, because it deprives fans and makes the game look silly.

There's no danger to batsmen. Although when it is gloomy

batting against a red ball does tend to be difficult. When the lights are on, there appears to be more extravagant movement – swing in the air and nip off the surface – and a pitch invariably looks quicker. So, the lights give us more cricket. But it appears the bowlers are licking their lips.

The Future of International Cricket

Linked to this, my first thought when I heard Colin Graves, the ECB chairman, moot his idea of four-day Tests was that we'd be looking at one hell of a long day in the office. Graves floated a proposal for each day to contain 105 overs – rather than the current five days of 90 – but if players are struggling to bowl 90 overs, how on earth are they going to get through 105? I would be airing 'Start the car!' shortly after midnight when everyone else in the ground has gone home.

If Graves knows of a way to accelerate the action, then fantastic. But I fear broadcasters wouldn't like the change in their schedules if this proposal ever came to fruition. And you have to ask: do the public actually want to be there all that time? They were quite happy with 11am until 6pm. Nowadays the final over of the day regularly begins at 6.30pm. Back in 2005, Channel 4 brought play forward half an hour to guarantee *Hollyoaks* started at that time in the evening. They didn't want to break their evening schedule because the viewing figures were telling them that the cricket could not compete with a teen soap like that.

With good viewing figures comes premium advertising revenue, and it was one of their most popular shows. A show like that was worth big money to them. That summer Wrigley's chewing gum became the programme's sponsors. Previously, Nescafé had held a one-year contract to put its name to *Hollyoaks* in a deal worth £9.5 million. You could see why, from a financial point of view, they would have wanted to do all they could to protect that kind of income.

To be fair, they probably couldn't have forecast exactly how many would be watching England v Australia matches that summer. When England edged into a 2-1 lead at Trent Bridge, viewing figures peaked at 8.4 million people. More than half the people who watched TV that day flicked on the cricket at some point. It was a perfect storm that the greatest series of all time was on terrestrial television. They hit some peak audiences. Prior to that extraordinary few weeks, I understand that there had never been as many as 2 million tuned in at any one time.

Graves did make a point about four-day Tests tackling the issue of poor fifth-day crowds, but my solution to that is quite radical: make the fifth day free for spectators. Some of the best days of Test cricket in England over the past couple of decades have been the final ones, and you might get some people walking in for nowt, then getting the bug and coming back for more.

I have good reason to recall Yorkshire throwing their doors open for the fifth morning of the thrilling Headingley Test against South Africa in 1998. Play only lasted half an hour or so, but 13,000 came through the doors and it was inspirational for the players as they secured an historic first home win in a five-match series for 13 years. Some might say it worked a treat because Yorkshiremen don't like putting their hands in their pockets, but I couldn't possibly comment.

As things stand, fifth-day scenarios can act like a magnet to knowledgeable cricket fans. Entertain, offer a chance to dream, and they will come. Think of the 2005 Ashes when the queues at Old Trafford snaked as far as the eye could see, or when a big last-day crowd at Lord's with, significantly, free admission for kids witnessed the turnaround triumph over

New Zealand that had begun with England 30 for four on day one. Or in Leeds in 2017, when those who parted with their cash got to witness a marathon chase completed by a youthful West Indies. If we are looking to 'reconnect' with the public, then what better way to introduce people to the game? As Dire Straits might have put it, 'Money for nothing and your kids for free'.

There is some fantastic Test cricket being played around the world. The days of sides playing for a draw, going along at two runs an over, and then having a dig if they have a chance of victory are long gone. It's not just England.

Concern over Test match attendances globally is genuine, but I do not believe it should cause mass panic here. It's people's prerogative if they don't go to watch live, but that doesn't mean they're not interested. Cricket is peculiar in that so many people follow it on TV and radio. People work. They haven't got the time to sit there for five days. They dip in and out. I never go to watch Premier League football live but that doesn't mean I'm not interested. I love it, if I am honest, particularly on my big-screen television and with the benefit of central heating. Just personal preference.

I believed the move towards four-day Tests might gather momentum when the new Decision Review System regulations came into force in October 2016. The 'out' zone increasing by 25 per cent meant a lot more not out decisions being overturned, and matches have become quicker, naturally reducing their timeframes. But the incoming Test Championship appears to have saved the prospect of a uniform change until 2021. Like everyone else, I hope the round-robin system provides the context to re-engage those who might have lost interest.

AB de Villiers went public in advance of announcing his international retirement in 2018 about how he believed players will turn their backs on Test cricket unless 'something is done'. It wasn't enough to save him, but we need others to remain on board. It is such a brilliant product.

What gives me hope is the regeneration I discovered in the 50-over game while in New Zealand just a few short weeks before de Villiers called time with South Africa at the age of 34. To me, of the three international formats, the one that needed looking at was one-day internationals. For some time my preference had been for Test and Twenty20 cricket, to the extent that I would have gone quite radical and scheduled no one-day internationals other than a 50-over World Cup every four years.

That seemed a reasonable compromise in finding room for all three and not burning out the world's top talent. The format I'd ranked three of three was becoming rather too formulaic for my liking – the first 10 overs were always about taking a position in the game, the ball would then be knocked around for the next 25–30 overs before a bash for the final 10–15. But players and coaches opened their minds and the rule changes to its fielding restrictions inside the first 10 and final 10 overs have energised things and helped teams counterattack at various times of innings. Equally, bowling teams are increasingly trying to dismiss batsmen rather than contain them, and that has made for more varied games and spinners taking an increasing number of wickets. England's 3-2 win over the Black Caps was full of creativity and the games ebbed and flowed brilliantly from start to finish.

Finding a Balance

I am all for changes if they improve the game and, although restricting bat sizes in 2017 was a bit of a red herring, I am keen for an eye to be kept on the balance between bat and ball in future. Many grounds around the globe have redevelopments that have encroached on the playing area, and the net result has been that boundaries are brought in. Even at Lord's, where there is room, the rope's positioned 20 yards in from the picket fence, whereas back in the day it was quite normal to run fours and fives. It's not the bat size causing an uneven contest; it's the size of the boundaries.

That's not to decry that batting – particularly against the white ball – is increasingly a power game. Think of the Australian umpire Bruce Oxenford, who caused a stir when he began taking to the field wearing a protective shield strapped to his left arm. The self-made device was constructed using polycarbonate and featured a table tennis bat-shaped curve on the end to parry balls heading his way. Oxenford took action in the winter of 2016-17 when fellow compatriot John Ward was struck on the head and hospitalised during a match in India. It was first used in expectation of repelling the muscular power of Virat Kohli, AB de Villiers, Brendon McCullum and Aaron Finch in an Indian Premier League match.

It's a fearful prospect having a ball hit straight back at you with such velocity and perhaps highlights that there could be more done to make cricket less of a batsman's game, to the benefit of all. Take when James Anderson was removed from the England bowling attack for running on the pitch versus Pakistan in 2016. He was adjudged to have encroached three times, but I really hope the ICC revisit this soon because it detracts from the game and will restrict the supreme skills of left-armers like Mohammad Amir and Mitchell Starc in particular.

The thing is, when you talk to international cricketers they just do not see running on the pitch as a problem. It simply doesn't interfere with the outcome of the game. In fact, it makes it more interesting because it brings spin bowlers into it if more rough is created. Ironically, in the Edgbaston match in which action was taken against Jimmy, Yasir Shah would have been keen for him to carry on.

I would also be asking why players are tempted to tamper with a match ball when there are 20-30 cameras on them. My observation is that the Kookaburra ball used predominantly in Australia, New Zealand and South Africa just doesn't give the bowlers anything to work with. Unlike the seam on the English Dukes ball, which protrudes from the surface, the Kookaburra version is literally embedded. There is no use trying to pick it as there is nothing to go at, but you can see why teams are so keen to throw it in on the bounce in an attempt to scuff one side in the search for reverse swing.

Pitches

England's statistics tell the story, but it is not necessarily an Anglocentric one. Pitches are proving a problem in international cricket and it is an area that needs addressing, I believe. Since England won in India in 2012 only Joe Root, Matt Prior and Haseeb Hameed have averaged more than 40 away from home, and the last two played only a handful of matches. In the corresponding period, the big two bowlers (James Anderson and Stuart Broad) average just under 30 with the ball, Moeen Ali averages 51 and Chris Woakes, 57.

Look no further for why they're not winning. Another heavy Ashes defeat and subsequent 1-0 loss to New Zealand under the new captain, Joe Root, highlighted the need for greater variation in subsequent bowling attacks. Thankfully, I believe Ed Smith, the new national selector, gets it – to be successful on flatter surfaces in conditions that do nothing for a battery of 84mph right-arm seamers, variety is required and that means a genuine pace option, a wrist spinner and a left-armer to offer a different angle. The choice of Sam Curran in Smith's second match bodes well in this regard.

My view is that groundsmen should just produce the best possible pitch, although it appears worldwide that home advantage is the norm. What would be wrong with aiming for the best possible pitch – an even covering of dry grass, pace and bounce – whatever the country? Doing so would accommodate fast bowlers, batsmen and spinners, not to mention stroke players – oh, and spectators, who believe it or not are quite important.

The International Cricket Council really must start working harder with cricket boards to get the best possible surfaces. Because we're seeing too many like the ones on their doorstep in the United Arab Emirates. On England's last trip there to play Pakistan, Wahab Riaz unleashed a 91mph thunderbolt which found the edge of Ian Bell's bat and landed three metres in front of second slip.

So much cricket is played that the pitches become tired, which makes it harder for fast bowlers, and I am not overly enamoured of the ICC policy of ensuring no home advantage in their global knockouts. I fear the 2019 World Cup will follow the pattern of the Champions Trophy last year, when I walked into the middle at Cardiff before a ball was bowled in the England v Pakistan semi-final and was met by a scruffy pitch: ultra-dry and dead.

Why the ICC oversee these pitches I don't know. Are they saying they don't trust the host country to produce a cricket pitch? These groundsmen are very competent and know the job inside out. There is no reason why you should play a big semi-final on a worn pitch. All that does is favour the Asian teams. I hope for the sake of a spectacle next year we do not see a repeat.

Love Thy County

Whether it is in international or domestic cricket, I am all for improving the product. So how would we do that in the English summer? Quite simply by having less cricket. Reduce the workload on fast bowlers, and get players fired up to play between meaningful rest periods.

We currently play 50-over cricket in a big block and they say it's because we play all these one-day internationals. I make that a no-no. Let's go back to playing a knockout in the style of the old Gillette Cup. There was nothing better than a competition with the minor counties in because, as a coach, you used to be worried when you were drawn against one of them away from home. You had no idea where you were going, what pitch you would be playing on, what your opponents were capable of, and you were up against it in a sudden-death scenario. Lose and you were knocked out. Just consider what has happened in the Royal London Cup over the past couple of seasons. Players are being left out all the time, showing the counties aren't really interested. You can also lose matches and scrape through into the latter stages, showing that losing doesn't matter. It should.

England players don't take part in the 50-over tournament in its current format as they are either involved in Test cricket or at the Indian Premier League. Set up the embarrassment of a giant-killing and go for quality not quantity by arranging the rounds to fit in the gaps in which the internationals are available.

Go into any boozer in summer and you'll be surprised how many people are talking county cricket, and the Championship, the competition that produces our Test cricketers, in particular. I really enjoy popping in and having a look at the next generation, keeping up to date with who's hot and who's not.

I love leaving those big mausoleum Test match venues behind and heading to a small, cosy festival venue – a Chelmsford or a Scarborough or even a Canterbury. It's intimate, there's a good crowd, and they love their cricket. And it's arguably more watched than ever this year on the evidence of viewing figures on social media at clubs like Somerset, who recorded 15,000 watch hours by those streaming their victory over Worcestershire in April 2018.

It is a much-maligned and much-loved competition. And competitive too – the 2016 season, when Middlesex claimed the pennant on the final evening, being a fine example. Such a close finish was testimony to what two divisions have done for the domestic game. More matches count than they used to.

Toby Roland-Jones made his name as the first double-barreller to play for England since Mandy Mitchell-Innes in 1935 with a hat-trick during that dramatic finale. He was playing international cricket the following summer before injury struck. But players who make that move in future should be accustomed to the matches possessing greater intensity, and that would be achieved in my estimation by scheduling fewer. Three divisions of six counties apiece would provide 10 matches a season. That would be my recommendation, and if you wanted to add title and relegation play-offs that would be fine. But there really is no need for more than 11.

Player Futures

In my day, with one or two exceptions, a player tended to play for one county for their entire career. Now they flit about from one kit to the next and hop across the world's Twenty20 satellites seeking the biggest paydays. Personally, I have no problem with some players opting to dip out of first-class cricket to focus solely on the shorter formats, although I would not like it to become an epidemic.

During the 2017-18 tour of New Zealand, I happened to be stood next to Alex Hales when he was being interviewed by journalists about his decision to follow Adil Rashid into a white-ball diet. He said that for the next two years he was focused on getting in England's World Cup team, so he was putting all his resources into playing one-day cricket. He didn't want to be sidetracked playing first-class cricket. Every available opportunity, he said, he would be up against a white ball. Then, in two years' time, he continued, 'I may look at it again.'

His point was that he was only 29 and therefore had plenty of time to make other career decisions down the line. His target was clear – he wanted to become one of the best players in the world. The gamble was whether or not he would be picked up by franchises. When I chatted to him afterwards, he said there were technical things he knew he had to work on, and he was also appreciative of the fact that he had to get better as a fielder and improve his all-round fitness.

Of course, there is also a financial side to it and players like Hales, Rashid and Colin Munro were maximising their income by specialising. But they are professionals and that doesn't bother me at all. The game is in a really good place with the three variations of the sport and it will settle down as to who specialises in what.

The importance of white-ball cricket is only going to increase as it now serves as the primary revenue stream for many major nations. For example, when changes are made to English cricket with the introduction of the new eight-team competition from 2020, the Twenty20 Blast has to stay because it forms the counties' main income.

The new city tournament will also provide crucial funds

to these counties, and in turn that will safeguard the future of red-ball cricket. In England, our constitution is for 18 first-class counties and their collective futures will be protected by modernising what we do with the shortest format. They will get the benefits twice, if you like, and all my information from being at the Indian Premier League this year is that the best players in the world will come.

There is a lot of scepticism surrounding the likelihood of attracting the world's elite, but at the time of year they are earmarking – the height of English summer – all the indications are that the leading short-format targets will be free. All this despite suggestions that the money will not be good enough to interest them. I would even hold out hope for India players being allowed to participate. Remember where you heard it first and watch this space. The ECB are developing something in the interests of protecting 150 years of first-class cricket in this country.

Do not doubt that the Championship is a playground capable of producing world-class talent. Look no further than Joe Root. I was at London's splendid Garrick Club in 2016 doing a Q&A when one chap very forcefully stood up and asked: 'What on earth is wrong with Root?' I replied: 'The lad with nine centuries and a Test average over 52, you mean? One of the top four batsmen in world cricket? What's wrong with him? Nothing.'

To be honest, converting starts has been an issue for him but what an issue to have. I have seen a few good players in my half a century in the game and he is right up there. I can't really judge the ones who came before my time, but I've seen the elegance of Colin Cowdrey and Peter May, the dash of Ted Dexter, the bloody-mindedness of Geoff Boycott, the bravery and skill of Graham Gooch and the silky touch of David Gower.

More recently we've had people like Michael Vaughan, who was the best in the world for a short while, and one I rated very highly in Graham Thorpe. Then there is the insatiable appetite and concentration of Alastair Cook. And how about the one I believe is the best of the lot to play for England in Kevin Pietersen? He could do things that others just could not, as far back as 2005 when he kept on slog-sweeping Shane Warne. He got you on the edge of your seat.

It was Thorpe, who is now working for the ECB with the next generation of batsmen at Loughborough, who first mentioned Root to me seven years ago. Thorpe, who doesn't say much, told me, 'He's going to be an absolute belter.' He wasn't wrong. What has impressed me most following him across continents since 2012-13 has been his ability to change tempo. It could be argued that bowling around the world is not what it was when the quality of Shane Warne and Muttiah Muralitharan lay in wait. But he has made hay with his stroke play.

Contrast that with two batsmen who first played for England around the same time: Sam Robson and Nick Compton. They're old-style. The game's left them behind. You can't keep on prodding the pitch these days. Take Compton. He was as thorough a top-order batsman as they came, with bags of experience in the county game. Robson was picked after a mountain of runs in county cricket, some no doubt made on challenging surfaces and in testing circumstances. He then moved to the top level and looked at the pitch after every ball as though it was going to explode.

Root is coming up on KP's shoulder. He ticks all the boxes. The great players pick up length fractionally earlier than the rest of us, which Joe does, and he's a good build now he has filled out the body of his youth. He has to believe this imbalance of 50s to hundreds – only 13 transformed in 53 at the time of writing – is just a phase, like players getting out in the nervous 90s. It must be incredibly frustrating for him, because he never looks out of form, and then – bang! – he's suddenly out. But I'd be more concerned if he kept getting out for five, rather than 75.

If there is anyone Root can learn from it's his Yorkshire team-mate Kane Williamson, who went past Martin Crowe and Ross Taylor as New Zealand's most prolific centurion with number 18 during the most recent meeting with England. He just seems to flip between each format without a problem, and without losing any of his pizzazz.

The Making of an England Player

What I have come to appreciate covering England home and away is that, although they are using the most up-to-date techniques in preparation, things are not so far removed from when I enjoyed my fleeting spell on the international stage in the mid-1970s, or indeed when I returned as coach. As players, we were all naturally fit. We played every day, for a start, and would carry all our gear around with us. The players of today don't hit it any harder than some like Ian Botham – who once plundered 80 sixes in a season – and they don't throw it in to the wicketkeeper any harder from the outfield than some of our guys did. And the boundaries were a lot longer then.

Nor did the level of detail in the leaked Ashes menus of 2013-14 surprise me. The sort of foods the backroom staff requested were exactly as I would have anticipated. And not new, either. When I was England coach we had two guys, in Wayne Morton, the physio, and Dean Riddle, the fitness coach, who did much to bring in a new awareness of the benefits of fitness and correct diet. I would send them into grounds both home and away to ensure that they were clean and tidy, armed with a set of guidelines that we wanted them to follow. We would say, 'This is what we want as an England team' – just as Andy Flower and his side clearly did in Australia with their order of tofu, quinoa and mung bean curry in an 82-page dietary dossier.

Players such as Alec Stewart and Jack Russell in my time would be very careful and fastidious about what they ate. Alec once had chicken breast, mashed potato and broccoli 43 days on the trot at the 1996 World Cup while Jack famously had his daily Weetabix and baked beans double and, in a way, they were trendsetters. Pasta was introduced and players slowly began to eat more healthily and prepare better.

These days, players will be told when they can have a drink or eat anything outside the norm. They are very well rewarded and have to behave accordingly. But what they are doing is nothing different from elite athletes or, say, cyclists.

I am not sure Shane Warne ate anything other than pizza and chips, but it didn't seem to do the great leg-spinner any harm. In fact, his genius led me to hire locum coaches for the 1998-99 Ashes, in a precursor to what has happened during Trevor Bayliss's England tenure. As a head coach, I always believed I was a facilitator and that meant introducing drop-in specialist coaches every now and again – they would come in for three matches, a couple of weeks, a tour, whatever length of time was suitable for all parties. The modern way is for specialist coaches or consultants to come in for stipulated periods. Under Bayliss, Paul Collingwood has come in on a 100-day-a-year fielding coach contract, and they use Bruce French on a similar-length deal to work with the wicketkeepers. Sometimes in the cases of Mahela Jayawardene, Daniel Vettori and Shane Bond their agreements are only for a few weeks.

It can prove very helpful to get different voices in and

around the dressing room. There's nothing to fear in this process from the senior coaches. Players receive a lot of advice and other information and reject a lot of it. But if something sticks with them from a session or a series of sessions that tends to do good.

Vettori, Mushtaq Ahmed and Saqlain Mushtaq are among those parachuted in to work with young English spinners in recent times; while in anticipation of combating Warne, I asked another Pakistan great, Abdul Qadir, to come and help prepare us in the nets throughout that tour. Abdul was living in Melbourne and was available to bowl, and I believed the opportunity to study a top-class operator at first hand was an invaluable one for our batsmen. Few in the history of spin bowling have possessed variations as hard to read, and my view was that getting brains switched on to picking his notoriously deceptive googly would only have a positive impact. It might give our batsmen a bit better chance when we headed into the Test matches.

The other one I engaged was Peter Philpott. He was one of a rich line of Australian leg-spinners going back through Clarrie Grimmett, Bill O'Reilly, Richie Benaud. Peter played eight Test matches for Australia and wrote papers on the nuances of leg-spin. I knew him from his time in the Lancashire League with Ramsbottom and East Lancashire. So I would get him in as a bit of a leg-spin theory tutor before every Test match. As it was, due to injury keeping Warne out of all but one of them, the prep turned out to be for his very capable understudy Stuart MacGill.

I had done a similar thing as Lancashire coach when I discovered West Indies fast bowler Malcolm Marshall was available for a short coaching stint. He had finished up playing for Hampshire and was up in the Northern League turning out for Preston. We brought him in to work with a group of fast bowlers including

Peter Martin, Darren Shadford and Glen Chapple, and his level of expertise proved invaluable. He passed on some of the tricks of the trade of fast bowling.

His advice when numbers nine, 10 and 11 came in to bat? Hit them on the hand! 'They don't want to be there,' he would say to our lads. 'Remind them of the fact.' Pace can blow a tail away and, as Marshall said, 'that's a chance of three wickets'. There was a reward just around the corner if you were prepared to step it up. Malcolm's career was similar to that of Andy Roberts and our own Jimmy Anderson. All of them began as out-and-out pace bowlers who refined their skills. The best evolve to survive and they were bowlers who developed their own raw talent. The message going round the county circuit like bushfire in each case was 'this bloke's rapid'. The umpires are great observers and they get excited when someone with something a bit special springs up. Later in life Anderson became an artist, turning himself into Rembrandt. He was Banksy at the start. Both styles have great merits. Ninety-mile-an-hour pace is a weapon any fast bowler would take. But as time passes by, they realise the best friend they've got is the cricket ball. They learn what they can do with it. Where to position the seam, the different release points, how to use the shiny side to promote swing.

I always wanted to provide the players with as much information about opponents as possible and so, not long after being appointed England coach, I went on a scouting mission to Pakistan at the end of 1997 to watch the West Indies ahead of England's tour of the Caribbean. I did so armed with a Sharp Viewcam.

Manchester United used them through their main club sponsorship and I jumped on the back of that. It gave us instant replays which have become commonplace on players' smartphones and iPads 20 years later, although our process was rather more cumbersome. Finance was always a problem then and we were forever being told we couldn't afford the things we wanted at the ECB, so I had to be creative in acquiring the necessary and it meant lugging a load of cassette tapes around.

Train in Spain

England are looking at moving with the times and developing a training centre at Desert Springs, the resort in Almería, Spain, where they prepared ahead of the 2015 Ashes series. On that trip they went through intense fielding drills and got to know their new coach, Trevor Bayliss. Something about the place enticed them back several times since. Presumably not the nudist beach just down the road where the squad ended up innocently enough during an afternoon bike ride. Although I do understand Mark Wood revisited the area in the correct dress code later on the same day, on two wheels rather than mounted on his imaginary horse.

The facilities have been developed over the past couple of years and the intention is that more meaningful practice can take place in the winter months when the British weather prevents anything other than indoor nets or sessions in heated tents at Loughborough's national performance centre. They will need a similar infrastructure to that of Loughborough at their new home – a place for the physios, conditioning coaches, medics and nutritionists to carry out their work.

The plan of Andrew Strauss, England's managing director, all sounds very new, of course, and the fact he is looking to improve player development with increased work outdoors on grass is forward-thinking. However, it does rather remind me of my own career once more. As coach of England, I also wanted to access the best facilities possible in the off-season and do some level of warm-weather training. Medha Laud, one of the most brilliant people I ever worked with in cricket, was that well connected in the world of sport that she was able to secure a week at La Manga.

So we went to work primarily on fitness and bonding in Spain, and later travelled to Barringtons, a spa and leisure complex on the Algarve developed and owned by the former squash player, Jonah Barrington. Graham Gooch, who was a selector at that particular time, had an apartment there and they had introduced some cricket nets in addition to the golf, tennis, squash and football facilities already on site. We took the first team and emerging players from the Under-19 squad and got to know what made them tick, who wanted to get fit and who was focused on reaching the next level as international players.

Even then you could tell this was something that would be more prevalent in years to come. Places like this had great potential even though they didn't have cricket grounds. Both Desert Springs and La Manga – home of ICC Europe and a regular destination for Ireland and Scotland – do now, of course. With our climate like it is, it is thoroughly sensible to have a facility so close at hand, allowing players to be practising in sunshine just a two-hour plane journey away. It's a shrinking world and it makes perfect sense.

Of course, some of the early sets of academy players selected by England in the central-contracts era went to Adelaide during winter months, but having somewhere closer to home is much more practical. Talk was of developing Barringtons with cricket back then. But the finance was not there at the pre-ECB Test and County Cricket Board as it is now, and so there was always a consideration of how it would impact on the England team's annual budget.

There will always be those who question the benefits of being overseas ahead of a domestic season. Back in the mid-1990s, a benefactor offered Lancashire the chance to go to Jamaica for pre-season. The external financial contribution meant the trip was cost-effective, that we would get guaranteed outdoor practice, and intense practice at that, in readiness for the county summer. Critics of the idea were pointing out: when you come back to play here in April and May you are going to be on damp pitches, it's going to be cold and the conditions are not like for like.

No, they were not, but the benefits of being on a cricket field rather than indoors are huge. As well as batting and bowling in the middle, you can have a full-on fielding practice, put miles into the bowlers' legs on turf. It sounds such a mundane point to make, but throwing with force from A to B across any distance you choose is a real plus. As is hitting the ball in the air. You can't do either within a confined space or in an indoor school with a roof on.

The only downside to this Spanish retreat as far as I can see is you have to pass through those wretched airports crammed with middle-aged blokes in football shirts, Kojak hairstyles and the names of all their family members (often including some ex-wives) inked all over their misshapen torsos.

Airports are full of security now. You have to have everything checked and scanned – put your bag through, take your jacket off, remove your belt, just the way it should be. But if we are going to these lengths, why not have a breathalyser in the departure lounge? If you're over the limit, you don't go. Dead simple.

An extension of all this, of course, is for sporting bodies like the ECB to buy their own aircraft. Every year me and a group of pals club together to charter a plane to fly us from Luton to Spain and back for a golf trip. It's not that expensive, so you would think that a business with a multimillion-pound turnover might go a step further. Buy your wings and use them. They would pay for themselves in the long run.

Such a course of action is a lifetime away from where things began for me. In the days when a bus journey to a Lancashire League derby with Accrington seemed like a big adventure into another world. Forget a plane, no one in our first XI owned a car.

At the start of a journey that allowed me to appreciate cricket's intricacies and its potential to move with the times to meet them. The world was a much bigger place back then and I will forever be grateful for being given the opportunity to experience its four corners while contemplating the good, the bad and the mad of our sport.

And I hope you have not mistaken me for someone who peddles the line about 'how things were better in my day'. Yes, I have expressed my concerns about where the game is going. But throughout these pages I have tried to emphasise what is so good. I am not one to claim that the standard of cricket around the world has dropped. Nothing could be further from the truth, in fact. There seems to be a lot of doom and gloom about cricket and the fact that it is dying, that support is dwindling and that the prevalence of Twenty20 is somehow doing irreparable damage to more established forms.

But, as long as we sort out the conduct issues and remember that the essence of cricket is a parable for life – of fair play and kinship – we already have established audiences keen on it in all its forms. A loyal following who are watching a product that has never been better – whichever your cricketing denomination.

I have been involved in the professional game since 1965 and I want to tell you before signing off that cricket has never been healthier than it is right now. Over half a century I have seen some of the greats, and the likes of Virat Kohli, AB de Villiers and Joe Root compare favourably. They're right up there with the very best in history. Whenever they're in town there isn't a spare seat.

That tells me others retain the excitement I experienced when I made my first pilgrimage to the Accrington Cricket Club bar. They say the goal of any cricketer is to leave the game in a better place and I am certain I will when I raise my final glass to it. I leave you on a positive note. Cheers!

ACKNOWLEDGEMENTS

To those who have made this journey in cricket so memorable – team-mates, opponents, commentary box colleagues, friends around the world – a big 'thank you'. To those who have played a part in the production of this book – Ian Marshall and his team at Simon & Schuster; Neil Fairbrother and Phoenix; the ace scribbler Richard Gibson – you've all done very well . . .